HHB

The
SUNSHINE
SOLDIERS

by
PETER TAUBER

ℋℋℬ

Higganum Hill Books : Higganum, Connecticut

Revised Edition, First printing, June 2002
All rights reserved
including the right of reproduction in whole or in part in any form

Copyright © 1971, 2002 by Peter Tauber

ISBN 0-9635185-6-9
Library of Congress Control Number: 2002103753

Cover illustration by James Montgomery Flagg, (1877 – 1960) Published as the cover for
Leslie's Weekly, July 6, 1916. Later a recruiting poster. All rights reserved.

Published by Higganum Hill Books
P.O. Box 666
Higganum, Connecticut 06441-0666

Email: HigganumBook@Juno.com

Printed in The United States of America

The first edition of *The Sunshine Soldiers* was published as SBN 671-20844-6
by Simon and Schuster : New York, 1971.

FOR MY MOTHER AND FATHER
AND THEIR GRANDCHILDREN
LIKE PARENTHESES AROUND THIS BOOK

The incidents depicted in this book are entirely real and occurred just as they are described here. The events were recorded by the author as they happened. All dates, places, quotations and attributions are as accurate as possible.

Many of the individuals featured in this book read the author's first draft as it was being written, during their common tour of duty in Basic Combat Training. The reactions were varied, but in no instance was any objection ever raised to the journalistic purpose, accuracy, intention or substance of the work.

The names of all of the characters and their unit identifications have been altered to preserve civilian privacy and because some individuals are less innocent than others.

When a recruit arrives he is plunged into an alien environment, and is enveloped in a situation without relief. He is stunned, dazed and frightened. The severity of shock is reflected in 17-hydroxycorticosteroid levels comparable to those in schizophrenic patients in incipient psychosis and which exceeds levels in other stressful situations. The recruit receives little, or erroneous, in-formation about what to expect, which tends to maintain his anxiety. . . . Basic Training is unique in American society.

> ---Peter B. Bourne, "Some Observations on the Psychosocial Phenomena Seen in Basic Training," *Psychiatry*, XXX, No. 2 (1967), 187-196.

I urge you all to take notes. They will come in very handy later, even if you don't understand them now

> -Colonel Lawrence F. Thorne, Commanding Officer, --------- Basic Combat Training Brigade, May 12, 1969.

v

vi

CONTENTS

PROLOGUE

THE ESCHATON, I learned after four years of forgetting it on exams, is "the end of time." It refers to the closing of one historical cycle and the beginning of another through an apocalyptic event, such as the intervention of God in human history. So much for everything I learned in college.

Everything I learned in high school: a body at rest tends to stay at rest unless acted upon by an outside force. My body was usually kept from resting by parental force.

I was resting comfortably, confident of my immortality and supported by the notion that I still had time before I would have to take myself seriously, I still had exhibition games before the regular season began, still had time to be nothing before that awful day when I would have to "be something."

And while I was trying to learn the word "Eschaton" I fought the holy wars of adolescence as editor of a college humor magazine and a soldier in a noble political battle for the right to have women in dormitory bedrooms, always presuming reality to be largely irrelevant to my existence. But reality and the expiration of my automatic student draft deferment were beginning to overtake me.

Thus I found myself on a cold and greasy floor in an abandoned kitchen at Fort Totten, Long Island, with two dozen other

Army Reservists, trying to make sense out of what we were being told by a sergeant.

"All right, you mens, listen up", he shouted in the silent room, his words reverberating painfully from the tiled walls and floor. He read off a list of serial numbers--ER10910529--46. Mine was the last number.

"You will all be reporting to Fort Bliss, Texas, in sixteen days to begin ACK-DUE-TRAH."

"What's ACK-DUE-TRAH, sergeant?"

"Active Duty for Training. ACDUTRA, troop."

"How long is it?"

"Six months. If there is no more stupid questions we'll start filling out forms."

"Sergeant, do you know what the Eschaton is?"

"No, troop, and if it isn't part of the Army, I don't care."

Despite his lack of interest, I saw my entrance into the Army as a personal Eschaton. My time was ending. There would be no more watersheds before the rest of my life began. My virginity, such as it was, immunity, such as it was imagined, and invulnerability, as they used to say in Superman comics, had been lost.

I contemplated a cross-country jaunt I had planned with a girl I had met in Southern California--scratched. I contemplated my fetal career in newspaper journalism--postponed. I contemplated suicide--rejected.

Instead I flew to California, to wander from Mexico to Vancouver for two weeks, searching for a clue to my evaporating past, looking for some solid evidence of freedom to remind me who I was--and that I was young--when the Army wanted me to forget.

They sent me out to Fort Hamilton, in Brooklyn, on my last civilian day to pick up a ticket to El Paso, Texas, and I got there ten minutes before the place closed. I was given a talking to by the WAC who ran the ticketing section. Such breezy comings and goings were un-Army, she told me. I should have been there earlier so that I could wait a few hours, which *was* Army. I was carrying a briefcase and wearing a suit, and gave the impression that I had a poor attitude, that I was in the service of another master--myself. I acted, she told me, as if I were picking up theater tickets. I was, I like to think, and thanked her for the metaphor. She yelled at me for being a lowling with pretensions of individuality, and I gave one last protestation of my disintegrating civilian dignity: "Not yet, lady."

"That's 'Sergeant.'"

"That's 'lady,' lady. I'm not one of your little beasts yet. I'm still me. I'm here for my ticket, that's all. If you don't want to give it to me, it's your decision, not mine.

When they mustered me out a few months later I was the last to be ticketed, because an Army clerk felt that I had the wrong attitude--exactly the same as his: hatred of the Army. He told me that an attitude like mine would make getting along in the outside world very difficult. The WAC at Fort Hamilton had said the same thing about getting along in the Army.

All this was happening to me because there is this war, somewhere in the Far East, and the world gives you a limited number of alternatives for dealing with it. You can hit the trail for Canada and never look back. You can go to jail for your moral reservations and let buggerers and car thieves beat up on you for being less decent than they. Or you can do what a fellow I know did: actively protest it all by lying down in front of a troop ship. And if you don't drown, you can go to jail for "interfering with the workings of the Defense Department"--which is an overstatement if I ever heard one. Or you can go the pink-panties route, or scribble on your induction notice "deceased." Or you can try for a deferment as a conscientious objector, if at age three you started keeping carbons of letters you've written to random clergymen about how terrible war is, and can communicate the problems of "existentially coming to grips with transcendent values" in terms that your draft board can understand and appreciate. Or you can be lucky enough to be born with an incapacitating handicap. I tried putting in for a medical deferment on the basis of a jaundiced abdomen, weak vertebrae, wobbly knees and a markedly poor history of relations with authority. I submitted my junior high school detention record as corroboration--to no avail. And so my decision became: in or out. And there was no way out that I could live with and no way in but compromise.

There is a middle road, said Gautama Buddha, between pleasure and pain, so I sought the middle road of the six months' Reserves. To qualify for the other kind of weekend war-making, the National Guard, it helps to have a) political connections, b) minority-group status-but only in the three months immediately following a ghetto massacre, or c) a great desire to smack your fellow citizens around and clean up after sewer strikes.

The Marines have Reserves, but you have to be able to swallow the Marines to join. The Navy and Air Force have Reserves, but their initial active-duty hitch is unconscionably long. The Coast Guard has Reserves, but God only knows how to get in. I think you have to be born into it. But the Army. Ah, the Army Reserve.

Like the hottest places in Dante's hell, it specializes in accommodating those who in times of moral crisis preserved their neutrality. They offer you a better shot at staying alive than anyone else, for a pretty cheap price. All you pledge is six months of active duty in a dull but safe U. S. Army base and two weeks of annual summer training for six years, both of which are tolerable, given the alternatives. What *is* dear is the liberty also bargained away. For six years you must remain available in case your body is needed to plug a hole. And once a month for a weekend, or one day every two weeks, or one evening a week-- or variations on that theme--you must don the green, shine your brass, polish your boots and present your ass. There, men who get their charge by ordering other men around will order you, threaten you and make sure you have a haircut--all of which keeps us free from the atheistic Communists. Not much more goes on.

And so one January morning, stoned perhaps, and certainly reluctant, I did the deed. I took the oath. But I might easily have not It was a toss-up to the wire. Faced with unacceptable alternatives, I could make no choice. The moral question could only be answered satisfactorily, I thought, by mortifying the flesh in Canada or in prison, and I didn't have the stuff for such martyrdom. The physical question, I feared, was too great to leave to logic, itself the servant of conclusions demanded by the gut. If I was to lose a leg or my life, it would not be for faulty logic. That would be too much to take. So I decided, as Beau Geste might have, to do it all for love: to stop my girl friend from crying. My parents, convinced I was crazy, didn't care why, so long as I joined the Reserves; to remain immobile by dint of existential confusion is, in our day, to get drafted.

I mumbled the oath, and a Reserve major, who was, in his secret identity, a guidance counselor in a New Jersey junior high school, said "you in the red tie, you plan to join us?" And I said "I do," but I didn't really think I did; not all that allegiance I swore to a policy and a President I would have preferred to fight; not all that fealty to the Joint Chiefs of Staff and Secretaries of Defense and Army. But he told me "congratulations" and I knew that it was too late. The devil had made his contract.

Once my father was in a war, and time and again I had imagined myself, like Telemachus, awaiting the day that I could prove my manhood through that same trial of fire. I learned of his war--he rarely spoke of it himself--through the movies that it spawned. They always ended with the sweet, sad scene of Johnny coming home from the hill. He would lay his duffle gently down and kiss his ma and girl and say, "Well, I'm home." But, you know, it is not like that any more, and maybe never was. Yet in my childhood such was the moment of manhood. Now I wonder.

I wondered too about the country I live in. I went west with Gene McCarthy to save a nation, but it didn't want to be saved -- not by me. I went to Coronado to see the military expose itself at the *Pueblo* trial, and learned of the smug, insular world the military has constructed.

I was aware that citizenship wasn't enough, that something in my blood, or perhaps in my father's, has made it necessary to earn the full membership in the club that should be mine by birthright. It is not a knowledge of things or even a series of deeds that entitles you to feel American. You have to feel the rhythm in your blood. Feel it strongly enough to detect its absence in others. You can memorize the baseball statistics and brush with the right toothpaste and live a childhood like Dick and Jane's. But I knew that the Cub Scout manual was not written for me, and that they would never interview my mother corning out of a supermarket, never have my father on "This Is Your Life." "It Could Be You," I knew, could never be me. I didn't live in Orlando, Florida, or Columbus, Ohio, or anywhere in Indiana, I lived in a foreign country called New York City and had a nose and a religion that would never let me be President.

In the land of the free we fight first for our individual freedom--or so they taught us in the second grade--and now I had bargained even that away. And I was trapped by circumstance between two other sirens. I must confess that I have edged in my life toward the American frame of mind and out of the New York provincialism. But now I had married myself to boys and men whom, for the most part, I had left the Bronx, the city, and my childhood to avoid. And that Americanness with which I had flirted, setting me slightly apart from the other Reservists at Fort Totten, was about to be inflicted on us all full force. I wanted to stay alive, so I joined the Reserves; but I wanted, unconsciously perhaps, to show the Army I wasn't just some candy-assed New York Reservist, to show the Reservists that I was an American, to show the *Americans* that I was an American. Yet to the Army we were all New Yorkers. Us and Them.

Despite having sponsored the compromise, my parents saw even this mild militarization as a tragedy, but a far milder one than jail or Canada, and I began to agree. As we waited at Kennedy Airport for the El Paso jet that would take me to the Army they ordered a massive dinner. I ordered three drinks. The boys at the next table, already in uniform, were smoking grass. My flight was called and I got up, acting manfully, telling Mom and the niece and nephews not to bother. But my father insisted on walking me. It is the ultimate imperative of fatherhood to put the boy on the plane, so I let him do it, because it gave a little order to a silly scene.

And there we were on our way to the Army, like the characters in the history they taught us, called from our farms to serve the American nation as it fought for its birth, called again to put down the savages, recalled to protect the fleet from British privateers, called to preserve the Union, called to start an empire, called to make the world safe for democracy, called to destroy evil incarnate, called to repel the aggressors. They went, never willingly but out of some notion of citizenship, or patriotism, or indifference. And I went because they had outbid me and made the price of resistance too high. To rationalize it all, I concentrated on the thought that maybe, just maybe, there's truth to the notion that to be effective in changing the course of the future one cannot avoid the common experience of one's generation. I'd done the antiwar thing, the drug thing, the student radical thing. But it had taught me not a thing about anything but where my own head was at, and nothing about the great gray landmass beyond the Hudson. I had traveled the American People's roads and eaten in their diners, and now, on a bad bet, I was off to see the farthest outpost of their common culture.

And I decided then that it was worth keeping my "faculties intact." So somewhere over the heartland, west of the Hudson, five miles in the air, trying to become an American and trying to remain free in the United States Army, I began to take notes.

THE RECEPTION CENTER:

Basic Bliss

ABANDON ALL HOPE

Secure in its sterility, the giant American Airlines 707, bound for El Paso with its cargo of Americans and its load of egos destined for the assembly line at Fort Bliss, sweeps into the air space over Texas, near the speed of sound, but silently. As further insulation against the un-American debilitations of sensation, each passenger has his own earphones transmitting anesthetic Muzak.

The music is strangely midwestern, but fully American. The faces I see are Texan, New Mexican, southwestern. People I know don't wear faces like these. But there are people I know sitting all around me on this plane--twenty Reservists from New York, scattered about the plane in groups of twos and threes as if they are trying to deny the larger kinship that our common association on a mimeographed sheet of orders commands. And even these people I know seem distant. We are all New Yorkers, and for what it may mean, a dozen Jews, one black, a few Italians, a few Irish and a few who escape neat categorization. All twenty are from New York, largely middle class, nearly all college graduates, with a common dislike of the draft-tempered by the New Yorker's trait of bargaining with fate and the future to "get a better deal." Some are accountants, some are in law, a few in real estate, a handful in business and finance, three or four in graduate school, a journalist and an advertising copywriter, and a majority who know who they are only by knowing what they don't want to be. They are all from the boroughs of Brooklyn and Queens, and I am from Manhattan by way of the Bronx, a distinction which is only significant east of the Hudson, if at all. I feel very apart right now--from everyone--and I am trying to find the reasons.

We are all bound for Army Bliss, in El Paso, to spend eight weeks in Basic Combat Training becoming soldiers, and from time to time I make a foray into their midst to listen to their talk. Some are wearing the incomplete pieces of their just-issued uniforms, impatient to begin their Americanization. Stories are swapped about the torturing and maiming of their friends who have "been in" already. Like campfire horror stories, they scare the tellers more than the listeners. The nervous laughter increases, until the plane rolls to a stop and it is replaced by bug-eyed silence.

THE RECEPTION CENTER

Rolling through the gates of Fort Bliss, I get a sense of beginning, like stepping through the looking glass and noting the frame. There is no depth.

We begin filling out forms at 1 A.M. and finish at five. We are each given two form letters to send home in prestamped envelopes, announcing our arrival to our no-doubt worried parents. I send them off to two friends, with a peace symbol drawn over the mimeographed message.

The Army lets us sleep until noon, and a false sense of security begins to grow among us. The next day is all forms and orientation. The food is good, the regimentation mild, the sense foreboding.

THE SCALDED TRACHEA AND THE CLEAN TOOTH
AS WEAPONS OF WAR

We learn how to have coffee and ice cream in a lunch hour that is three minutes long. You take equal measures of coffee and ice cream and toss them, in quick sequence, down your gullet, so that they can moderate each other.

Our first evening as soldiers is devoted to the science of brushing the teeth. We are given a lecture by a captain who shows us a film on the vertical, or "the up-and-down," method. Without any sense of irony, or even awareness, he proceeds to demonstrate the back and forth method. We are all seated at tables facing each other, practicing what we have just learned with a free, disposable toothbrush, a ration of one squiggle of toothpaste and a small paper cup filled with water. Each desk has been covered with a paper towel so that nothing will dribble onto it, and we are each given a large paper cup to spit into. Soon the giggles begin to reign, and spittle and toothpaste drip down the chins and onto the shirts of the men. Whole mouthfuls are shot forward as convulsive laughter pries clamped teeth open. A corporal walks around the room taking the name of anyone who has dripped onto a desk.

We are mysteriously marched in and out of the same class-room three times--a maneuver that gives me the distinct impression that no one is in charge, that we are ruled only by a vague sense of authority.

We are shown a film on the evils of AWOL, featuring Good Joe and AWOL Johnny "who couldn't take his mind off a little girl back home." I am not convinced that he *should* take his mind off her. Good Joe is a good soldier: clean, upright, brave, obedient--and stupid. Very convinced that you ought to behave well in the Army, because, well, you ought to behave well in the Army. Besides, the people who run the Army are good, intelligent, wise American leaders. Johnny is a sharp character. His politics don't quite come through, but for whatever reasons, he has little use for the Army, is a bit of a wise guy, and seems to think he has better things to do with his time than clean a rifle. He is obviously the kind of kid your parents didn't want you to play with, because he wants things to make sense and doesn't like to do things that have either a high boredom quotient or a low survival rate. The Army wants Johnny about as much as he wants it, but it's got him, and the way it deals with people who don't like it is to make life miserable for them. The logic is simple: It's a privilege to serve; if you don't want to serve, we'll make sure with even greater certainty that you do; if you still don't want to, we'll beat the crap out of you until you "change your attitude" and love us, maybe just a little.

So Johnny, driven to the brink by eminent good sense, goes over the wall. Those of us watching him support him with lusty cheers: "Go, Johnny baby. All the way. Make it, boy." The officer in charge of the indoctrination film snaps on the lights and growls at us.

When the film continues we find out that Johnny goes AWOL about four or five times and spends the larger part of his young adult years breaking rocks. He is repeatedly given new chances to learn to love the Army and consistently blows them.

He is finally awarded an Undesirable Discharge and discovers that he can't get a job because the outside world takes the Army as seriously as the Army takes itself. Johnny--and please make a note of *this--reapplies* to the Army to gain enough "good time" for an Honorable Discharge or at least a combat wound. But the Army declines the offer, content to have him pay for his crimes not only through the Army's own punishment but now through eternal damnation.

And so Johnny naturally winds up a drunk.

Good Joe meanwhile has spent his time policing up cigarette butts with patriotic fervor and is rewarded with an Honorable Discharge and the civilian rank of obnoxious clean kid. His evenings are spent playing checkers with Dad, sitting around the house in a starched shirt and a cardigan sweater, awaiting what he knows is sure to come: Johnny's nightly call for bail money.

Let it be a lesson to you.

WATCH ON THE RINDS

We are marched back to the barracks to mull over the indoctrination films we have seen, and the lights are snapped out at 8.45, but the talking doesn't stop until midnight, because we are sleeping sixty in a room, Texan and New Yorker, and we don't really know who each other is, although we know who we are and where we may be going. The Reservists, twenty of us, will spend six months in the Army and go back to New York. The other forty, mostly Texans and southerners, the Americans, drafted or enlisted, face uncertainty and perhaps Vietnam. We trade our boasts about money and power, tell about our subways and snow storms, our muggings and skyscrapers for their stories about what it's like to live in a world of trucks and cattle. There is some derisive laughter. I just listen.

I wake up nearly garroted by my dog-tag chain, which dangles from my neck, and in my groping sleep has wrapped itself around my arm.

I am assigned to walk fire guard, to make sure that none of the new recruits smokes in bed and burns down this week's shipment of flesh before the Army can systematically melt it down. This entails an hour of strolling around the barracks, and aside from the mental charge one gets out of being on night watch while others are asleep--a stimulant not to be belittled--it also gives me a chance to explore the barracks and compare them with the only other ones I've seen--Sergeant Bilko's.

We fall out at 3:30 A.M. Some of the new recruits, Reservists who have been to meetings, have pieces of uniforms that have been issued by their home units, and in their rush to look like true troopers, put them on, and look, instead, like the German Army in retreat. We are introduced to Specialist 4 Douglas, a returned Vietnam veteran, who looks clean and all-American. He wears a shiny helmet liner pulled down over his eyes, like a grenadier's hat, and a tailored, neatly starched uniform. Specialist Douglas needs a few men to march at the head of the platoon for a few days, and a few Reservists, itching to get a small junior-leadership position, volunteer that they have had previous military experience. One is chosen to be "platoon leader" and immediately begins to believe he is a General. At odd moments he calls urgent meetings of the platoon to discuss our "mission"--to march to the infirmary to get shots--and give us a brief pep talk. Or he finds it necessary to have a "conference" with Specialist 4 Douglas about "the men," who worry him. The other junior leaders begin to shirk all duties, such as helping clean up, under the general rationale that they are "unbecoming to a leader."

Lights out at 8:45 P.M.

Lights on at 4:00 A.M.

WHERE I LIVED AND WHAT I LIVED FOR

We're here in a place called a Reception Center because the Army knows that it is well advised not to thrust us raw into the meat factory. We have to be softened up a bit first. So we spend three days in a pleasant, clean, Spanish-looking concentration camp, like rats being exposed to a psychologist's maze for the first time: sniffing around, checking to make sure that it's non-lethal, building our illusions and rationalizations until we are ready to cooperate and they can lower the boom.

The Army's processing procedures are remarkably efficient, which is as it should be after nearly two hundred years of trying. Not to say that anything is accomplished, just that we are herded from place to place with great speed. Aside from a general sense of imprisonment, the atmosphere is otherwise pleasant. So pleasant that it hangs like a bad lie. Everything is too easy.

For reasons that have only a little to do with anti-Vietnam politics, I like my hair. It does nice things for my face. It is straight and clean and fine and spills around my ears and curls onto my collar. I can shake my head and feel it swirl in a downbeat rhythm; I can toss it back with a shake of my head. But among the things that my hair also does is drive the Army nuts.

I am standing on line with fifty hairy recruits ready to be shorn, None of us needs delousing, so the Army's glib reply that the baldy as a health measure is insufficient. Shaving the head is simply one of the fastest ways of separating a human from his civilian identity. We are shot forward in waves toward waiting Mexican barbers, who grin sadistically. In twenty seconds all of the hair on my head is removed.

I am photographed, fingerprinted, shot full of vaccinations, fitted for a uniform, and am beginning to forget who really owns my body.

KID McDONALD

I get into a nearly violent fight about Vietnam with a seventeen-year-old redheaded enlistee named Billie McDonald. Young McDonald, as full of his years as I am mine, pale of face, fresh of cheek, freckled and breakfast-cereal-ad cute, insists that Vietnam is where we ought to be lest we have to fight the Reds in California next week. I stifle a dozen jokes about which parts of California are worth defending and, instead, quote Walter Lippmann: "That theory is a scurrilous insult to the United States Navy." Strategic mistake. McDonald doesn't know who Lippmann is, and no one else does either, but the reference sounds snotty. McDonald offers that Nam is good for the economy. Where do I begin? It's no use arguing economics with him or trying to recite the "plight of the cities" litany to Texans. An opening emerges when he offers that a good healthy war keeps the population down. I suggest disease as a less expensive alternative, but he doesn't appreciate sarcasm.

I am asked why I don't take off my uniform and go to Canada if I don't think that America has the right to fight whomever the hell she wants without having to take a lot of crap from her goddamned citizens. I suggest that I wear my country's uniform because that's what a good citizen does, but a good citizen who loves his country needn't stand by silently when his country does something stupid. A good citizen kicks and screams and doesn't let it get away with being less than it can be.

Some of McDonald's friends object to my assertion that there are some things one should be willing to die for and some things that one should not. I discover, as lines begin to form between the Pinks and Red-White-and-Blues, that among the things I'm not willing to die for is--principle.

THE CHRISTIANS ARE INTRODUCED TO THE LIONS

Our at-bat drawing near, we leave the on-deck circle of the Reception Center and are marched to a parade field, where we observe a group of recruits--they are called a "class," or a "cycle," as one cycle comes in and goes out eight weeks later, while seven more cycles come in in the meantime--that is "graduating" from Basic Combat Training this day. They look oddly purposeful, in step, and serious. Someone nudges me and asks, "Don't they look sharp?"

After the parade we are turned over to our new captors, and I begin to get the sense that things are as bad as we imagined they would be. We are seated in rows, on our duffle bags, preparatory to a short bus ride to our new "homes," listening to a sergeant bark for several minutes in an "Oh-boy-do-you-ever-deserve-what-you're-going-to-get-for-having-been-born-civilians" monologue. Eight weeks of this lies in store.

He turns to greet two drill sergeants, who are dressed in khakis and wear the drill sergeant's Smokey-the-Bear campaign hat. They all jolly for a few moments about how we're going to get the shit kicked out of us. I see a horrifying vision of running the high hurdles or a steeplechase, with a drill sergeant bearing down on me from behind as I lag asthmatically, kicking me when I slow up. How does he keep up the pace?

In appearance the two drill sergeants are a study in opposites.

The larger of the two is Drill Sergeant Dave Wilson, a huge, bronzed blond with a linebacker's build and close-cropped hair. He slowly removes his sunglasses and his hat--with the air of a man taking off his jacket to give a beating to a cripple. I suck in my breath with awe. Now he is fingering a pair of wire-rimmed glasses as if, I imagine, they are all that is left of a peacenik he has devoured. He tries to put them on, and then grins madly, his teeth on edge.

The other one, apparently Wilson's superior, is a short cherubic-faced Negro named Field First Drill Sergeant Tom Rawlins, who has a soft voice, but who speaks even more vividly about the tortures awaiting us.

I am trying to figure out what they stand for. Does Rawlins drive himself and his men harder to show the white sergeants that he is just as big and tough and American as they? Does Wilson, who appears to be the archetypal California Golden Kid, ride herd on the easterners because he is confident of his Americanness? Who would kick harder as they chased me over the hurdles? I decide that you could, with a smile and a twinkle, make Rawlins unconsciously aware that you are on his side, a co-conspirator in his efforts to prove his manhood; let him know that you accept him and that he doesn't have to prove anything to you. But Wilson would have to be talked to. You would have to let him know that you don't like Pinkos or college kids, that you like California and that you too hate things that you can't figure out. But you would have to talk to him, and you might not get him to stop kicking you before you could get a word in.

Our names are called off and we are loaded onto cattle trucks for a half-mile ride to our new home, the side of a mountain called Logan Heights, where we will live for eight weeks in Basic Combat Training. I begin to feel what I sensed was the common feeling among the Reception Center cadre: there is no world beyond the Army, no Army beyond basic training, no time beyond now.

THE FIRST WEEK:

Basic Combat Training--the Real Thing

WE arrive on Logan Heights, home of Charlie Company, in which we will undergo Basic Combat Training, after lunch on Friday, get called to attention by a waiting group of sergeants, get screamed at for nothing, hear "at ease" after an hour and are successfully terrorized.

I am standing behind my duffle bag, every muscle squeezing desperately, hoping that the new sheets I have just been issued don't slip off the top of my bag. If they do, I will be the first one to call attention to himself in a group of people all trying to petrify themselves into anonymity.

Another company pants by, running in step as a drill sergeant calls cadence. They have sweated through their tee-shirts, and their heads bob as they run. Twenty yards behind them a whale of a recruit stumbles forward, lurching to keep up, falling further behind. On his tail is a small, slight drill sergeant with wiry muscles that bulge through his tee-shirt; he looks like every hood I've ever known. The fat boy runs a jagged route, spinning to his right and his left as he goes, his head lolling from side to side, drooling and wearing an expression of imminent death. From time to time he closes his eyes, as if to pray for a merciful tumble.

Fifty yards past us he falls. We can hear the sergeant yelling at him as he wallows on the ground, "Git up ya' fat muhfuh, git yo ass off the floor." But the fat boy, who must weigh what two of us do, just lies there. The sergeant yells some more and tries to pull him up. The next thing we hear is a scream. The sergeant is standing over the fallen boy and is kicking him in the stomach and backside, sometimes prodding, sometimes letting go with a field-goal kick. Screaming sobs fill the air, wails of torture and pain. The sergeant takes off his pistol belt and begins to whip his prey. The boy holds up his hands to protect his face and the sergeant kicks them away. The boy pleads, then cries and screams for the sergeant to stop, but the sergeant keeps beating him. He screams a curse at the sergeant, who kicks him in the ass for it. The sergeant drags him to his feet, and he goes, being pushed, no longer screaming.

After they shaved our heads at the Reception Center they deloused us further by having us mail home all our civilian clothes, obscene magazines, guns, and knives longer than three inches. I managed to keep a copy of *Existential Man*. Now, having witnessed my first beating, I am looking out from the inside of my velvet-smooth skull, imagining myself as I once was, in a coat and tie, with hair and power. But I no longer feel the weight of my hair, and I can look down and see my fatigues and boots. And as the fat boy's screams fade, I sense a loss of power.

We are assigned bunks, settle in, get rearrangement assignments, resettle, and at midnight, the middle of our night, get roused to pack and move again.

A drill sergeant, walking guard in the middle of the night, wakes me to tell me that my head is not in line with the feet in the next bunk and that I am violating the sleeping regulations. He picks up my mattress and rotates it until I am facing the right way.

The next morning we spend three hours filling out information cards that I am sure will never be used. We are asked whether we have ever sung in a glee club, what sports we like, what our hobbies are, and what we do for a living. Like the cards that asked us what organizations we belong to, they can only hurt you. If you say "church group," nothing happens. If you say "SDS," they beat up on you. If you say "Center for the Study of Democratic Institutions," they question you for security.

The weekend passes with nothing more than heavy exercise, seemingly pointless work and only a few minor brutalities. No one is killed. No one strikes back. Lots of spit and polish gets applied to anything that will take it.

TIME WARP

The most striking feature of Logan Heights is time. It doesn't seem to flow here as in the real world. It stands still until something happens, and then much of it is past. Events do not seem to build and develop, but instead, explode and disappear. Personalities surface like shooting-gallery bears: they pop up, get shot and fall down. In the life I have just left they glide along like the gallery ducks until they get shot or fall over the edge.

GETTING "ORIENTATED"

We are welcomed to the ranks of men by Colonel Lawrence F. Thorne, who commands the brigade, looks like Eichmann and sounds like a scoutmaster. He is to deliver the Great Orientation Lecture, and we are to give him, in grateful appreciation, before the fact, great homage. Prior to his arrival we are told to stand when the band plays the Colonel's fanfare. A trumpeter coughs through his mouthpiece and two thousand men leap to their feet, realize their mistake and sit down as the band begins the fanfare. Half the men jump up, see the rest still sitting and jump back down; random groups leap up, and leap down. Confusion dampens the effect of martial order as cries and counter cries of "Hey, stand up, stupid," "No, wait till he gets here," "He is here," "Are we up or down?" "What are we supposed to do?" greet the Colonel on his entrance.

"Thank you, men, you looked pretty sharp there," says the Colonel. An aide leans into the microphone and says "Taaaake *seats,"* cracking the word "seats" like a whip. I guess we are supposed to leap down as we are supposed to leap up, diving for the seats like foxholes, but the men turn lackadaisically around, put their seats down and settle into them over a period of about ten seconds.

"Ten-hut." We rise, in batches. No good. Again. Better.

"Take . . . . .*seats"--and* after three tries we do it as it is designed to be done—"smartly, men, smartly."

Colonel Thorne speaks, as four others have done this weekend, on the folly of AWOL. The other warnings came on separate occasions, three after we had learned that men had gone AWOL, and one after we had heard that one had slit his wrists.

Thorne tells us about the need for teamwork and discipline. He cites the New York Jets and how well disciplined they were as my mind flashes to Broadway Joe's revelations on how he trained the night before the Super Bowl with a bottle and a girl. Thorne doesn't seem to be able to end his speech and is heading for a painfully long fade-out when he suddenly takes an abrupt step back from the mike and sits down. Half the men leap to their feet. Half applaud.

A guest lecturer from the local YMCA invites us down. He shows us slides of the facilities they have, including a game room constructed by local boys, with materials, he says, that were stolen from construction sites of private homes. He discloses this with an inflection that says, "Heh, heh, heh, isn't that wonderful how resourceful boys are? Boys will be boys-- they'll be on our board of directors someday."

A Catholic chaplain talks about the "wholesome and creative activities offered at the *Y,"* offers to baptize any of us, and tells us how fortunate we are to be sitting where we are, for reasons that escape me the moment they are spoken.

A Protestant chaplain talks, interminably, and then, like a cheerleader for the Army, teaches us the "Caisson Song." We sing it about ten times, until it can be stood no longer, and he mercifully ends it.

A rabbi fails to show up.

Four more officers warn us of the dangers of AWOL. One mentions the name of the avenue we must cross to be AWOL--it is called Dyre; but the irony seems lost on the officers.

Colonel Thorne rams himself at the microphone again and gives a short "Count on me" statement. "Let's be pals, troops," he says as he bursts off the stage like Batman. We leap almost to our feet when Lieutenant Colonel James Treandley assumes command of the show and sits us back down. As we sit he barks, "Ten-hut." Up. "Take   *seats."* Down. "As you were, men."

Treandley introduces himself: he is the Battalion Commander, and, in our lives, God--unless Colonel Thorne is around, at which point he becomes only Gabriel.

Lieutenant Colonel Treandley becomes the third person to tell us that Treandley is spelled like "'friendly' with a t," making three people who spell "friendly" "freandley." He shares the intelligence with us that "this is the best battalion in the U.S. Army."

And with that, he concludes, " you are orientated"

MONDAY AFTERNOON AT THE PROPAGANDIST'S

The Army's cinematic explanation of the drug scene seems to have replaced the traditional venereal-disease slides. No more full-color blowups of infected genitalia before lunch. No indeed. Sex is out, because drugs are farther out. *Trip to Where?,* a film about LSD, begins with a Russian roulette game which ends with a gun actually being fired at some poor acid head's head. That'll shake 'em up, General," I can hear the jodhpured studio man say. We settle down to a half hour of freaky music and light-show effects, which the movie tries to imply are horrific. The fatigue-clad audience begins to groove on the welcome vibrations; the soldier next to me whispers that he has been stoned since he took the oath a week ago, and has three days' supply left On the screen an LSD freak-out party leads to an obvious *sexual* liaison between Good Joe and Clean Suzie, bringing lusty cheers from the audience. The announcer, who has remained silent for a half hour, breaks in to tell us that "you are beginning to see the dangers of LSD-now let's look at the medical facts." The main danger he has in mind, it seems, is Sex. Someone is always forgetting to pass the word to the Pentagon.

After intermission another film, starring Sonny Bono, of Sonny and Cher--looking pretty stoned--discusses pot. Am I supposed to believe that he is against it when in his day he freaked out more fifteen-year-old girls from afar by his manner than anyone but Mick Jagger? Sonny comes clad in a traditional bearskin vest over a simple polo shirt and seems to be having some difficulty focusing his eyes. Entire affair has the vague sense of those "Hi, I'm Hugh O'Brian for the Heart Fund" ads-- earnest and stultifying. The action in this film is at another party, and as the kids shake their fannies in some 1950's jitterbug they toss off the common "myths" about inhaling *Cannabis sativa* vapors. But before the film can rebut the assertions the lights get snapped on again because the entire brigade has to get up to march somewhere and stand for a half hour doing nothing.

After lunch we watch two hours of gore and glory, which in- spire me less than the drug flicks. An instructor, at the end of a film on the Army's role in American history, asks why the Civil War was important, and calls on a southerner, who replies in terms of tactics, supplies and maneuvers.

"The history of American liberty is written in red on its en- emies," proclaims a film. We are told the story of the "screaming eagle," a mascot taken into battle during the Spanish-American War. Fifteen minutes of questions follow: "How did they feed it?" "Did it live in a cage?" Like the third grade at the zoo.

TO VIETNAM, PRO PATRIA

Private Doby is a six-foot-four-inch, skinny, shy, nearly illiter- ate rural Louisiana Negro. He has been in the Job Corps, he has been in three separate federal programs designed to push him toward a survival-level literacy, and now he is in the Army. He has been summoned under a McNamara brainstorm called Project 100,000. Each year the Army rejects approximately 100,000 men who have not come up to the military's mental or physical standards, but now they draft them anyway and try to give them some training to bring them up to a useful level.

Private Doby cannot read or write yet, but he is testimony to the Army's facility for doing whatever it wants whenever it gets a chance. Despite the money it has been given to train Doby in the rudiments of civilization, such as reading, counting and printing his name, the Army has simply thrust Doby in with the rest of us and said, "He's your responsibility, boys." They no doubt have spent the money on public relations.

There is something about Private Doby that draws me to him. He is large and smooth-skinned, radiating beauty and gentility. He seems to feel no animus, no bitterness at his lot, no hatred and no suffering. He just does what he has to do and is at peace with the future. He is not, for all his lack of education, stupid. His speech is slow and lyrical; his images are pungent and earthy.

Private Doby asks the sergeant, with an unsarcastic honesty and simplicity that only he seems capable of making believable, if, as the sergeant says, we have never lost a war, how come we haven't won in Vietnam yet. The sergeant offers that we are try-ing to "fight a polite war."

Across the aisle is Private Martinez, a tall, skinny Mexican with a perpetually dirty face and a daffy smile that gives him a beclouded look. He is missing two upper left front teeth, and, together with his preposterously protuberant ears and GI haircut, looks like a cross between a tall Mexican hairless dog and a swarthy Alfred E. Neuman. He rises to ask a question, and, seemingly aware that he is ridiculous, grins all the way up, looking around, as the laughter begins. "Sir, Private Mar-tee-nez," he announces in a central-casting Mexican accent; he is an extra in the American Life movie.

Gales of laughter make him grin more widely, and he tries

again. "Sir, Private Mar-tee-nez. When I sign the paper I ask the man that, and he say that the reason is they are using Chinese tanks. Is that true? He tell me it was." In the midst of the roomful of guffaws the sergeant answers that, yes, it is true.

Private Martinez seems to see the Army as a strange privilege he is being allowed to partake of good clothing, good food, fresh air, equality. He is a Mexican national, I am told. He lives in a border town in Texas and was drafted.

When the "Greetings from the President of the United States" came to Private Martinez he knew what the next episode in his life was going to be. He didn't know the alternatives, and no one wanted to tell him.

ILLEGAL GRASS

I am racing along a parched patch of dust between two slivers of pavement when a sergeant screams at me, "Keep offa the grass!" I look around, bewildered. Anything not paved is grass.

CAHIERS DU CINEMA

Like everything else, our first taste of Basic Rifle Marksmanship is celluloid. We watch a film showing an actual bayoneting several times--slow motion, stop motion, and every way but from the inside out. The faces around me are wincing and turning away each time, missing what seems to me to be the finest antiwar movie that ever slipped by the Army.

During a less action-packed film, on the application of foot powder, Private Pepper falls asleep. He and a cohort, who aided and abetted by sitting next to Pepper without waking him, are forced to stand, then kneel, holding chairs over their heads, then outstretched in front of them. It is precisely the same torture described by the U.S.S. *Pueblo* crewmen as "inhuman," and its effect is the same in El Paso as it was in Korea. It is painful and senseless and makes the victims hate their captors more. Anyone who has taken a little behavioral psychology could tell you that it doesn't work either.

SHORT ARMS

A hygiene discussion turns to venereal disease. There are no slides. Many of the men look somewhat vacant as the lecturer discusses "veneral diseases" until he clarifies the subject by mentioning that they are also called "the clap," "the crud," "the crabs" and such. With recognition all around him, he becomes increasingly crude. His analysis of *how* the diseases are contracted is limited, geographically, to Juarez, Mexico. You just can't get them anywhere else. He looks embarrassed every time he makes a reference to male genitals. So he makes a few silly jokes and dwells more on female genitals and their uses. The main reason for avoiding VD is that "when you go home, you don't want to give it to your mom and dad, and brothers and sisters. You mens which are married, you don't want to give it to your wife and kids."

A lieutenant comes in and explains the symptoms of spinal *meningitis* to us, asking whether any of us have felt similar pains. Fort Bliss has just emerged from a scandalous near-epidemic of meningitis; scandalous because the hospital, in true military manner, told the first victim that he was a malingerer and sent him back to infect the other troops. Half of the room say that they feel the symptoms--general fatigue and headache. I detect a weakness in the Army's armor and note it for future reference.

WAR AND PEAS

I am assigned to serving duty in the mess hall and amuse myself by singing antiwar songs so that I don't lose my mind trying to concentrate on scrambled eggs. In some unconscious administrative burst of Joycean creativity, the mess-hall gods assign me to dishing out peas at lunch. I fill each tray with a "Peas be with you, brother," or point to the condiment rack, asking "Peas in our thyme?" Three people out of 1,500 laugh.

GUARDING THE PEACE IS A LONELY BATTLE

A trainee in his seventh week of basic training tells me that the most important thing in the world is a letter from home. Our company mail clerk is on duty one hour a day, after dinner. He reads the name on each letter, flings it skyward and lets it disappear into the swirling mob that clusters about him. Trainees away on KP and those who have gone to the after-dinner sick call, have to wait until the next day's hour; trainees in the hospital don't get their mail until they get out or until they have orders cut assigning them to the hospital. No one goes to the evening sick call any more. As I dive for a letter with my name on it, under the feet of reaching, clawing trainees, I begin to understand what it's like to be a hog at slop time.

THE DRILL SERGEANTS

The Army didn't have drill sergeants until the early 1960s. It had special instructors and platoon sergeants, but never cultivated the special brutalizing and demoralizing breed of sergeant that made the Marine Corps training famous. But now, complete with forest-ranger hat, special drill-instructor badge, and extraordinary prerogatives--'Yo' ass belongs to me, and only incidentally to the U.S. Army, when I'm tru wi' it,"--the Army has its own. And they are a study.

Our platoon's drill sergeant, Bill Razor, has been a drill instructor for six years. He has been to Nam and come back a hero, for what he claims was being "a crazier ass than anyone else." He is tough and wiry, about five-foot-six, and thirty years old. He has thin, sandy hair and wears an RAF mustache. He looks the way I imagine a Belgian mercenary would, and has a look in his eye that speaks of the soldier of fortune. He calls his wife "my 120-pound pussy." He looks as if he could, and might, kill you without thinking twice or blinking once.

Drill Sergeant Roger "Bronk" Conboy, assistant platoon sergeant to Razor, is twenty-two years old and also a Vietnam hero. He is a former hot rodder and rodeo rider, who drives around in a beat-up pickup truck. He still has the look and demeanor of a tough kid, but his toughness is softened somewhat by his fondness for screwing around. He was introduced to his wife by mail while he was in Vietnam. She was the sister of a friend of his, and they wrote each other while he was in the jungle. He married her a month after he got back. A month later he acquired a girl friend while hanging around an El Paso high school.

Blond, massive Dave Wilson, who greeted us all earlier, appears to be sadistic, constantly dropping his platoon for push-ups at random moments. I get the feeling that he thinks he is enhanced by his punishment of others. On guard duty in Vietnam he heard something moving in the bushes and fired. In the morning they found a goat with thirty-seven machine-gun bullet holes in it.

Drill Sergeant Harry Brown. He is huge. He is beefy. He is Mexican--no, Filipino. Or Korean. Maybe Japanese--maybe Chinese. He is scary. He swallows all of his words, so that his ordinary speech sounds like marching commands. All of the AWOLs and the rumored slit-wrists were from his platoon. If Wilson is a sadist, Brown is a maniac, and you can see his mania in the glint of his eye or the way he rolls his shoulders and expands his chest in slow, deep, sighing breaths. I finally learn that he is Hawaiian. His utter confidence and impenetrable toughness on top of his genetic indecipherability make him appear a living version of Oddjob.

Drill Sergeant Bill Robinson looks like a black Van Heflin, with a touch of James Earl Jones. He speaks in a deep, nearly unintelligible growl, and wears a constant frown. His motivation seems to be not the sadism that one detects in the other drill sergeants but a desire to produce "men," as he understands the term, by the best means he knows. He tries to be friendly and introduces each of his instruction periods with a joke. "Before I came in, my mom and dad were in iron and steel. My mom ironed and my father stealed."

Drill Sergeant Vernon Grbr, pronounced "Garber," likely lost all softness when the vowels fled his last name. He is mean and short, skinny and distempered, with eyes that seem to sit in the farthest recess of the skull. His eyebrows are stringy and matted, and with his sunken cheeks, they give him a wild look. He speaks in seven-word bursts, like a machine gun or a teletype. He looks like a hanged tomcat

THE EVENING BREEZE

I find four of my platoon mates crying themselves to sleep. Another is nabbed before he goes over the hill. One goes out to make a phone call and never comes back.

THROUGH A DOOR, HEAVILY

Seldom in an epoch does a figure come along who validates the myths that men live by. Churchill made the English believe their history. Hitler made the Germans believe their legends. Kennedy raised American rhetoric to the point where we believed the promises the past had made to us. Private Norman Peyser works in a more subtle way: he makes men believe in the myths and stereotypes they hold of others--like Stepin Fetchit. He is short, fat and sweaty, dark and ugly--a mole rules his nose- -without a trace of common sense or intellect. He is babyish and seems to have no sense of social grace. To the delight of the drill sergeants, he is a New York Brooklyn Jew and a perfect target for their animus. Were he just a little lovable, he would pass for Sergeant Bilko's Dwayne Doberman.

It is not just that Private Peyser is without muscles. He seems to be without bones as well. His skeletal structure is amorphous; his face formless, pasty and lumpy. He is a Pace College dropout who tells half the world that he is a Rutgers graduate--in the presence of the half that knows he isn't. He is a teller in a bank and calls himself "a banker." He cannot stand up straight. His uniform hangs like a sack as his pants slide down from his undefined waistline. Buttons fall off his uniform with determination, his belt comes loose and his laces untie. He stumbles, he trips, he never tries, and is already receiving relentless ridicule and punishment.

I get the sense that he is one of those poor souls, as we might all be, who doesn't understand the codes and gestures that are used in nonverbal communication. He seems to be moving out of phase, in imitation of life, like a man watching other people's feet while he dances, always one step off the beat, flinching from shadows. Simple things like walking through a doorway or bending down gracefully escape him. If I am trying to become an American--trying to pretend that I too feel the rhythms that make the Americans from Texas flow and feel as they do--and if the rest of us from New York are trying to be a little whiter, trying to become more Connecticutized and Manhattanized, then we must see Private Peyser as one who is still trying, unsuccessfully, to become what we are trying to leave. He is one step behind--the selves we might have been had we not been tempted to cross the River. He is the stereotyped middle-European Jew who is a stranger in his own country.

The simple life-tasks and survival lore escape him. We laughed, and knew that it was wrong, when he failed to tie a box with a piece of string. He watched the other men tie the boxes by drawing the string across itself, flipping the box over and pulling the string tight. But he was watching and not seeing, so he girdled the box and pulled the string and saw it fall limp. Again he tried, making a ninety-degree turn with the string, and was amazed, looking paranoid when it wouldn't pull tight for him. Four times without variation he tried this maneuver as the rest of the platoon burst into convulsive laughter. Sitting cross-legged on the floor, like a bewildered bullfrog, as tears of laughter rolled down the cheeks of the other trainees, he tried again and failed, until his own tears fell. "He's a comic genius," a trainee whispered to me. "No one could be that dumb." But he was and he had to be shown. And he had to be shown that the head of a bolt did not screw into the threads of a bore.

The first day in camp he broke his glasses, which bob on his nose, and had to wear a pair of space-man prescription sunglasses instead. But the teasing from the sergeants grew so great that Private Tommy Romini and I spent an hour rebuilding his other glasses with string and a pencil and aluminum foil. Within a day they had fallen under his feet and he had crushed the lenses.

For making no effort during physical training, for being grossly overweight, girlish and immature, for paying no attention, for being consistently out of step, for picking his nose, for being in a dimension removed from the rest of our reality, for having a fly that won't close, a bed that won't stay straight, boots that won't stay shined, for having flies buzz around his head like a sweaty horse, he is called "Piggy" and "Porky" by the drill sergeants--when he is not being called "Bitch." Drill Sergeant Razor has him spend each evening crawling on his belly in the low-crawl pit, a 40-yard sand trough that must be crawled on the stomach in 30 seconds.

He collapses, crying, his second night in the pit.

He shouldn't have to be in the Army anyway. We don't treat him like a citizen, but like a captured savage from a precivilized culture. He is not allowed in the club, so why must he defend it?

SITTING ON THE DOCK OF THE BAY

Private Meadows, pronounced "Meeders," has been a steelworker, a steeplejack, a truck driver and a chemical worker. When he tells this to an inquiring sergeant, who bears a bronze star for valor in Nam, the sergeant asks him, "You got some kind of death wish?" He is sitting with me on the back steps of the platoon billets, and we are staring at what I believe is absolutely nothing. But he is watching the trucks roll by on Dyre and tells me, "The thing that hurts most of all is seein' them Diesels roarin' down yonder whilst I have to jest set here."

THREATS

Someone passed a little wisdom to me before I came in: "If they threaten you with anything, don't listen to it. If they wanted to do it to you, they'd just do it. If they threaten it's because there's a reason why they can't do it to you right then and there."

The Company Executive Officer, a forty-year-old ex-sergeant, Second Lieutenant Tanner, threatens Peyser with the Special Training Company, which is to basic training what the Black Hole was to Calcutta. It is a camp for fat boys and incorrigibles. As a matter of economics, it is also where they hold the ones who can't read the final exams and those who haven't enough strength to stand up after eight weeks. For the fatties and feuders, though, the training is intensified and the regimentation stiffened. The word is that the Marine Corps would be favorably impressed by the training program.

YOU GOTTA BE A FOOTBALL HERO...

Private Clem Carson is chosen by the sergeant in charge of the company's training to be the Trainee Field First Sergeant, the trainee in charge--sort of a player representative, or a trusty, or an appointed captain of the team. So Private Clem Carson becomes Trainee Field First Sergeant Carson and is entitled to wear a set of sergeant's stripes and be a Big Deal. He has been chosen because he weighs 250 pounds and much of it is still muscle, left over from his days as a tackle at Iowa State College. He has a face that looks like a clenched fist, and in general seems to have a lot of Neanderthal blood. When he does a sit-up it is like the take-off of a Saturn rocket. He rises slowly, by inches, gaining strength and speed, until at a critical point he bursts forward with an explosion of energy, and is, if not in orbit, at least sitting upright. He has been working for VISTA for the past two years and living on an Apache reservation. He is going back to live there as a member of the tribe after he gets out of the Army. He has been unable to move his bowels for six days, and is walking around bent at the waist like a bear from the pain of backed-up crap.

PREVENTIVE DETENTION

A medical specialist sprays a room full of sick patients with DDT to kill some ants he has spotted. He leaves a choking cloud of gas in the room as he locks the door behind him on his way out.

FS AND Q'S

One of the two kids who run our company is Second Lieutenant Horne. The other is First Lieutenant Mott, the Old Man, the Commanding Officer. Their aggregate age is not quite forty. Lieutenant Home is an ROTC jock who looks as if he is nine years old. He spends most of his time asking questions because he doesn't know his way around. He meets me as I come back from sick call, and I snap to attention, mentally noting that he has more acne than I. He also has an impish face accentuated by a chipped front tooth that gives him a look of positive cuteness, like a little boy playing soldier.

"What do you say when you greet an officer?" he demands.

"Oh, hello, sir," I reply.

"That won't do."

"Uh, good morning, sir," I snap off smartly.

"Don't you have some sort of motto or something that you're supposed to shout out?"

"You mean a company saying that we yell out when we see an officer, to show that we're tough and battle-ready, sir?"

"Yeah, something like that."

"No, sir."

We are in fact supposed to snap to attention and shout:

"Charlie Company, first on the Hill, sir." But the less young Beep-Beep knows, the better.

Drill Sergeant Robinson begins a lecture with another iron-and-steel joke: "My wife thinks I'm Rock Hudson. She wants to tie a rope around my neck and drop me in the Hudson--I mean she wants to tie a rock around my neck and drop me in the Hudson."

Lieutenant Tanner, the Company Executive Officer, delivers a lecture on military courtesy. He displays the Army's official insignia: a group of unidentifiable symbols with the inscription "This We'll Defend" beneath them. He hedges when I ask what the symbols are and mean. Nor does he know just what it is we're so willing to defend. But we'll do it, damn it. Just like in Vietnam. Let 'em figure out what it was all about later. Let's win the damned war first.

Tanner stresses the parallels between military and civilian courtesy. I mention that I had a civilian fondness for ignoring fools and sons of bitches. Tanner insists that the Army harbors neither in the ranks of officers, and that if I know what's good for me, I'll salute anyway. Period. End of parallel.

Private Weissman, a National Guardsman from Cincinnati, inquires in a series of questions that take fifteen minutes whether he can get into West Point and how he can go to OCS. He has just graduated from the University of Wisconsin and has no intention of doing anything but take up fifteen minutes of Lieutenant Tanner's time, which makes him a minor hero in the company as we all parade out for our water break at the end of his questions.

THE BLACKS

All of the blacks seem to be playing a southern rural stereotype, sittin' and laughin', playin' dumb and talkin' about sex. One cool hand who arrived with an Afro has become meek and submissive. I think that he senses greater power behind the Texas racism than the southern styles. The white southerner betrays his own fear, and consequently his vulnerability, by his insistent racism, but the white Texan is more sanguine and secure and subtly superior.

Martin Reisterton, a Long Island black Reservist, has been having an identity crisis since his arrival. For months now he has been trying to fade into a predominantly Jewish crowd, and to that end he has become Oreolized--black on the outside, white on the inside. In fact he is more from the Jewish ghetto than many of us. He is from Kew Gardens, Queens, is middle-class and has predominantly middle-class aspirations. During the year before we arrived here I watched him in our Reserve unit as he switched with the fashionable currents, from his comfortable materialism to a verbal black-powerism, and now he is assuming pretensions of illiteracy as he tries to fit in with the southern blacks.

THE RETURN OF GOOD JOE

We watch a film on the uniform starring a pair of pants and our old pal "Good Joe" from the AWOL movie. The story plugs away at why it is important to keep your uniform neat, and after several minutes of attempted justification, gets to the meat of the issue, which is, like everything else in the Army: because if you don't, they'll break your balls.

So again we have a guy who can't take his mind off a little girl back home for long enough to shine his shoes. The dramatic tension is supplied by the question of whether he can shine them well enough to win a pass and see her. No, he can't, and in failure learns a great lesson. From that moment on he takes his cleaning with great seriousness and purpose, until, at long last, he sees his girl, along with his mom and dad, at his "graduation" from basic training. They look like Mr. and Mrs. Lyndon Johnson and Luci. But never mind. He has learned to take good care of his uniform and to love doing it--and that, after all, is what is important in this life.

NOW HEAR THIS

The mess hall continues to post, without fail, each day, the previous day's menu.

THE "LIBERRY"

We are supposed to scream and yell when the company enters a building or a classroom, as a demonstration of our aggressiveness.

So here we go, howling like Comanches, screaming bloody murder, two hundred soldiers in full battle gear, with rifles and bayonets, until we are all inside and have captured the reading room of the post library. The librarian tells us about all of the services the library offers, and then she tells us that we can't use it because we're in training. While she talks the drill sergeants look bored, roll their eyes, yawn, fool around, and finally stalk out in a gesture of contempt. Drill Sergeant Brown joins the others on the street in front of the library when he is finished quietly breaking all of the librarian's pencils.

While she talks to us I wander back to where a trainee is listening to a record through some earphone. He lets me listen for a few seconds: Sergeant Pepper! He tells me he gets stoned behind the PX and then comes in and gets quietly freaked on records that he has stashed in his barracks. He tells me that he kept a few joints hidden in the library, between the pages of a book on why we are in Vietnam, and for three months no one found them.

THE NATURAL

Private Sanders has become the spit-polisher for the barracks. He is a coal-black Texan, and someone decided that by a genetic determinism he would know how to spit-polish a boot better than anyone else. I watched him polish a pair, and it wasn't so extraordinary. But when his were compared with one of the New York Reservists'--a pair that were attacked with love and dedication, a pair that shone like black gold, in fact one of the great pairs of polished boots of our era--the Negro from Texas was judged to have given his a superior polish.

RIFLES

Rifles were distributed today. First thing we are told is that they are "rifles," sometimes "weapons," and *never, never* "guns." The much-talked-about phallic symbolism is not exaggerated. Suddenly, docile and lugubrious trainees come alive with pretensions of potency. One particular charade involves placing the rifle between the legs like a monstrously enlarged erection.

A mnemonic device is introduced to break us of the habit of calling rifles guns. It seems that a rifle is a rifle, and a gun is between your legs. "This is my rifle, this is my gun. One is for killing, one is for fun."

My rifle has a plastic stock, to make it lighter in the jungle, but that only adds to the sense of unreality. A certified weapon of death is in my hands, and it resembles nothing more than a highly stylized Christmas toy.

Lieutenant Home, Beep-Beep to the troops, has been acting like a kid who's inherited the Army, and has been wandering around trying to find a role for himself. He arrives at Physical Training, walks around kicking anyone who can't do the exercises and insulting the weaklings. Finally a Reservist asks him to give a demonstration of the correct push-up technique. It is either push-up or shut-up for Beep-Beep. Beep-Beep shuts up.

I AM A CAMERA

The buildings here on Logan Heights seem to have an air of permanent impermanence, as if no one really wants to admit that Basic Combat Training is here to stay. All of the structures are two-story yellow flat-top cheese boxes. The older ones have wooden sides with parched, flaking paint that cracks and fades; chipped shingling on green roofs, broken windows and litter less streets compound the impression of a ghost town that once was important but now is forgotten.

The mess hall is one of the newer buildings, like our barracks. It is made of yellow cinder blocks, with poured cement floors and an aluminum roof that glistens in the relentless Texas sun.

On the roof of the mess hall is a massive air-conditioning housing with bolt and rivet holes that look in their random configuration like the aftermath of a machine-gun attack. Perhaps a comment on the food by a light-weapons unit? The food continues to be bland, greasy, overcooked and heavy--and served with a snarl. But we wolf it down.

THE FRONT LEANING REST

"There are only two kinds of rest" yells a drill instructor, " 'at rest' and 'front leaning rest." ' The front leaning rest is the "up" part of the push-up. You hold the prone position, with your arms supporting your weight, until your strength begins to flag and your muscles quake. It is used as a quick-torture device: "Drop for twenty and hold in a front leaning rest, troop."

We are holding in the front leaning rest, two hundred of us, at the end of an exercise period. The drill instructors are screaming at us to get our backs straight and backsides down. The longer we hold, the more drop out of the position. We begin to scream at each other as the drill sergeants tell us that we'll remain in the front leaning rest until we all do it correctly. The pavement has been baking in the hot sun all day, and it rips and burns the palms of our hands until the pain of the flesh is as bad as the pain in the arm muscles. The drill instructors tell us to kick anyone whose ass is up, turn on your fellow man if he is too weak, because he causes your suffering. All our humanity breaks down as the strong arise to kick the feeble. I hold until I can hardly bear it, and I too turn on the weaker ones. For some reason I recall the fourth article of the Code of Conduct, which we have been forced to memorize in all its defunct majesty: "If I become a prisoner of War, I shall keep faith with my fellow prisoners . . .

and take part in no action which might be harmful to my comrades." I think of this as I kick the ass of a skinny seventeen-year-old kid who lies face down on the scorched cement, shaking and crying. One good kick relieves my suffering not at all, makes me no stronger, no more fit, but aware of the weakness of our commitment to the bonds of civilization.

NEWSPEAK

In the military, it seems, you can pretend you never said some thing if you add a quick "as you were" and correct yourself. Thus commanders who find that their pronouncements are superseded by new orders from "higher up" can simply wipe the slate clean with an "as you were" and amend the new understandings to the current truth.

Or, when giving a lesson to the troops, a verbal slip can be erased by the quick addition of an "as you were" followed by the correct words, leaving the listener to patch up the air by canceling out the appropriate vibrations and suturing up the remainder until it makes what passes for sense.

Thus when Drill Sergeant Grbr announced, "It is the mission of basic training to beat, *as you were*, to teach candy--assed, *as you were*, civilians how to kill, *as you were*, to fight for the glory, as *you were*, the defense of the Army's Way of Life, as *you were*, the American Way of Life," we were supposed to put the sentence back together and make it make official sense.

CPA STAN

My bunkmate is a CPA from Brooklyn who lives at home with his parents and tells me he joined the Reserves because he had just entered a training program with an accounting firm and didn't think that there would be a job waiting if he were drafted for two years. Would there be a world?

He spends an hour making his bed to the precise specifications: measuring and pulling, smoothing and tightening until it is "GI." When he returns after lunch he finds that the bed has been tossed off its springs by the first sergeant during this morning's inspection. When the first sergeant finds something that is not "GI" he leaves his comments like an autistic child's temper tantrum. Beds are thrown off their racks, sand is poured on the floor, lockers are ripped apart, clothing dumped from hangers.

My bed, which was the object of three minutes of straightening, not stripped, but merely pulled tight and smoothed, somehow escapes the giant's wrath and passes.

METAMORPHOSIS

We are given another hour to play with our rifles, and I, inadvertently, unconsciously, let the hour of rifle play serve the purpose the Army wants it to. They want us to grow familiar with the weapon, to regard it as another toy, to be comfortable with it. They know that there are those, like myself, who resist the brainwashing by remaining strangers with their weapons, who see it as an object and something quite apart from themselves. After an hour of casual play I unceremoniously pull the trigger and find that I have crossed the line, just that easily. Were it a hard trigger, my will might fail as my strength was tested. But it was easy, and in the absence of any suggestions to the contrary, I became one of the trigger-pullers.

I am watching two trainees play with their rifles in an increasingly auto sexual way. Finally one decides to rape the other with his muzzle.

THE INEQUITIES OF THE UNIVERSE AND WHAT I DO ABOUT THEM, PART I

The chow line is broken down into Reservists and draftees for reasons that are important to an accounting office somewhere in the Pentagon. The Reserves line is shorter. I stifle my guilt. My price is getting lower.

MILITARY JUSTICE, AN OXYMORON

There is no justice in the military. Oh, there are hints of East-of-the-Pecos customs to keep the libertarians at bay, but when they want to get you, they've got you. When you're accused, the only question that is really open is how much of a penalty they are going to mete out. What you are charged with, when you are charged, is a specific crime, yes, but in a larger sense you are being charged with the inability to fit in or the failure to get away with it with the smoothness of the others. So indictment is all that really counts.

The Company Commander talks to us about military justice for an hour, citing all the protections that the Army gives you once they get on your trail. They give you a lawyer "at the Army's expense"; they give you a choice between a summary judgment by the officer who is accusing you and a full trial by a group of officers picked by the officer accusing you. Several Reservist lawyers get up and moan at the bar about the subtleties of justice that are missing and the subtleties of injustice that are present in the military command-justice system. The Commanding Office flatly denies this without bothering to answer the charges. Peyser asks a question that has already been asked and fully answered.

The Army doesn't like to talk about its problems--like the Presidio and Fort Ord court-martials. Only the Navy has problems. The Army doesn't want to expose us to the suggestion of crimes against the Army.

THE RETURN OF KID McDONALD

Kid falls asleep three times in lecture and is forced to do five-minute stretches of the front leaning rest each time. He is beginfling to feel his manhood is less involved with soldiering than he thought. He begins to move imperceptibly toward the dovish. He is seventeen and has signed up for three years.

THE TIES THAT BIND

The chain of command is a little confusing. Directly above each of us is our drill sergeant and assistant drill sergeant. My drill sergeant is Bill Razor, and his assistant is "Bronk" Conboy. Directly above them is the Field First Drill Sergeant, a master sergeant or sometimes a staff sergeant, who runs the training of the entire company. The only noncommissioned officer above him is the First Sergeant of the Company, usually a master sergeant or a sergeant first class, who is in administrative control and acts for the Company Commander, out of an office almost as large. I have never seen our first sergeant, but it is rumored that his name is SFC Theodore Bower and that he will be made a sergeant major and moved to Battalion HQ--if he doesn't die of cirrhosis first.

Field First Drill Sergeant Rawlins is a mild, cheery, easily confused, round-headed, bald Negro. He is tolerant of nearly any form of insolence or ineptitude as long as it's couched in the guise of stupidity. But he gets stern with the Negroes who foul up, and slaps and scolds and bawls them out. I sense that he doesn't quite know what to do about the Reservists.

Sergeant Razor begins referring to all the Mexicans as "bean vendors."

CPA Stan engages the Commanding Officer in an earnest discussion about the military death penalty, how it is administered and where. Private Martinez inquires "what kind of death?" The Commanding Office replies that he thinks it is the same as the civilian kind. Martinez seems satisfied. CPA Stan is not. "Is the penalty the same," he asks, "for killing an enlisted man, as for, say, killing a Commanding Officer?" "What did you have in mind?" "Oh, I just want to know my options," replies CPA Stan.

AMERICANISM

I am in the midst of a group of Reservists from New York, and we are trying to survive our fate: being thrust in with Texans and others who feel their Americanhood and sense our lack of it. We are trying, beyond all, to avoid being beaten up by our comrades, to avoid being chewed up by the system, to avoid being cast off by America. We are trying to become Americans by going through the wringer with the Texans, perhaps by watching their style and learning their rhythms, by surviving the common hardship of American boys, so that around the great cracker barrel we too can say, "Yeah, I've been there, I'm a Vet-trin." And I, for reasons that betray a dissatisfaction with my genealogy, I suppose, have learned to some extent the mannerisms of the out-of-towners, the upstaters, the westerners and middle-westerners. I have traveled and studied the people of my country as if they were foreigners. And now it is paying off. One of the New York Reservists tells me that he thinks we're all like Negroes in a small southern town, and asks how come I seem to be getting it across that I'm just a little bit whiter than the rest of the jigs. It's working and it's a lie, but no greater lie than half of our deceptions that aim at survival.

As the end of our first week of basic training approaches we are told that there will be a test on everything that we have learned. We are then given copies of the test--with the correct answers marked--to study.

MOTIVATION

The drill instructors introduce a set of prison-yard exercises: duck walks, bear walks, frog jumps, belly crawls. All are certified to be counterproductive and tear more muscles than they build.

Peyser is brought to the middle of the exercise yard and made to work until he collapses on his knees, his back bent over, his head and forearms on the ground. Six drill instructors stand over him, their necks red, their starched uniforms contrasting with the dusty, broken figure on the ground. They are fifty yards away from me, so all I can see is the veins on their necks straining as they yell. I can see their mouths open as they shout, but hear no sounds. It looks like a scene from the cover of the *Police Gazette.*

The desert wind blows hot in the face and tosses sand onto our parched lips. Swallowing is difficult. The faces I see are black with dirt and sweat, eyes are glazed, mouths hang open. Off we go on a two-mile run.

Peyser is called into the Executive Officer's office. It is the last we expect to see of him.

Kid McDonald is forced to do twenty push-ups for calling his rifle a gun. He repeats his mistake three times without learning, for a total of sixty push-ups. Kid McDonald moves a little more toward the dove position.

Private Peyser returns from the Executive Officer's office looking pale. He has just learned that the Army can keep him in basic training for two years if he keeps messing up. Sudden resolve wells in Peyser's eyes.

THE EXAM

"We're a little late," says Sergeant Bazor, "so the first five answers are A,C,C,B,D."

Questions six through ten he mumbles through, garbling every answer except the correct one.

"Sergeant could you repeat question seven?"

"Certainly: B."

RANDOM NOTES

The company cramps have given way to a mysterious on-slaught of company diarrhea.

I continue to pray that the food will be seasoned with saltpeter.

The grease and oil of a shouldered weapon in the boiling sun smells like my childhood electric trains.

People are pulling rifle triggers as they point their rifles at each other in soldier play, defying all known safety laws. The Army smiles.

PRIVATE NELSON

We are sitting in an empty barracks, being taught about the M-14 rifle, because it is too hot outside to do anything but sweat. Two drill instructors enter from opposite sides of the barracks and, with their M-14s set on fully automatic, fire off clips of twenty blank rounds apiece at each other over the heads of the class, giving off a deafening sound that reverberates from the concrete walls and terrorize the class.

We are all frightened out of our wits except for Private Robbie Nelson, a Jewish New York Reservist. Private Nelson is a graduate student at M.I.T. and one of the few well-adjusted New Yorkers. He is coping well. He isn't transfixed with fear, because he is too busy screaming with pain. He is sitting to the right of the path of one of the drill instructors as they enter with rifles blazing, and directly in the path of the searing hot copper shells that pour from one of the weapons. Four shells in the first second strike him on the neck. Sixteen whizz over his head as he keels over in pain.

Drill Sergeant Welch, who rides to work on a brutish Harley-Davidson and sky-dives on his day off (and yearns to go to Vietnam, because he thinks he is tougher than all the other drill sergeants, but has no official medals to prove it), comments on the wounding: "Well, I finally got me one."

Private Nelson is advised by Field First Drill Sergeant Rawlins that he really hadn't oughta go to the dispensary about his neck, which is beginning to look like an exposed intestine, because other aspects of his health might suffer as a result.

A FURTHER REPORT ON THE INEQUITIES OF THE UNIVERSE

Field First Drill Sergeant Rawlins explains at great length why he thinks Reservists, National Guardsmen, and anyone from a city is stupid: because they know little about guns and killing. He runs a little test to prove his theory. He has us strip and re-assemble our M-14 rifles after having given us only verbal instructions. The Reservists and Guardsmen and city boys finish well ahead of the good country Americans.

SYMBOLISM 103

Drill Sergeant Grbr makes a direct simile between the rifle and the male reproductive organ, almost artfully.

Another instructor explains, in serious detail, how one can, when lonely in the jungle, pull back the bolt of the M-14 and rape a rifle. Careful now.

Drill instructors continue to fire random blanks in classrooms despite Private Nelson's now-oozing reminder of the dangers. Drill Sergeant Brown, strutting down the aisle, grinning like Oddjob, fires a few blanks at sleeping trainees. His safety retainer comes loose and flies across the room, nearly hitting a trainee. He grins and stalks to the back of the room, a weird glow about him, his rifle on his hip, his eyes glistening, firing like a madman. He is undisturbed by the other drill sergeants, who ignore each other's aberrations with mutual tolerance.

We watch a film on how to keep the rifle steady. The film keeps slipping. Blanks are fired at random during the performance.

Notes from the Underground: Someone has carved a very neat little peace semaphore on my desk:

Peyser tells me that he's going to try to get the chaplain's intervention in his "case."

THE SLOW CHANGE

We are assigned to a desert clean-up detail, digging weeds out of the desert floor with picks and shovels, like a prison detail. In the process we kill several wild desert flowers, some of which are quite beautiful but have to be chopped down for efficiency. We can't stop to check out what is friendly and what is not. And that, I suppose, brings us to the question of Vietnam, which we have avoided for yet another week.

At lunch I found myself discussing each of the drill sergeants in strictly scatological terms. It is as if I had forgotten all metaphors and adjectives, all similes and adverbs. And slowly we all can become killers, I suppose, whether it be with language or as a person, of language or of persons.

And slowly, measurably, faintly but thoroughly, the Army, the world, America and the universe mark us, other men and ourselves, and work their evil as we work it on each other; and we are different.

THE BIG PARADE

We drill until we resemble one of those parochial or military high school marching bands, all patent leather and spangles, cutting and spinning in a precise martial ballet. Like, perhaps the St. Helena's Day parade, without the pom-pom girls and kids in blazers, featuring the St. Bartholomew's drill team and marching band. We do this daily to prepare for the Friday retreat, when we will all parade before Colonel Thorne, to let daddy see what we have learned this week.

This afternoon ten companies form up to parade before the Colonel, three battalions strong, an entire brigade of America's fighting best. The public-address system, mounted on the back of a station wagon, breaks down during "The Star-Spangled Banner" at "o'er the land of the   braaaammmpppp." An aide-de-camp pulls some wires on the subversive thing and it is stilled. Reservists giggle. The Regular Army and draftees are tense.

Salutes get messed up, and a rag-tag drum and bugle corps, complete with a drum that says "El Paso Senior High," consistently misses the beat.

A dust storm begins to blow as a martial record begins to skip. Colonel Thorne begins to speak: "Nothing, nothing, nothing, nothing . . . . and don't go AWOL." As we pass in review I see that the Colonel is saying something to the troops that pass before him; no doubt something to inspire them in their mission, some marvelous charge about being on the front lines of freedom. As I pass I hear him say, "When the drum beats, step with the left. Look straight at the Reviewing Officer."

THE GOD SQUAD

Signs are placed about the barracks advertising chapel services and suggesting that if we know what's good for us we'll go. The Catholic and Protestant insignia is the crucifix. The Jewish insignia is the Ten Commandments tablets, with the individual commandments enumerated, from left to right, in Roman numerals. Holy, holy, holy.

Friday religious services are attended because of the promise of two hours of freedom from sergeants, which coincides as well with two hours of scheduled barracks cleaning.

The chapel is neat and small, with dreary drapes hanging on one wall, while another wall of concrete and pipes stands bare.

The chaplain is a short, cherubic-faced man, wholesome beyond belief, with thinning blond hair brushed straight across from right to left. The rest of us have learned, without ever consciously appreciating it, to brush our hair from left to right. Is this another sign of a man out of phase with his culture? He has transparent eyebrows and pale blue eyes and a rosy complexion, which upon close survey reveals acne scars that trace a thin line of aggrieved adolescence from jawbone to ear. He is mild and soft. He speaks with an apologetic inflection and looks nervously about the room, as if he knows it is not his art and not himself that bring in the flock, but only the storm outside. He and his God must be saddened in these hard times. He leads us in responsive reading, which, as ever, drones on without meaningful expression or appropriate speech patterns, losing even its hypnotic quality after a point and dissolving into mumbles. Private Nelson and I decide to do something about this and begin to read aloud as if our lives depended on it, if not our souls. Every imploring of the Deity is filled with rising verbal passion, each "My God" a two-word crescendo, until the chaplain looks up horrified, seized up in the fear that perhaps he has a bunch of religious fanatics in his midst who will soon swoon with the weight of heavenly unction.

Rapidly he closes the group-participation portion of the services and moves swiftly to a brief sermon, which springs from a parable about two parents who erect a memorial window to their dead son, and another two who erect one to their living son. "And why," he asks, trying to lead rabbinically into the subject of charity, "do you think these parents built a memorial window to their live son?"

"Because," yells CPA Stan uncontrollably, "He's just become a doctor!"

Quickly the chaplain draws the service to a close and leads us to the Promised Land-the back of the chapel, where there is a pagan display of food. Private Rackles, a Catholic from Cincinnati, who is fat and being starved by the Army, leads the charge. He is taking me for wine and wafers on Sunday.

After seemingly ceaseless preliminary prayers we dig into the Mogen David wine and salami, gorge ourselves with Pepsi, rye bread and bologna. And girls?

Four girls, who, as these things go, are ugly as, well, sin. In fact, that may be, in several senses, the reason for their attendance.

We are driven home by Mrs. Beadleman, who lives in El Paso, and whose son Emmanuel is a private in our company and marked as a schmuck. He is an eighteen-year-old kid who enlisted and wants to make the Army his career.

In the car Emmanuel spends his time pinching and feeling his sixteen-year-old sister Janet; she spends hers whining. Mrs. Beadleman talks disjointedly, complaining a little, selling her daughter a lot. She pulls into a hamburger stand and is about to let us order when she asks us, "Is this off limits?" We tell her gleefully that it probably is, and she pulls the car out and drives us straight back to the base, the carhop's tray still attached to her window. She nearly cuts a sergeant in half as she sideswipes him with it. I stare straight ahead. Mrs. Beadleman offers us Janet for no other reason than that we are ethnically qualified. "She's gone out with soldiers a lot, and I don't mind it a bit. But I want to tell you that she's very well brought up and that if you don't keep your stinking hands to yourself, she'll break 'em off." Janet adds, "That's right. Why only last week a soldier tried to kiss me and I knocked him down." Seven soldiers crammed in the car stare straight ahead

I ask Janet about the three other girls at the services, whom I talked with for lack of anything better to do, all the while sustaining a stream of anti-Vietnam War chatter, to their obvious discomfort. "Oh, they're WACS."

"Why don't you boys all come to our house Sunday," says Mrs. Beadleman. "Manny can arrange it with the chaplain, and we'll all get together with some records."

"This is where we get off," I cry, a good half mile from our company area.

SHOWDOWN AT THE COMPANY C
CONSOLIDATED MESS HALL

Three companies collide, without drill sergeants, outside the mess hall, shouting epithets at each other. My team spirit is at an ebb. I can't remember just why Charlie is better than Alpha or Bravo, and what makes it worth getting a black eye for. Private Nelson whispers to me, "Send for the marshal, there's agonna be a shootin'." "Why," I implore, "can't there ever be peace in the valley?"

Private Terry, a white-racist Georgian, answers every Negro-- answering only the Negroes--who shouts something about being a bunch of "muh-fuh?" with a cry of "What side of the street does your mother work on, boy? What's her price?" Private Terry is a tough cookie, about five-foot-seven and 150 pounds.

Private Parson, a six-foot-three-inch Negro with a steelworker's build that stretches his fatigues taut over his chest, breaks ranks and walks up to Private Terry.

"What you say about my mama?"

Private Terry stares at him nervously, his Georgia upbringing welling false courage behind his icy blue eyes.

"Go back to your company, boy," says Private Terry.

Private Parson looks at him and says, "Maybe you didn't understand. I'm gonna ask you one time only to apologize. I ain't been called a boy since I was ten."

Georgia Terrys do not let black Parsons tell them to apologize. Georgia Terrys do not get taught manners from black Parsons. Private Terry, in crisis perhaps, suicidal perhaps, sticks to his guns and his life patterns, as the only thing he can do.

"I said scram, boy, back where you come from," he answers, doubling the ante, pulling the control rods out of the uranium pile with a half-scared, half-brave smile.

Private Parson looms nearer, and the rhythm of their dance sweeps us forward in time and we expect a thunderclap of a black Parson fist, catching Private Terry in the mouth, twisting his head and spilling him to earth.

It does not occur, and we are snapped backward into reality and see Private Terry and Private Parson standing chest to chest, daring each other to explode, toeing the line of bluff and bravado, courage and crap. Sizing each other up, feeling for the other's guts, they nod, mutter "Okay," and at the same time both take a step backward and start to laugh, as do we all.

Like men adrift in a lifeboat, or souls sharing a common alcove in purgatory, we make a little room for each other's sins as the week ends, since not to do so would only make things hotter and more crowded.

THE SECOND WEEK:

Where the Boys Are At

THREE CHARACTERS

Private Martinez, of the glazed expression and Vietnamese future, has just purchased a Polaroid camera and has been taking pictures of the other trainees. They jump in and out of their various uniforms, climb into full battle dress, stage combat scenes and strike martial poses for the folks back home. Martinez has been selling his pictures at fifty cents each, and is twenty-five dollars in the hole before he realizes that he is selling below cost.

Private Todd, a tattooed, web-toed farm boy, is shaped like Herblock's caricature of The Bomb. His personality is surprisingly convoluted, displaying by turns intelligence, the casual bigotry of his native Kentucky, humor (flashes of quick wit and long, involved dirty stories), thickheadedness, subtlety, and enough guts for a battalion. His size and weight make the training exercises doubly difficult for him, yet he punches his way along until he is overcome and passes out (twice) or falls down (thrice) or pukes (once). This week another facet of his personality emerges. After noting that Private Todd seems to enjoy walking around the barracks naked, goosing the other trainees, wrestling guys in underwear, spinning long sex stories, detailing his romances with calves and sheep, and standing well inside the social distance when he talks to you--gazing deep into your eyes--CPA Stan whispers to me, "The next time he gently touches you while you're talking to him try not to let on that you know he's queer."

Private Dorpf, an egg-shaped bullet-headed braggart, who arrived at Fort Bliss wearing a baby-blue blazer over a white turtle-neck, somehow managed to survive doing so. He has bribed his way out of the less attractive aspects of Army life, and has thus stayed far from anything requiring effort. He is not afraid to be ridiculed for going to sick call every morning, because he knows that if he keeps it up, the Army will weary of light jobs and buckle at the knees. For ten days he has complained of asthma, and at every opportunity has begun to wheeze and make himself a medical nuisance. We laugh. We tease and joke. And now Private Dorpf laughs last. The Army, knowing that it can ignore real ailments by refusing to recognize them, knows also that it can rid itself of a pain in its own ass by imagining Private Dorpf's ailments to be real, and has awarded him an Honorable Medical Discharge.

THE DROPOUT

Our drill sergeant, Bill Razor, has begun to warm up to us, and we seem to have befriended him, as well as having adjusted to him. He dropped in a few times over the weekend to reassure us that things weren't as bad as they seemed, to tell us not to be too worried or scared, and to give us a hint or two on how to get out of work without attracting hostile attention.

Bright and early Monday morning he and we are summarily informed that he has been promoted to Battalion Headquarters. We are introduced to our new drill sergeant, Dave Wilson, who blows hot and cold. This morning he blows chilly, recommending that we greet him with fifty push-ups. It looks to be a long eight weeks.

Physical Training takes on aspects of fun as we are moved into a new phase of it where we are allowed to use our newfound skills against a "partner" and attempt to beat him to death in "dual combat." Trainee Field First Sergeant Clem Carson, Cro-Magnon former tackle for Iowa State, is matched against Private Norman Peyser. Peyser steps on his glasses, and then falls to his knees as he approaches the hulking Carson, like Patterson before Liston, or Liston sinking after Clay's phantom punch. Private Todd pins his opponent with what looks more like a rape than a pin, arises and blows lunch all over the pavement.

FINITUDE AND INFINITUDE: VARIATIONS ON A THEME BY SØREN KIERKEGAARD

We are formed into a column and set to marching with our rifles on our shoulders, then double-timing, our rifles held out in front of us, toward some unknown destination. Quickly we move past all familiar points and the limits of our previous travels. No one knows where we are bound except the drill sergeant at the head of the column, and he gives no hint by the rise and fall of his cadence. With no fixed aiming point, one can envision only an endless death march. We have been trained to obey all orders with maximum vigor and to trust in the order-giver's desire to preserve our lives. But like Columbus's sailors, we foresee an open-ended trip off the end of the earth. Grumbling begins, and a curious mutiny spirit begins to spread. Evidently men will soon fall out and refuse to march until they are told how far and to where. The necessary sense of finitude and enclosure has overcome us and its absence, the dread feeling of endless pain and nothingness, the sickness unto death, has filled us with fear and trembling. Existentialism goes to war.

But no. Before the revolution can begin we make a quick turn into a building, without a lost step or a break in our pace. And there we are, face to face with a TV set. Mecca.

The man on the tube spends the next three hours reading the ten pages in our field manual on how to pack a field pack, which is no more inane than the fact that we could have watched him read at our own company's TV, thirty yards from the barracks.

We are encouraged to jog back to the company area, well over a mile, in full battle dress, our mess kits rattling in our empty packs, our canteens jangling against our bayonets--two hundred men clattering like a frontier peddler and his junk wagon.

We stop in front of the barracks and practice what we have become most proficient at: looking stupid and doing nothing. "This is the kind of work that many of us have a born talent for," explains CPA Stan.

As we struggle with our field gear in a protracted practical exercise in pack-packing, it becomes clear to me that just as the Army's stupidity is brilliant on one level--everything is so mechanical that the dumbest recruit ever recruited can understand and learn (I mean, even the clothing has sewn-in instructions.)--it is altogether too easy to be an accidentally good soldier.

Standing in the midst of a platoon of regulars while these supposedly facile soldiers struggle with their equipment, it becomes apparent that, like Political Science or English, the non-credit course in killing can be absorbed without any effort. That's how clever the Army is. They've seen to it that those of us "too smart" to give it any effort don't have to.

THE I OF THE STORM

The result of this morning's inspection looks like the aftermath of a boiler explosion in a whorehouse. Beds and mattresses are strewn about, clothing lies in confused heaps, blankets are strung from the rafters. And there in lone splendor, untouched by the giant's wrath, sits my bed, still made, safe on its springs. My clothing hangs undisturbed in my locker.

Why? Does someone suspect that I'm here as a spy? As a journalist? As Christ's vicar? Why does the wave break around me? Was it I or some cosmic luckiness that placed my bed and locker where they would escape the holocaust? My confidence in an egocentric universe begins to crumble as I decide that maybe they're testing me, or maybe they've learned that I'm dying of leukemia and don't want to spoil my day. Maybe they've discovered that my secret weakness, like Superman's fear of kryptonite, is an aversion to being singled out, separated from the safety and anonymity of the group. Maybe they're expecting me to crack, like Raskolnikoff, under the weight of self-consciousness. Maybe they're trying to get the group to turn on me. Maybe they just forgot. Whatever, they've won. The first thing I do upon reaching my bed is quickly strip it.

POLITICAL SCIENCE 007

We are listening to a drill sergeant explain at length about guarding Government Property.

"Excuse me," asks CPA Stan, 'but whom are we guarding it from?"

"Why," answers Drill Sergeant Grbr, "from the people."

"Well," continues CPA Stan, "I mean, couldn't you wind up killing them? How would it look if the government of the United States killed its own people because they wanted to enter Government Property? I mean, the government is the people and owns the property *for* the people. It just can't go around blowing their heads off for using their own property."

"No sweat," answers Drill Sergeant Grbr. "We don't use ammunition on guard duty. Only at missile sites."

"Suppose," interrupts CPA Stan, "I want to pet one of my missiles,"

"Suppose," answers Drill Sergeant Grbr, "you just sit down." Martinez wants to know if you shoot at a Russian spy whether you might not blow up a missile and a nuke. Drill Sergeant Grbr opines that that is the price you have to pay to keep the Russkies at bay and keep their atheistic hands off our missiles.

A dozing trainee, picked off at fifty yards in the midst of two hundred others by a well-aimed rock thrown by Oddjobish Drill Sergeant Brown, is forced to do a front leaning rest, while Private Stein, having dropped his rifle, is forced to embrace it and kiss it; like having dropped a Bible. Phallic symbolism does a back flip.

Private Stein is a six-foot, red-haired, robust basketball-playing National Guardsman kid from Cleveland, who might have a lot of things going for him if only he'd permit them to. When he is not whining and complaining he is moaning about how tired he is. The first day in camp he told me that he had never been away from home before and didn't know how to make a bed. I showed him, and when I looked up to see if he had understood, I found that he had escaped and was outside playing basketball.

QUESTIONS OF THE DAY

Six people ask me the same question: "Does anyone know we're here? Does anyone care?"

On the way to bayonet practice Drill Sergeant Wilson asks Peyser whether anyone has ever told him that he looks like a walrus.

We are lined up at the bayonet training field in groups of righties and lefties. Why, in a company of 200 men, with 80 Negroes and 30 lefties, are there only two Negro lefties? What does that say about matriarchy? Is it a product of a belief, hammered in at too-early an age by authoritarian mothers, that the world would not make room for them? Were they told that the burden of proof was on them if they wanted to play in a hostile world? How does it affect them now? Is it true, as I have always believed, that every man tries to make the world safe for the little boy he once was, that he hopes to have his childhood instincts proven correct and the bogey-man buried? I always hoped that "they'd prove" that batting cross-handed was a superior way to hit a baseball and that vegetables were bad for you. Will we someday see--or are we seeing--a revolt of Negroes who are telling us that they're tired of accommodating the world, that they want to be lefties, want to be themselves, that the world can go to hell if it can't make some room for a little boy's ego to live in peace?

Private Roberts, a muscular, cheerful, left-handed Negro, with feet the size of flippers, who has been chosen to be assistant platoon leader in my platoon, defies the standing instructions forbidding anything but cold water in canteens. He discovers that Kool-Aid, canteen plastic and solar heat make a toxic mixture. Private Roberts' personal revolution gets quelled by a stomach pump.

DAVY CROCKETT GRINS DOWN A B'AR

The night fire guard discovers me sitting on the back steps of the platoon billets well after the bed check.
"What are you doing here?" he asks me.
"Nothing."
"Oh."
Score five points for the "psych" method of internecine warfare.
Five minutes before the nine P.M. bed check I realize that today has been my birthday.

SHORT THRUST

We are out on the bayonet-practice field trying to master the arts of "short thrust," "long thrust and hold," "vertical butt stroke," and assorted other movements that seem gleaned from captured World War II Japanese films of Samurai warrior pageants.

This class is the most popular to date, as the public-address system wires have gotten crossed with someone's radio lines, and our instructor's orders take on a contrapuntal rock 'n' roll rhythm. The drill sergeant disconnects the PA system, and continues to shout his orders a *cappella* into his lifeless microphone.

We are told that, like karate, proper bayoneting requires a lusty shout to convince your adversary that you are marching to a different drummer and not about to be logically persuaded to drop your spear in favor of a panel discussion of the issues. "You've got to let him know that you're a mad-assed mother-fucker," shouts Drill Sergeant Brown. "He's got to think that you're dangerously crazy." The short, lusty word "kill" is recommended, and would indeed frighten any English-speaking foe into respect. As for non-English-speaking combatants, any visceral grunt is acceptable. I choose "Sorry!"

Private Doby asks Drill Sergeant Brown a question and is laughed at instead of answered. "How far away do you have to be to bayonet someone?" Drill Sergeant Brown estimates that one rifle length is sufficient. "I mean," Doby adds, "when do you stab a guy and when do you hide in the bushes instead?" Drill Sergeant Brown suggests that we all take our water-and-salt-tablet breaks.

The heat of southwestern Texas as we approach the summer solstice has become so intense that the Base Commander has ordered every company to carry around blankets and pillows in case of sunstroke and heat prostration. A giant water bag is re-filled every hour and we are constantly urged to take salt tablets. Anyone caught with his hat off--courting sunstroke--is liable to a stiff sentence of front leaning rest. But despite the heat, boredom and exhaustion, the most verboten verboten in Basic Training is falling asleep in a class, even though one is required to sit in the hot sun, still and silent, for up to an hour of dull instruction. The penalty for being caught napping is interminable push-ups.

And yet, involuntarily, sleep cheats its way across the con-sciousness and daydreams become more and more vivid until a shock wave ripples up your spine and you realize you have been dozing. A jolt of fear snaps you awake as you pray--in a microsecond, as if you have found yourself asleep at the wheel--that you can open your eyes before disaster overcomes you. But at every free moment, as the eyelids sag and the muscles slacken, scenes of liberation trot past the mind's eye. Memories of happy times, travels, youth and freedom, and everything else that makes the world beyond Basic Training so attractive dance a seductive ballet in the mind. Visions of liberty play like un-penned puppies in the universe behind the eye.

Sleep has taken on a greater importance as a release mech-anism than for physical rest, and is the most important leisure activity besides reading mail. "I wouldn't care who wrote the laws if I could write the ballads," said Thomas Jefferson. I wouldn't care who owned my ass if I could have my dreams, say I.

THE ULTIMATE WEAPON

Among the Army's arsenal of weapons perhaps none is more potent than "the automatic repeating mess menu." It can reduce a battalion of fighting men to a diarrheic disaster area. We have had spaghetti in various disguises three times this week. And I am here to tell you that, yes, there is such a thing as "spaghetti soup."

BABES IN ARMS

Young Lieutenant Beep-Beep is still unable to figure out what to do with his time, so he acts like a disciplinarian, looking to the drill instructors for approval. They are, in relation to his three months' tenure, hardened veterans, battle-toughened pros. When they are not around, he buddies up with the New York Reservists, as I suspect we represent the secret wise-ass in his soul.

Private Stevens is a baby-faced, pouty seventeen-year-old black kid from the slums of Houston, angelically pretty, who insists that his civilian occupation was: pimp. He is full of noise and jokes with forgotten punch lines, improbable sex stories and unfulfilled plans to go AWOL. The little boy in him is near the surface, close behind the "aw gee's" and "sheyit, yeah's," hard by the urine-soaked sheets of his first military morning, railing against the fact that he has volunteered to be a paratrooper. You look in his face and you see smooth cheeks and hopeful eyes. You can see little lines of fear and distrust too.

It is us against them, us guys against the Army and its monitors--the ones who take it seriously and want to aid it in oppressing us. Us guys discover an empty barracks, Barracks #4, which we convert into a clubhouse where we can smoke, nap, fool around, and be far from the eyes of sergeants.

RESPECT THE UNIFORM, NOT THE MAN

Saluting evolves into a meaningful thing on one level as privates pass each other on the road and trade snapped-off salutes to other privates, saying, "I *do* respect you. I'm suffering with you." A tip of the hat, a salute, a "V" sign or a black-power fist is the correct response. Friendly gestures, freely offered, easily earned.

And to those who don't earn it, but demand it as a right, the game becomes: Make 'em work for it. Find an officer driving with his left hand on the roof of his car and right hand on the wheel. Snap one off and watch him swerve as he switches hands. Find an officer with packages and hold your salute until he feels compelled to stop, put his packages down and return your salute. Ever hear of someone court-martialed for saluting too much?

LIFE AGAINST DEATH

Again we are marched two miles to watch a TV program that we could have watched in our own company classroom. Entering in a state of near exhaustion, two hundred trainees attempt to fan themselves with their hats, but abandon the effort when they realize that they are waving hot, fetid air into their faces. The tricky maneuver called "opening a window" is not included in the Army's survival manual.

In an unbelievably strong stench we listen to a lecture on field sanitation. Drill Sergeant Conboy describes the primitive Vietnamese sanitation methods to the accompaniment of loud, derisive, perhaps patronizing, laughter from the trainees. Is this why we are in Vietnam? Has American hypercleanliness brought us to this pass? Is it anal retentiveness that has made us play the cop? Is Norman 0. Brown right? Perhaps it is the white man's burden to bring pay toilets to the savages.

We are privileged to view another TV tape, which, after five minutes of trainee protests, the drill sergeants reluctantly admit we saw last week. The channel is switched and we watch yet another instructor read from our field manual. Something familiar grabs me, and I finally realize that the Army's TV-tape theme, played before each lesson, is an uncut version of the old Flash Gordon theme; no more ironic I suppose than Goebbels turning a Harvard fight song into a Wehrmacht marching tune.

Private Stein, hopelessly bound to logic, asks why, if the Army makes such a fetish out of field sanitation, it refuses to let us wash before meals, and indeed, has us do push-ups in the dirt outside of the mess hall. He is instructed by Field First Drill Sergeant Rawlins to carry a bar of soap with him from now on wherever he goes.

THE FINAL SOLUTION

"All Jewish personnel, fall out," yells Field First Drill Sergeant Rawlins as we line up in the early afternoon.

"If they have Stein pass out bars of soap and tell us to take showers," CPA Stan tells me, "make tracks for Mexico."

"Your chaplain is coming to visit you," Field First Drill Sergeant Rawlins tells us, "so all of you men will report to the Day Room. And take Pisser and Beagleberger with you.

"Beagleberger" is Emmanuel Beadleman, and "Beagleberger" is what Field First Drill Sergeant Rawlins thinks is an accurate pronunciation of his name. "Fonebone" is what he is called by the New York Reservists because of his striking resemblance to a Don Martin caricature. At lunch today he planted himself at a table occupied by Ronald Woodling, Howard Lee--two black trainees--and myself. "Well, what do we have here," he said as he wriggled his ample rear into a seat, "two browns and two Jews." I uttered my first real live threat of violence, offering to stick a fork down his throat, because I had worked too hard in my lifetime at being me to let loonies like him typecast me. Lee and Woodling said nothing, but when Fonebone got up, Woodling muttered, "We are watching the world's greatest single cause of anti-Semitism take a stroll."

Private Pisser-Peyser, the consensus pick to cop the title from Fonebone in the stretch, listened not at all to the first day's instructions on operation of a rifle and let his pudgy little thumb wander across the path of the rifle bolt as it slammed forward when he pulled the trigger. He now has four fingers and a foot on his left hand.

As we enter the Day Room I notice that someone has graffitiized its welcome sign. "STOP--and wipe your feet" now reads "STOP--The War--and wipe your feet." On the Day Room bulletin boards are two maps. One bulletin board says "Commanding Officer's Board" and has a map of the whole wide world. The other board says "Enlisted Men's Bulletin Board" and is less expansive. It has room for only an outsized map of Vietnam.

The chaplain arrives late. "How else would we know that he's Jewish?" suggests CPA Stan. He is largely ignored in favor of a Coke machine. He really has nothing to say except for some mildly paranoid things about how we're "their guests" in this Army, and we have to stick together because of "them," but not rock the boat. "Maybe we've outstayed our welcome," I suggest, "and should all go home."

CPA Stan asks whether he is called Chaplain Captain or Captain Chaplain. He doesn't know, he says, but suggests that "Rabbi" will do.

He is a bland and pleasant young man, surprised to hear that there are Jews in Chagrin Falls, Ohio, when Private Barrett tells him that he is from there. "That's what they say in Chagrin Falls," Barrett replies.

Captain Chaplain Rabbi is from Pelham Parkway, the Bronx,

by way of Yeshiva University, and is in the army because he thinks it's his ethnic duty to "represent his men."

"Your parents must be proud of you," offers CPA Stan. "I, uh, don't know," he stutters as he leaves, blinking his confusion, inviting us down to services, offering his aid if "they don't let us go."

"He needs our help," says CPA Stan.

LOVE CHILDREN

I have become the brigade tennis champion, because even though I showed up for the team tryouts in my combat boots and fatigues, no one else in the company, battalion or brigade showed up at all, except for the fellow who sat next to me during the drug films and he, bless his soul, is still stoned.

PRIVATE RICARDO

Private Ricardo is a tough, hoody little Mexican-Texan, not at all like Private Seguera. Private Seguera complains that his business is falling off now that he has been drafted. His business, he explains, is that he is the major fence for merchandise pilfered from Houston homes by a band of teen-age housebreakers he has trained. Private Ricardo gives me a hostile stare that questions my manhood when he asks me what I think a particular car has under its hood and I answer, "An engine?"

"How big?"

"V-S?" I venture.

"No. Cubes!"

"Oh, yeah," I feign, "uh, 327"--which sounds right.

"327? Only Ford makes a 327."

"Oh, isn't this a Ford?"

"Naw, it's a GM. 'sgotta be a 328."

"Gee," I marvel, "what's a little cubic inch?"

"Everything."

During a lecture on "the NATO round," a 7.06-mm carbine

round for M-14 rifles, I ask the sergeant giving the class what a millimeter is a measure of (Is it the diameter of the round? The length? The circumference?) and he says he doesn't know, but that it might be the weight.

Private Ricardo, who has been moving on a collision course with just about everyone, has become suddenly mellowed lately, his pugnacity notwithstanding. His wife has taken a job on post under her maiden name, and he has become the sole possessor of the Day Room men's room, every night from 7 P.M. to 9 P.M., where he entertains his wife and at least fifty trainees who huddle silently by the door.

GREAT DAY IN THE MORNING

It is entirely possible, in the civilian world, that "a big day" will end at 3:30 A.M. Today is a "big day" and it begins at 3:30 A.M. I think the Army believes that we have wasted three and one-half hours already.

We have gotten up early to get a good jump on the day, because aside from the usual instructional periods, we have to take the first three Physical Combat Proficiency Tests. We will take one this week, one in our fifth week and one in our eighth week. Then we will take a "final" to determine whether we graduate or not.

The test, called the PCPT, consists of five events that test the muscles and skills needed for combat.

The first event is "the low crawl," a torturous and dusty trial that involves crawling on the belly--the chest and head may *not* rise above the sand--through a sand trough of forty yards. The trough is filled with coarse sand and rocks, and has a body-wide groove worn down the center, which only makes it more difficult. But at least ours is better than Alpha Company's pit, which is all gravel. The pit must be crawled--twenty yards one way, twenty yards back--in less than 30 seconds to get the minimum number of points needed to pass. I do it in 45. Private Peyser does it in 86. A slithery Texan does it in 23.

The second event is called the "run, dodge and jump," and consists of running in sand, dodging around hurdles and leaping over a pit. Two round trips must be made in 25 seconds to get the minimum points. Private Peyser lands in the pit each time he tries, and after three attempts gets his time down to 50 seconds, but still can't make it over the pit. I finish in 30 seconds, which is about average. A mercurial Negro does it in 20 seconds.

After two events my watch says 8 A.M. I assume my watch has stopped. The sun is pretty low in the sky. It could very well be eight in the morning. I decide that my sense of direction is screwed up and it's really 4 P.M. But it is eight, and the day, it is obvious, will never end.

The third event, now that we've been loosened up, is a series of overhead bars, ten feet off the ground, that must be traversed--a row of 13 must be traveled up and back until a minimum of 36 have been done--in one minute. The first bar is reached by standing on a pair of fixed stilts and reaching up. Several of the smaller Mexicans have to be lifted up by friends. Once they get up there, three of them scramble along as if they could swing forever. One does 96 bars, one does 100, another does 76--the maximum necessary--and drops off well before the minute is up. I do 54 as my arms and my minute expire simultaneously. Private Peyser reaches up for the bar and misses, nearly killing himself. He is hoisted up, like a piano going into a third-story window, and grabs onto the first bar. He holds it for about five seconds, takes one hand off to reach for the next, and crashes to earth.

The fourth event is a course of 150 yards, up a slight gradient-- but it feels like a hill--which must be run in less than 50 seconds (again, only to get the passing score) while carrying someone of one's own weight. Peyser, paying the penalty for his useless fat, has to portage a two-hundred-pounder, all the while protesting that he only weighs 135 pounds. He finishes, after falling, dropping his passenger, walking and staggering, in two and one-half minutes. I twist my knee--honest--and fall across the finish line in one minute flat, gashing my arm and gaining about three pounds of subcutaneous gravel. A Texan lopes to a 45-second finish.

Finally, nearing exhaustion, forbidden water, we are led to the mile track, where, in full fatigues and boots, we attempt to run one and one-quarter miles in less than 8 minutes. As we run, trainees faint, collapse, quit and start walking. Strategically placed drill sergeants kick the laggard ones. Peyser walks for half lap, and then falls down when he is kicked. I feel asthma coming on after two laps, and blast a little inhalant down my throat. I feel faint and tumble to the ground. I hear a rumble of feet and see an approaching drill sergeant half a lap away. I reach into my first-aid kit, in fear for my health, and take out an ammonia smelling-salt ampoule. A quick whiff and I am off again, ready to finish, propelled on the wings of fear, and of course, love of country. I finish in about 10 minutes. Field First Trainee Clem Carson keeps slugging through the cloud of dust of those who have lapped him, never stopping, never quitting, and finishes in 14 minutes. Peyser finishes in 16 minutes. A Mexican does it in 6 minutes 45 seconds.

Private Stevens becomes the only Negro to fail every event, mostly for lack of effort. Field First Drill Sergeant Rawlins scolds Stevens like a father, and Stevens breaks into tears.

It is apparent, as I lie here gasping for breath, that it is psychologically easier to run two miles, in formation, keeping in step, one step at a time, than to run one mile individually, where all the demons of fatigue and pain have no counterforce to oppose them.

At the end of the PCPT, trainees lie about in heaps, like the survivors of Bataan. Some are out cold, some are twitching. Some are throwing up.

MISSING IN ACTION

We are paraded past the personal property of one of the trainees who went AWOL. It is scattered about, rifled and muti-lated. A picture of his girl friend in her high school graduation dress lies on top of the heap, as does his unopened mail from home. The juxtaposition of her picture, her return address and his parents' return address seems like a little overdone Psywar Hollywood-fade-out stuff; fade in on J. Edgar knocking on his door.

THE TRUE BELIEVER

Two New York Reservists are relieved of their command of eight-man squads for excessive friendliness with the troops-- calling them by first names. One is replaced by Private Tommy Lawson, an arrogant Hitler-Youth type from North Carolina. Lawson is in the National Guard and is as athletic-looking as he is arrogant. Like Captain Queeg, he addresses his men as *"Miss- ter,"* or sometimes "Sol—dier!" He believes that he is commanding us by right of genotype. As I look at my fingernails he approaches me and screams in my ear, "You're at *Parade Rest,* Mister! Now drop for twenty." I turn and look at him with wonder. "Where the hell do you think *you* are, West Point?"

"You're in the Army, soldier. I'll have your stripe for this."

"Oh, mercy," I protest, looking to CPA Stan for aid, "the man wants my mosquito wings."

"Don't look at me for help," says CPA Stan. "I knew you were a troublemaker the minute I laid eyes on you."

"Lawson," I implore, "I promise not to misbehave, sir, if you'll do me a favor."

"I don't make deals," he says, stealing a line from Batman.

"Well, just this once, hey? I'll behave if you'll look up the word 'popinjay' when you get home." His malevolence is distracted by Private McDonald, who in his patriotic fervor is filling his canteen with ice water in the mess hall.

"Who said you're allowed to do that?" demands Lawson.

"No one . . . I . . ."

"You've got KP, soldier," screams Lawson.

"All of the platoon water coolers are broken."

"You'll be too when I'm through with you," asserts Lawson.

"Lawson," says Drill Sergeant Conboy, having watched the show for ten minutes without saying a word and now, like a prison guard calling off his Doberman pinscher after it has chewed its prey to bits, "kiss my ass. Shut up and leave these guys alone." Peyser waddles over to the water cooler and fills his canteen.

PATRIOTISM

We are sitting in the blazing sun, and it occurs to me that anywhere else on earth one might, quite reasonably, get up, go indoors, lie down, and quit for the day.

Drill Sergeant Grbr tells us that "next week we'll be inspected by some congressmen and senators. Just a bunch of loafers, I call 'em." I am angry. But then I realize that I might call them that also, and reject his calling them that only because he is in the military; and the truth of an idea should not be dependent upon the character of its sponsor.

None of the cadre men--privates, corporals, specialists and sergeants attached to a particular unit *for* administration--seems to like the Army, but they dislike it the way farmers dislike the government. They damn it, but deem anyone else who does likewise a traitor.

We are taken to hand-to-hand combat, and half the company sustains injuries at the hands of the other half. The first position we are taught is how to fight while lying on the ground.

The Catholic chaplain walks up to me, notices my name-strip on my uniform, and the dressing on the hand I injured in the PCPT. "How's the hand, Tauber?" "Oh," I reply, "it's--" He is gone before I finish, and I address my words to the Holy Ghost, "--painful."

We are taught how to catch a kick with our hands, or ward it off, and the technique actually works in slow motion. It is suggested that a quick kick with a steel-toed boot would shatter one's mitt. Drill Sergeant Welch clears up the problem, though.

"How many gooks have you ever seen in combat boots?"

"Never saw a gook, drill sergeant, and never hope to see one."

"You'll get your chance."

It is deemed an honor in drill sergeant circles to kill "gooks," like plucking a white feather from an eagle, and it is deemed a duty in larger military circles to want to kill them.

We've been running and jumping for Cong and Country for 14 hours now. Collapse is imminent. We are told that we may have the evening off to prepare for Saturday's foot- and wall-locker inspection. CPA Stan spends an hour hunched over his underwear with a ruler, making sure that it is folded and rolled so that it is 8 inches long, no more, no less. The edge of absurdity is blunted by the seriousness with which the entire venture is treated. There is not an article or item that one can possess that does not have precise dimensions and an exact position that must be conformed to.

"Maybe," CPA Stan says, looking up, "if we head off the Viet Cong in Texas with neat underwear, we'll never face the awful day when they get to Jackson Heights."

KILLING TIME

At five in the morning, when the sun is barely up, the best way to hide from Physical Training is by showing up for formation, slipping back into the barracks and catching an hour's sleep under your bed.

At six in the morning there is no place to hide. In full battle dress we are trucked, like an advancing army rolling through Italy, across the New Mexican desert for rifle practice at the MacGregor Range. We sit sleepily on our field packs, like paratroopers awaiting the green light. Our M-14s are between our knees, helmets over the muzzles, making each seem like a grave marker, as we sit sadly and quietly behind them.

We slide past squat, lifeless homes, into the desert, over the ambiguous dust that is here Texas and there New Mexico; no

difference can be perceived. Could one tell the difference
between American and Canadian soil? American and Russian?
earth rocks and lunar rocks?

A sign tells the distance to Alamogordo, New Mexico, and to
White Sands. In the lifeless desert, on a creaky bus, cramped and
drowsy, we see these and other names from another age flash
past.

We roll on past a house of chipped and rotted slat boards
called The Primitive Baptist Church, through the desert, so
barren that the phone company uses wee-short poles, on toward a
sign that welcomes us. "MacGregor Range," it heralds, "the Free
World's Largest and Foremost Air Defense and Missile Range."
We are unloaded at one of the many training areas. Nothing
grows in the sand out here but rifles and grenades, radar and
missiles. And but a short distance to the north a mutant, which
they called Baby Boy, was born, at a site named Trinity.

We are instructed in the safety regulations of the rifle range,
paramount among them being: Don't smoke in the latrine.
Legend has it that a trainee lit up in the hooch last year and set
the old outhouse on fire. When he was released from the hospital
he was put through basic training again. For most of us, being
put through basic training again is a compelling enough reason
not to smoke in a latrine, far stronger than the possibility of
burning it down.

The order of the day is "quick kill," a Pentagon-Vietnam
phrase for instinct shooting, eye-hand coordination enabling you
to shoot from the hip or raise your rifle and fire without the
disruption of aiming--a simple, easy method of, well, killing
quickly.

Quick kill. Like "body count," this facile locution is the way
we incorporate murder into a bureaucratic system by
manipulating diction. The linguists say our language and culture
are mutually determining. What does it say of us, then, when we
talk of surgical strikes, kill ratios, free-fire zones, pinkvilles, and
pre-emptive interdictions? The debasement of language either
leads to or follows a fallen ethic. The hearts and minds of the

people, my pacified ass.

The method of quick kill is simple. We are all issued BB guns, and simply work at plugging little metal discs that are tossed in the air. In three weeks we will be allowed to shoot at each other with BBs in a mock attack.

Our BB guns are all unmistakably labeled "Daisy Air Rifle," which I note with the glee of discovering a local Decency League president in a bordello raid. I have always suspected Daisy Air Rifles. Their cutesy ads on the back pages of comic books about how to prove yourself a real Dad-and-Johnny-type American kid were the first hints.

Aha! Now we find them, not just in bed with the Army--the only product to be presented in its straight commercial form-- but, great guns, a *sponsor!* Daisy Air Rifles! Like the Boy Scouts, who are permitted to use the base facilities free of charge, they are co-conspirators with the Army, not a whit less innocent, in the creation of the schisms in America. Daisy Air Rifles, the Boy Scouts and the Army are the ones who caused the generation gap and college riots. They are the ones who began labeling some of us real Americans, and some of us not. Daisy Air Rifles. D.A.R.

FRUITS OF WAR

The Fire Control Officer has an Irish name, a Chinese face and a Spanish accent. How many wars created his line?

GET ALONG

After chow we are informed that anyone found with live ammunition, or even empty shells, will be tried for a serious violation of the Uniform Code of Military Justice. A cascade of live rounds and empty shells hurtles from every direction into a pile in front of the instructor. We are lined up and searched, amid grumbling by many whose fascination with weapons and shells has been frustrated, and who might, in other contexts, find an outlet in the Army. Nothing much is discovered except for a hash like substance on the person of a Mexican, so just for fun we have to low-crawl through the sand for ten minutes.

After two hours of purposeless waiting because someone forgot to send for the buses, listening in fear for my life to Private Stein explain to Sergeant Bronk Conboy why Jews are superior to everyone else, the buses finally come. Conboy seems to be not at all fazed by Stein's declarations, and doesn't seem to care that some of us think Stein is full of crap. "Well, what the hell," says Drill Sergeant Conboy, poking a friendly finger in my chest, "I ain't never met a Jew before. But I also ain't met one who could ride a horse and rope, neither. So"—still playfully poking my chest and belly---"it's hard to see how you Jew-boys could be superior to me, right?"

The buses leave, and we learn a military trick in budget cutting. The Army doesn't believe in wear and tear and depreciation. Any tension between humans and materials must be borne by the humans and absorbed through regenerable muscles and energy. On the way back to the base a two-hundred-pound ammo case sits in the lap of four trainees so that it won't rip the rubber stripping on the floor of the bus.

El Paso enjoys its first rainstorm in four years, which CPA Stan interprets to be a sign from God. "If it keeps up, and you see a pillar of smoke in the distance, head for it--we'll beat the Egyptians to the river," We are marched through rain and lightning to get haircuts, and once more we become artificially bald and purposefully humiliated.

SICK CALL

Time was when sick call was a haven for the weary soldier and a place where a little tenderness crept between the floorboards of military existence.

But sick call begins at 6:30 in the morning and we have to fall out at 4 A.M. Until sick call one must, unless convincingly unable to stand up, run two miles in boots and fatigues, clean the barracks and report for all details or KP. The two-mile run is an exercise in group pressure. No one thinks he can do it, but you are dragged along by your fear and a sense that the others don't seem to be having as tough a time as you, so that you'd better make it, unless your pain is greater than the imagined pain of a drill sergeant's boot.

Sick call entails waiting outside of the dispensary until 7:30, when the medical people show up. Then it moves inside with no talking and no sleeping. Anyone caught closing his eyes, no matter the ailment, is forced to stand at attention for five minutes and then do 35 push-ups. I am told to do 35 push-ups, and upon completing them am told to do 35 more, correctly, saying, "One medical specialist, two medical specialist" and so on. I struggle through it and get up, but am told to get back down and get up correctly, saying, "I have done 35 push-ups, medical specialist, and promise not to sleep, may I please get up?" I promptly fall asleep and am sent out to run ten laps around the dispensary.

I am laden with writing paper, mindful of the usual four-hour wait. Private Romini, one of the New York Reservists, is carried in with heart palpitations. A medical specialist tells him to sit and wait his turn--wait until the heat-rash and blister cases have been handled. Private Young and I drag him to the doctor's door and thrust him through. Private Young is whispering, "Look, if you wait, the palpitations might go away, and you'll be up shit creek then. Keep palpitating, boy, just a little longer." The doctor calls an ambulance, and Private Romini is well on his way to a discharge.

"You're lucky you got him in there before he died," says a sleepy-eyed soldier next to me through clenched teeth. "If he'd expired in here, you mighta had to carry his ass back to yo' company area. I hear tell of one old boy passed away right in the middle of the old obstacle course. Sergeant yelled to his buddies, 'Drag his ass offa my course.'"

"Get out of my office," screams the doctor as a whimpering

buck private slinks out of his examination room. "You're a goddamned faker. You've had a complete medical and there's not a goddamned thing wrong with you, so get your stinking ass out of here. I don't have to take any crap from a private."

My complaint is barely traceable asthma, and my allegation of it has obviously put my life on the line. After eyeing my reasonably white Anglo-Saxon face, my records and my faint smile, he speaks: "You're the third honest person I've had today."

"Aren't you going to look at my chest?" I ask.

"Oh, yes, of course. But the major thing is that you're telling the truth. You might be able to get out on this. But it's not worth the odds of recycling. Wait until Basic is over and try then."

Exposé: If anyone ever says that to you, my friends, remember that I told you here that they will later say, "Well, looks like you made it through basic training with asthma, so we guess you can make it through anything." The best way to get a medical out of the Army is to start falling down the very first day and not stop until you are safely nestled in the bosom of your mama.

When I return to the unit Field First Drill Sergeant Rawlins notices my writing paper sticking out of my shirt.

"What's that?"

"Writing paper."

"You took writing paper to sick call?"

"Yes."

"Why?"

"To write on," I reply, but he is not satisfied. "Well," I explain further, "there was the usual four-hour wait."

"So you wrote."

"I wrote."

His wrath is redirected as Private Watts walks into his office bearing a note with a dentist's signature that says: "Abscessed tooth and three adjacent teeth removed. Twenty-four-hour bed rest." His mouth is swollen and lopsided as if it had been hit by a wrecker's ball or as if a cancerous jaw had been excised.

"They give you anesthetic?" I ask.

He shakes his head mournfully, holding what is left of his

mouth closed.

"What you doin' with assessed teeth?" demands Field First Drill Sergeant Rawlins.

Attempting to answer, Watts opens his mouth, and says "Weff, fargnt, muff mow wi imfmtd" as blood and pus and infected matter pour from his mouth onto Rawlins' desk. Rawlins utters a short shriek as he sees Watts's guts cascading onto his paper work. "Get outta here. Get into bed. You too, Tauber. Scram."

WHOOPING IT UP AT THE GENEVA CONVENTION

A class on the Code of Conduct begins with a movie from which we learn that "The American fighting man has been captured in nine different wars." CPA Stan whispers to me, "You'd think he'd get tired of it."

Describing the horrors of prison-camp life, the movie narrator tells us, "Then there's the food, if you could call it that." Sort of like basic training, eh? "Captured GIs in Korea were forced to listen to an explanation of the Korean war--from the Communist point of view." Sounds reasonable. But no. We learn that the North Koreans "blame the Korean war on Wall Street warmongers. The techniques of Korean captors include: skilled interrogation, artful propaganda, assured humiliation." It still sounds like basic training.

My mind turns to Commander Bucher, out there in the North Pacific, facing, among other natural hazards, crazy North Koreans. Whom do you think he'd resent more as the North Koreans bore down on him, the Koreans, who could be expected to do exactly what they did, and are thus like typhoons, or the U. S. Navy, for sticking him out there defenseless and ill-advised? I think about the unacceptable alternatives we place on men like Bucher: Stand fast and watch your men die one by one, or refuse to crack, refuse to denounce your fictive aggression for the sake of face and politically determined loyalty. One could reasonably expect fourteenth-century bishops to watch their priests be tortured, to go to the stake themselves before they'd renounce God, but what of twentieth-century man? What do you demand of a man when you put him in a situation where you have determined the price of cracking, where it is decided that whichever course he picks he will hate himself forever? Who has put him in the situation in the first place?

Another movie is trotted out from the Army's endless repertory. We shall, like Korean prisoners, be ready to say anything when they are through destroying our minds, I fear. This one features an all-ethnic cast--like Sergeant Bilko's platoon--getting captured behind Korean lines. The Army is running scared. The only ones to crack under enemy torture have anonymously WASP names and faces.

You can look into these Korean-era faces until they seem hollow, devoid of personality, no longer rooted in an era-faces that might have been in the Civil War-nineteen-year-olds whose names are scratched on aging gravestones in all those Gray and Blue cemeteries. Fathers' wars and sons' wars, part of coming of age in America. This last-name business of the Army begins to come clear; it is not Tommy or Peter who lies arotting but only another Atkins, another Tauber--a family's taxes to the nation paid. There is an anthropology to this that I understand as I look into the blank stare of McDonald, seventeen years old.

Emphasizing the need for teamwork, the announcer cites the universal experience of our high school football teams. My high school didn't have a football team. But we did have a chess team and a math club. It took me until I was a sophomore in college to climb my way back into the company of the kids who had high school football teams, the all-American kids, who knew the place was made for them.

Brief mention is made, after an elaborate explanation of the Geneva Convention, that everyone we have fought since its signing, or are likely to fight, does not recognize it. CPA Stan immediately suggests we declare war on Great Britain so that we can fight somebody who'll play fair.

Lieutenant Beep-beep is discussing some dilemmas of prison-camp life.

"Here are two situations," says Beep-Beep. "The first is that three privates have an escape plan. You're a thousand miles behind enemy lines. All previous attempts have failed. The captain, who is senior officer, says 'No.' What should you do?" Everyone except me agrees that the captain is a chicken-shit. "Accepting the premise that the Army needs your body," I say, "and is thinking of the long run, one must accept its power, exercised through its officers, to deny you the privilege of embarking on suicidal adventures on your own authority." But the class sentiment is for a headlong dash through unknown territory. Even young Beep-Beep casts himself as a hero. Surely we have had a surfeit of Ronald Reagan films.

"Our second situation is simpler," says Beep-Beep. "You've got a man who you think has been spilling your escape plans to the guards." The multitude agrees that accidents will happen, and a knife in the shower room is accepted as the accidental ultimate. What about doing it legally, I inquire, standing squarely in the jailhouse door as the lynch mob nears, on the balls of my feet, ready to run when my arguments and commitment to justice run out. Legally? Too cumbersome, they agree. One last plea for justice and mercy: "Who knows for sure if he is an informer, or what torture they've used? Who knows that it's not a trick to divide you? Who made you God? I'd hate to sit on your court-martials when you got back to the States."

"Commie-lover," yells CPA Stan.

"Pinko-stinko," shouts Private Nelson.

"Fuckin' Korean," screams Private Lawson, the only one not kidding, as he leaps at me. The vigilante spirit prevails. Good Daisy Air Rifles! *We* know who *we* are and who is not one of *us*.

Interposing himself between Lawson and me is Private Doby, who succinctly puts it better than I: "You ain't no court. You can't go round killin' folks. That's lynchin'."

"But he's an informer," says Lawson, clawing at me from within Doby's giant grasp.

"But it still ain't right."

"Stinkin' Korean Commie," hisses Lawson.

LATER LIFE

"All right now," hollers Drill Sergeant Grbr, "you'll be using left-face and right-face a lot in later life."

"How did we ever get along without them," muses Private Nelson.

"Peyser," says Drill Sergeant Grbr, "show us a left-face." Peyser insists that he can't do it.

"Show us twenty push-ups, then."

"Can't do that either."

"How many can you do?"

"It depends."

"On what?" asks Grbr, exasperated.

"On whether you count the one going down as one or one-half."

"It's only one-half, Peyser."

"Well," Peyser replies, proud at having at least come up with an accurate answer, "one-half, then."

ESCAPE AND EVASION

All of the Jewish personnel have been banished to services by order of Field First Drill Sergeant Rawlins. "The less men around, the less can go wrong on inspection," explains Rawlins. "Peyser, I don't care if you're Jewish or not, or whether you want to go or not" eyeing the lumpen sad sack and the fifty-pound log he is required to carry around to build up his nearly nonexistent muscles--"you're going. And take your log."

When we return, after hours of wandering around the base, browsing through the PX, lingering over coffee--just like in the real world--and pondering Chaplain Captain Rabbi's rambling sermon on the unanswered question, "What kind of fruit did Adam and Eve really eat?" we return for an unexpected surprise.

In our absence my platoon, since it has the most Jewish personnel and half a dozen others with Jewish-sounding names, like Roman Catholic Private Rackles, who could escape without suspicion, has consequently left behind the fewest personnel to be inspected. We have had the least go wrong and have been given passes to continue wandering the base. Like Yossarian, who took immense pride in the Officers' Club that he didn't help build, I am pleased beyond words at the result of my lack of effort and my disciplined absenteeism.

So that the next weekend we might get real live Liberty Cards, they have us fill out a form for national security clearance. The last ten spaces are for "criminal convictions, non-traffic," and I watch in horror as a Texan labors over it for ten minutes. Finally he raises his hand. "May I have an extra piece of paper?"

We are told, after reading a list of 300-odd subversive organizations, like the Lithuanian Anti-Fascist Friendship League, not to admit past or present membership in SDS. But the word is out that membership will disqualify you from national security clearance needed to be sent overseas and the privilege of toting a rifle through the swamps. SDS's amorphous membership ranks are swelled by at least twenty chicken-assed Reservists.

CHARLIE COMPANY AT EASE

Private Todd refuses to get out from under Private Thurmond's sheets, but says politely that, no, he is not, when CPA Stan asks him whether he is a homosexual.

Private Williams' cousin, a cadre man in another company, spins a series of pointlessly anti-Semitic jokes as I sit listening, amazed. "This guy from New York told me them. Says he's met a lot of Jews."

Private Yates, a tall white from Uvalde, Texas, remains inseparable from his black bunkmate. "It don't matter that he's a nigger," he tells me as they stagger home drunk on 3.2 beer, their arms around each other, supporting each other in their lurching fatigue "We're all poor, so we're all the same."

Private Williams tells a series of Rastus-Eliza jokes while Private Yates's buddy, black Private Sanders, sits and listens and laughs at the Negro phallic myths.

Private Martinez is fined for soliciting-selling his Polaroid pictures at a loss.

I read another letter from my mother, defending herself and the creed against *Portnoy's Complaint.* I ponder how to tell her I like her without at the same time bad-mouthing masturbation.

CPA Stan lies on his bed thinking of his girl friend, who writes him daily and whom he loves more than his electric adding machine, and half-silently, half-asleep, tries to list for himself all of the swearwords that he knows, repeating them over and over as if he is memorizing them.

THE THIRD WEEK:

Yin and Yang

STRANGE INTERLUDE

The arm," shouts Drill Sergeant Welch, showing us his arm, "makes a forty-five-degree angle, like this, in the primary hand-to-hand combat position."

The angle resembles an arm signal, perhaps for a left turn. He is showing us how to get somewhere.

"Your fingers should be aimed at Charlie's eyes or throat." It is the turn, I realize, as suffocating heat presses in on me, like the one you make on Routes 5 and 20, traveling through Seneca Falls, New York, from Geneva to Aurora--the left turn north.

"Your first jab should stick old Charlie's Adam's apple into his throat, or shove his eyes into his brain."

North through Seneca Falls, then east and south to Wells College for Women, for springtime and freedom, leaving the world and its wars far behind; leaving now the desert floor and the pain in my stomach as I close my mind to the sounds.

"Pivoting on your left foot, you drive your right foot into his chest, or lower to his groin; that'll slow him up."

Slopes of un-mowed grass and tiny white flowers roll from

Wells College to Cayuga Lake below. Wooden footbridges were our playground then, and gladioli and peach blossoms filled the eyes and lungs with spring.

"You've got to wipe him out with your first few moves, 'cause he's gonna come at you like a grizzly if you just wound him."

The memory of journeys past the lakes, the familiar mile-posts and farms, captures my spirit.

"The right lateral heel stomp is a two-part motion: rising up on the left toe, bringing your arms up to your armpits, and stomping down, thrusting your arms down to give you added momentum. You should split Charlie's head like a grapefruit."

The smell and taste of the auto ride through the Finger Lakes, anticipating a chase or a ring-around-a-rosy with a teasing young spirit, drifting through flirtation into simple sexual play. The alluring vision of an unmet girl tossing an uncaptured smile-- leading with the eyes and cryptic at the mouth--makes me its prisoner for a moment once more.

"Drill sergeant," asks Private Martinez innocently, "what damage will the heel stomp and bayonet parry do to a human's body?"

"You haven't been listening, boy," says Drill Sergeant Welch, "or you'd know." Maybe we should all adjourn to Wells College for Women and study war no more. It would be springtime in Cayuga County this week. Maybe all the boys in the world can agree that they are tired of fighting wars for their Generals and can go to Wells College for Women. Maybe Martinez and I can find some common ground beneath a willow, lying in the laps of adoring young ladies. Maybe we can get Drill Sergeant Welch to come too.

THE BLACK AND THE BLUE

The world seems made of opposites this week: Texans and New Yorkers, death games and romance, "America" and American people, illusion and reality. I caught myself lying on my back last night, staring at the moon, bridging the distance through a sustained effort of will, traveling the miles by collapsing all distance behind a point of vision, dancing at last upon its craggy surface, separating, as I have learned to do, my body, which is a prisoner, and my mind, which crashes about looking for avenues to freedom. Last night I had to leave the earth.

The boys of Charlie Company, Texan and New Yorker, can all run two miles now in fatigues and combat boots, and though we grumble that the physical training is barbarous and pointless, we are a little pleased with our progress. But there are other aspects of training that please no one but the Army. We observe the second beating in two weeks of an Alpha Company trainee as he lies prone beneath a maddened drill sergeant. The boy is on the ground and is being pummeled. We watch, shocked: shocked that it is happening, shocked that we stand idly by like Kitty Genovese's neighbors, doing nothing, glad that it is not us. The boy rises to his feet, and is kicked to earth again. It is somehow a test of our fitness not only to accept pain stoically but to accept others' pain silently.

Alpha Company's reputation is that of a horror house, and we marvel at the administrative caprice that spared us the fate of its sorry members. All of us were spared but Private Dix. Dix--Mopey Dix we call him--came in with us, but his blood betrayed him, and he is in Alpha. The day we were to leave the Reception Center for Charlie Company, Dix and I were sent to the doctor's office--I to make a feeble plea for asthma, and he because his blood had given off a positive reaction to tuberculosis tests. He doesn't have tuberculosis, only some demon in his humors that does not like to be poked and prodded--befitting a Yale philosophy grad student like Dix--and gives a mischievous "yes" to TB tests. Further testing showed it to be an involuntary lie--a proud protestation of physical integrity, nonetheless. I managed to rejoin my group in time to be shipped out, but Mopey Dix, detained an hour longer, was put into another company—a skinny esthete adrift on the hostile seas of Alpha Company. The pressure has eased, if only a little. One of us "Rodneys," as trainees are called, was forced to do punitive push-ups for some fanciful insult to a drill sergeant--an Alpha Company drill sergeant--and having done 50, then 40, then 30, 20, and 10 push-ups while protesting "illness," collapsed, unconscious. His kidneys had split after about the first 75, and he nearly died. When his mother heard, not being bound by tribal laws of tight-lipped acceptance, she called her senator, who in all likelihood called Mel Laird himself, and faster than a speeding memorandum or a bureaucratic "As you were," the word came down: "No more physical punishment." We may never hear "Drop for twenty, troop" again. But the Alpha Company drill instructors are pretending they haven't heard--except the one who precipitated it all, who has been relieved of his platoon, awaiting reassignment.

Private Wessly, a nearly feeble-minded trainee in Alpha, runs into me, wearing two black eyes and assorted facial bruises. "What happened?" I ask.

"Oh, I went AWOL and stole a car. I got sleepy, so I went to sleep in the back seat, and the police caught me in the morning."

"What did you steal?" I ask.

"A motor-pool sedan."

"What did they do to you?"

"They may court-martial me, but they just sent me back to my platoon for the time being."

"How'd you get so bruised?"

"I didn't take a shower for a week, because they had me on KP every night and day. I'd finish at nine-thirty and have to be up by three in the morning. So the drill sergeant told the other guys to beat me up, and six of them jumped me."

"What about Open Hours?" I ask. Open Hours are an effort allegedly to "further democracy" by letting us go straight to the Commanding Officer, bypassing the chain of command, if we have a problem or a complaint. But don't you believe it. Whenever Open Hours are scheduled, we are scheduled to be off the base at the rifle range, and woe betide the brave recruit who dares to exercise his rights.

"Open Hours?" asks Wessly. "What's that?"

"DO THEY TAKE OFF FOR GUESSING?"

There is a feeling of impermanence among the trainees that alleviates the sense of imprisonment. Equipment labels still bear the names of those who've "gone before," as if they somehow had a greater claim to this equipment than we. Private Stein wears a pack that says "Pvt. Cattles." Last cycle? Or were they too timid to claim it for themselves as well? There are people, we think, who belong, and know they do, who didn't feel anyone would follow. Yet we know we are transients, and it makes us free. Maybe those people could also make sense out of the sign in the mess hall that says "Take only one glass of milk." It is next to an identical sign that says "Take only two glasses of milk."

We feel ourselves on a conveyor belt of time, bound to this place by the slowness of time, supported alone by our ability to survive. One hovers somewhere between a suspension of belief in time and a suspension of belief in what goes on here.

The signs on the rifle range are written for someone, I suppose, but they make sense to no one. "Here lies Fred/ He is Dead/ He didn't believe/ What was said." And, above an open grave: "Vacancy-For: The Day Dreamer/ The Unbeliever/ Know It All/ Sleeper/ Do You Qualify?"

I qualify today because I have been teamed with Private Peyser on the rifle range. Private Peyser, who, if Geppetto the puppet-maker's prayers were answered by the animation of Pinocchio, must be the dream of some chopped-liver sculptor come true, endangers my life on three separate occasions. His attitude is betrayed in the plaintive question he asks the range instructor as we are told about the "qualifying test" we must pass. "Do they take off for guessing?" he asks. "They" nearly took off my head when he loaded my ammunition magazine backwards, and I nearly took off his when I clobbered him with my rifle butt.

Ten trainees are standing at a table loading ammunition into magazines. Ten others stand at another table, unloading magazines, until by the end of the day the race is a draw. As many have been loaded as have been unloaded. If you have never been in the Army you probably won't understand why they didn't just switch tables.

"Cease fire" is called, and a private is carted away on a stretcher at another firing area, the right side of his face partly blown away, the result of a defective round exploding in the chamber. When it happens--and the odds are low--the round behaves like a mini-hand grenade. We have no alternative but to accept the odds.

THE CREED

"Yorile zawe'en o'depf," explains an instructor after lecturing three hundred trainees for forty-five inarticulate minutes. He tells us, from what I can gather, that he grew up in Throggs Neck, the Bronx, and he is, near as I can figure it, trying too hard to sound like a soldier. It reminds me of a letter I got from a former colleague just as I pondered Samuel Beckett's question in the play *Play*. "Does anyone know I'm here, does anyone care, can anyone hear me ask?" The letter told me to "watch out for Sergeant Gomez. There's always a Sergeant Gomez, but he may change his name from year to year. They're all the same, though." He had been in in the late fifties. "And don't forget your Rifleman's Creed, for God's sake," he implored jokingly.

The Rifleman's Creed, courtesy the U.S. Army:

"This is my Rifle/ My Rifle is My Best Friend/ There are many like it/ But this one is Mine/ I must fire my Rifle True/ I must shoot straighter/ than the enemy of My Country/ Who may be trying to shoot at me./ My Rifle and I are a team/ Together We are Defenders of My Country/ And are Dedicated to its Defense/ Unto Death, Before God, I swear this.--The Rifleman's Creed."

Like the Army's systems and customs, invented to save democracy in a crisis, this drivel is handed down like the Apostles' Creed.

The instructor demonstrates the handy-dandy Hide-UR-Face camouflage stick, pushing it like a cosmetics salesman. For all his trouble with the English language, he manages to glide over "camouflage" "technique, maneuver" and "appliqué" with fantastic facility. Ten camouflaged trainees crawl on the desert floor three hundred yards away so that we can practice spotting camouflaged trainees crawling on the desert floor. Two Mexicans on my left constantly scream, "I see heem, I see heem." When the crawlers stand up I still can't see them, but spot two platoon-mates who had been chosen as crawlers and decided instead to take a nap behind the instruction stands. One, who was supposed to be on his belly "three football fields away," comes screaming at us from behind, having had cross words with either a Gila monster, a scorpion or a rattler--he's not sure which.

The class in crawler-spotting is interrupted by "an event"--rare enough in the desert. A missile is launched at White Sands, to the north, and all activity and noise stops as everyone looks skyward to observe the swift, graceful flight of the rocket--as Dizzy Dean used to do if a plane passed overhead when he was on the mound. Silent seconds pass until, at its apex, the rocket gives off a noiseless flash and consumes itself. As if waiting for the first act to be over with, several dust devils, little twisters, dance across the rifle range, tossing sand and tumble-weed, ripping down targets and mercifully disturbing the peace. More fire follows, and maybe brimstone will be hard behind; heat lightning streaks from mountain top to sky and back. CPA Stan whispers to me, "God will soon speak to us in a still, small voice."

I *do* see God, and my entire life, flashing before me as Private Peyser falls over from the recoil of his rifle, pointing his loaded weapon straight at my head, even as he raises himself. I snatch the first opportunity--and his weapon--and knock him in the steel pot helmet with his own rifle butt.

THE SHOT

We are trucked to the MacGregor Range dispensary, where we will all be given penicillin shots to counter the wave of strep throat that is sweeping Fort Bliss. Our medical records are back at the base, and anyone who protests that he is allergic to penicillin is accused of malingering and threatened with court-martial. I carefully list the symptoms and treatment of classic penicillin reaction and am excused. Private Sanders, who is not believed, turns blue, then gray, then purple-then falls on his face, twitching. About 10 percent of the troops suffer immediate reactions, which, as I recall, is about the correct percentage of people allergic to penicillin in a random population. Later the figure will rise sharply after a forced march, until 20 percent lie moaning, half from leg paralysis caused by injections into the sciatic nerve.

Private Thurmond, from South Carolina, with an accent that is so thoroughly Mayberry RFD that he is called "Gomer," comes over to me the next day with glassy eyes and says, "D'y'all have any asprin?" I recognize what appears to be acute penicillin shock. There is no one else around to pronounce on his health--except for a drill sergeant, who is allowed to say, "He ain't sick, he's just lazy"--so I'm "it."

I take him over to the equipment shack and note that he has a fever, swollen glands, headache, dizziness, a tight chest and swelling in his joints, which are stiff and sore. I treat for shock, mop his brow, borrow some antihistamine from Peyser, who is afraid that he will succumb to pollen in the desert, and watch. A brief desert thunderstorm swirls outside, and the electric effect of the lightning, giving the desert a tan and amber glow, plus the soft boom of the thunder, like distant shells, make us feel like the remnants of a patrol, cut off from our unit, watching the world through a battlefield window, a wounded man on the floor. Outside, the rest of the company squat under their ponchos like little tents in a bivouac field, spread out like an open-ranks inspection of a battalion of frogs, to give the lightning a difficult target. Last year a trainee's bayonet or steel pot helmet attracted lightning and blew him apart.

An ambulance arrives for Thurmond and buses arrive for us.

We are whisked past "Temple Hills" billing itself as the "Southwest's garden spot," a long, endless flatland, without shade or greenery, crammed with jerry-built houses. Another sign, handsome wood, highly polished in the figure of the archer, proclaims "Robin Hood Park," standing in front of a trailer park, the trailers squatting in random formation behind it.

We are going home, and I shudder to think that Fort Bliss is home.

THE GIRL

A flatbed pickup truck stops next to us at a light in El Paso. A little girl in pigtails, blond and smiling, sits next to her daddy in the cab. I wave and smile, and she wiggles her fingers in reply, giggling and acting shy, nuzzling up against her daddy, peeking out to flirt some more. They drive off and I look at my-self, sitting in a drab green bus, a field pack on my back, a dented helmet on my head, my bayonet and M-14 between my knees, thinking of a little girl.

We disembark from the bus and I inhale a lungful of fumes. I am momentarily, joyfully, illusorily transported to New York-- too briefly. I breathe better for the rest of the day.

MAKE LOVE, NOT WAR

"Tauber," whispers Drill Sergeant Wilson to me during closed ranks inspection, "you're going to KP tonight, and do you know why?"

"Yes, drill sergeant," I reply.

"Why?" he asks, testing me.

"I don't know, drill sergeant," I answer.

"Why did you answer 'yes,' then?"

"Because you're not supposed to answer 'no,' drill sergeant," I reply truthfully.

"You lied when you said you knew why, didn't you?"

"Yes, drill sergeant."

"You're going to KP tonight for lying."

"Thank you, drill sergeant."

"For what?"

"For telling me why, drill sergeant."

"Oh, don't thank me, it was nothing. And you're going at lunch also because you got shoe polish on me today."

"You bumped into me, drill sergeant."

"That doesn't matter," he says softly.

"I can't go at lunch because I'm playing in the tennis tournament, drill sergeant."

"Oh, okay." He shrugs, unconcerned, as if the terrorization, not the actual punishment, was the point. "That's okay, then. Good luck, Tauber."

"Thank you, drill sergeant," I answer.

"But don't forget to go tonight," he urges, like a mother reminding a child to brush his teeth, *con Gleem.*

"I won't, drill sergeant."

"Tauber, fall out," says Field First Drill Sergeant Rawlins, annoyed. "You're not going with us to bayonet because you're playing in the tennis tournament."

"Yessir."

"Yes, sergeant."

"Yes, sergeant. Yes, field first drill sergeant."

"Tennis is a girls game, Tauber."

"Yes, field first drill sergeant."

"Are you going to play in girl's shorts?"

"No, field first drill sergeant, in combat boots."

"That's good."

Things are going better for me on the whole in the company -- even with KP and all--than in the tournament. My first-round opponent is the recreation officer of Fort Bliss, a tennis amateur well known in the state of Texas, who came in second to Lieutenant Arthur Ashe of the West Point faculty in the all-service finals last year. The Army has seen fit to draft the finest athletes in the nation in a vainglorious effort to teach its officers to be gentlemen and turn its officers' clubs into country clubs. The officer half of my brigade's entry, noting that I am about to be eliminated before I even tie my sneaker laces, inquires whether I'd like to be on the archery team, as a way of getting out of some more work.

After returning nearly half a dozen of my opponents serves, and getting one game all the way to deuce, the match ends 6-0, 6-0,6-0.

I am teamed in doubles with Lieutenant Davis, an ROTC officer who claims that he became a member of ROTC by the grace of a case of Scotch five days before his draft board was to pluck him from graduate school.

We lose to Lieutenant Colonel Treandley. It should be noted -- to scrape something out of this dishonor--that Colonel Treandley runs from the knees down, and has a great alcoholic nose, red and bulbous, looking tender to touch and streaked with distended veins. His eyes are fierce, like his tough crew-cut hair. I'm glad we lost. I'd hate to meet him in the locker room.

Lieutenant Davis and I, the Custers of the courts, retire to the Officers' Club steam room for the rest of the afternoon, he to relax, I to salve my sunburned scalp and breathe the better air of freedom.

Lieutenant Davis invites me to spend the next day hiding out in his Day Room, and I accept without hesitation.

The Day Room is filled with sergeants who challenge the relevance of writing letters to defending freedom, but seem convinced when I say I'm waiting for a summary court-martial by the Commanding Officer. A radio is blasting Elvis Presley trying to sing "Gentle on My Mind." Something that sounds like music spills from the local radio stations and continues to be the worst that Country and Western can offer. After every few songs they put on some motel-Muzak tunes in the name of "pop." Perry Como croons the praises of See-Attle like a chamber of commerce talent-hunt winner:

> Like a beautiful child
> Growing up free and wild,
> Full of hopes and full of fears,
> Full of dreams to last the years,
>   Is: See-Attle!

Lieutenant Davis drives me to the Officers' Club, where we both hit the whirlpool and sauna and reflect on the wisdom of the Army's simplemindedness. It has ordered us to report to the tournament, but not necessarily to win. I put my fatigues in a bag, steal a towel that says "Officers' Club," and, in my borrowed tennis whites, go off to visit friends on the base, getting treated like an officer, or at least a Human, because my towel has two embroidered words on it.

THE BIG INSPECTION

We await Colonel Thorne for two hours in our spick-and-span barracks, getting sweaty palms and losing Private Sanders to a nervous stomach. He makes it to the door moments before he would have spoiled three days of floor buffing and seconds before Colonel Thorne steps through.

"Good God, there's vomit in your front yard, drill sergeant. Check to see if any of your men are sick."

"Yes, Colonel," replies Drill Sergeant Wilson. "Men--"

"Later, drill sergeant, after I'm through. Where's your other drill sergeant?"

"He's on his truck, Colonel."

"Oh, I see."

Drill Sergeant Conboy is parked out back in his flatbed truck, baby-sitting for all the garbage and contraband that the Colonel's eyes would be offended to see. But the Colonel knows, and maybe the Joint Chiefs know as well, that you can't shine shoes without filthy rags, that dirty mops are part of the business of war, that our laundry bags would be nearly full by this time of the week, that we wouldn't have such a sparse collection of "personal" items and that the inspection, like the Army itself, is a large vestigial joke.

Colonel Thorne and Lieutenant Colonel Treandley move around the barracks like twin locomotives, leading a train of lesser officers. Occasionally Thorne stops in front of a Smith or Rodriguez to ask if they have any brothers who were once in this outfit. Junior officers take elaborate notes on everything, like court reporters.

As Lieutenant Colonel Treandley passes me, I flash a quick "cheese" smile, and he stops dead in his tracks, his eyebrows arched over bugging eyes, searching my face for an identifying clue before he explodes. An eyelash before the detonation he looks enlightened and says, "Oh, yes--Tauber."

My tennis racket sits atop my field equipment and catches Colonel Thorne's eye. "What's that, uh, Tawber?"

"Colonel Thorne," intercedes Lieutenant Colonel Treandley, "Private Tauber here represented the brigade in the singles tournament."

"How did you do, *Tawber?*" asks Colonel Thorne.

I recite a brief, uncalled-for history of my byes and defeats. "Well," says Colonel Thorne, commenting on my defeat, which came only three hours before his elimination from the doubles, "welcome to the club."

"Thank you, sir. A pleasure to be a member of the same club as you." Colonel Thorne blinks twice, hops back on the train and is gone.

"Say," asks Drill Sergeant Wilson, "did you ever go to KP that night I sent you?"

"Yes, drill sergeant."

"What did you do there?"

"I arranged plastic flowers for two hours."

"You ever go to the stockade?"

"Not lately."

"Well, you came as close as any man can with Colonel

Thorne."

I don't want to tell Drill Sergeant Wilson that at KP I made an elaborate bandage on my hand to avoid washing pots, that I simply walked away from mopping a floor, and that I am wrestling with my psyche over whether it is good for the soul to do dirty details or whether they should be avoided. At times I think it is a necessary rigor to do unpleasant chores, to develop a little spine. But when faced with KP, I realize how hopeless the development of my spine is.

TEXANS, NEW YORKERS AND OTHERS

It is obvious that much as we New York Reservists are provincial and narrow, our Texas cousins are even worse. We are bound by the geocentricism of the Hudson, safe in our self-confidence, convinced that the world is measured relative to us. But we are playing in the Texans' ball park, and their assertiveness seems to grate in proportion to our discomfiture.

We try to meet them halfway. An evening is spent attempting to explain that all non-Texas accents are not the same. Several excellent imitations of Philly-teeny, Montreal-canook, New Yorksnooty, Brooklyntypecast, Chicagobreezy, California-mouseketeer, Bostonbrahmin, and Virginiagentleman are offered to no avail. They are indistinguishable to the Texans. I try to talk about Country and Western music with them, as they seem oblivious to pop, rock and any kind of folk. But they don't seem to know their own music either.

I have noticed that Country and Western music is the same from truck stop to truck stop, a culture borne, like pollen, along the back roads by the diesels. The jukeboxes at the twenty-four-hour truck stops five miles from Geneva, New York (where an "all-nighter" devoted to a final in comparative political systems could be fortified by some eggs and coffee) are the same as those at the Fort Bliss PX or a diner in Rocky Mount, North Carolina-- equally distant from the Fillmores East and West.

CPA Stan is busy telling Texans that if they ever come to New

York we'll show 'em where it's at. "You can stay at Tauber's place."

My squad leader, from Lookout Mountain in Tennessee, emerges as a leaping, screaming, raving bigot, lacking the subtlety of say, a Bull Connor, pouring it forth in simple, direct statements that spill easily from a self-satisfied, blond, blue-eyed southern Baptist face.

His bunkmate Gomer Thurmond is admired by the other southerners, because he has been to college for a year. He tells me that his "sock-alagy prefesser" at Central State was "ranked fourth in the country in sock-alagy; and my bah-ology teacher was ranked seventh." If you make the top three for two years in a row," says CPA Stan, "they retire you.

Billy Hickock Cavendish, a tight-skinned, wire-haired tough guy from Arkansas, decides that he's gonna skin him some dudes, and so he breaks out a deck of cards to show the boys something about a game called poker. CPA Stan and two other accountants from New York hustle him out of $150 in three hours.

Drill Sergeant Wilson pulls me out of bed at two in the morning to come up to the Charge Quarters to help him sit watch. We start to talk, and it's sergeant to private until he inadvertently tells me how old he is--twenty-three. I stop cold.

"Oh no, man," I say, in the flush of realization, "we got this all wrong."

"What are you talking about?" he asks.

"Hey, don't you see? We ought to be in this together. You're as old as I am, but they've got us on different sides. Man, we ought to be *pals,* out having us some *times.* Why are you trying to make me afraid of you? We ought to be *friends.* "

"Hell, I don't know," he says.

"Well, fuck it. I won't pull any bullshit on you, and you don't give me any crap, okay? And the two of us, well have a good time out of this Army yet."

"Sounds good," he answers, as if he was looking for a reason why it didn't sound good, but, unable to find one, will accept the reasoning.

We talk until well after breakfast, telling jokes, talking about women and sharing future plans. We're not so different.

Drill Sergeant Conboy relieves Drill Sergeant Wilson, and I am passed on like an inheritance, which is fine with Conboy, as he says he wanted to talk to me anyway. He too seems eager to begin dealing with friends and is receptive to being treated like another guy.

He shakes his head imperceptibly as he tells me about his year in Vietnam.

"You lose the kick of killing people after a while. I knew a guy who used to walk up to little bitty babies with a flame thrower and, WHOOSH, light 'em right up." In excited detail he tells me what it's like to see a man's chest blown away, to see friends' bodies blown apart, to be routed by an attack as you sleep and have to fight in the jungle in your underwear, to fight while stoned on Vietnamese pot, to have your very own whore, whom you know to be a V.C., and to kill her in a staged raid on her village. I listen to the stories with growing immunity. The horror and depravity don't faze me anymore; nor do they faze him, he sadly admits.

Drill Sergeant Welch, who believes that he is Steve McQueen, and sky-dives and snares women with imaginary war stories, finds a commando raid of trainees has loosened the bolts on his motorcycle engine. When he starts it, the engine falls off on his foot. He finally fixes it and discovers that someone has filled the gas tank with sugar and ruined the insides forever.

Preparing for the Saturday inspection, many of us work off our tension by singing and doing quickie scenes from musicals. The Texans, across a cultural chasm from the singing and dancing New Yorkers (and Kentucky Private Todd, who seems to know the score from every simpy, flowery musical love story) stare their hostility.

Several of us, who could have escaped to go to services, stay to help clean up, at the request of Drill Sergeant Wilson, to show the other guys that we are "part of the team." Peyser and Stein, who make pests of themselves and whine about their civil liberties and how they are doing everyone a favor-by messing up more than they clean up are rewarded with KP. "To 'The Pits,' Norman," is Drill Sergeant Wilson's curt command. "The Pits" are the grease traps, and they are disgusting. The rest of us get passes, to make up for a holiday--Memorial Day--that managed to escape us in our furious barracks cleaning.

Private Miller shows me a wallet photo of his wife. It's a Polaroid snapshot, and she, in fine color, is absolutely naked, holding her breasts in her hands. Pvt. Thomas commissions Private Rodriguez to take his picture with Pvt. Martinez' camera to send home to Mrs. Thomas. Thomas poses for several shots, naked, holding his testicles in his hands, hoping perhaps that such a reminder of the nature of his love will keep Mrs. T. from straying. Martinez, who has been fined for soliciting his pictures at a loss, is told that subletting his camera is still living dangerously.

"Danger," he replies in one of the all-time great three-way puns, "is my business."

Private Lawson, who plans to make the National Guard a career, tells us a "funny" joke about a Negro riot, prompted by CPA Stan's baiting statement that "it must be great to be able to beat up on college students and minorities." Deep in the bowels of the joke, protected by convoluted syntax, unwrapped and presented like a secret, is a word. He looks around quickly before he says it, checking to see if the coast is clear, and then lays it on us, putting it out front and sliding swiftly on to the next word without a hitch in his stride-right past "nigger" into conventional politics.

"I don't know what you looked around for, Lawson," I tell him.

"I don't like that word. You should have looked at me."

He looks at me quizzically, half smiling, squinting to see if I am as unabashedly hostile as I seem, his smile fading as he realizes that I am willing to betray the white race from within the country club locker room. I challenge someone like this every day. I knew what he looked around for. He sought a little freedom. Freedom to be Mr. Lawson, crude and straightforward, as even I would like to be. He can do it--as long as no Negroes are around--while I, alas, cannot until the whole Army goes away. CPA Stan found himself on the back of a Texan the other day, swinging his fists, showing him that he "was just as fuckin' tough as you are."

AMERICAN NOTES

Someone mentions Vietnam and World War II in the same sentence and I shudder. From time to time the thought creeps up on you that you are training to fight World War II, and the Army, despite its stupidity, violence, craziness and insult, seems almost reasonable. But soon you hear the words "Charlie" and "gook," and you realize that it is a different war and a different America; a war that represents all that is wrong with this different America. "Charlie" and "gook" are words that have led us to Saigon. It's so simple. All the talk about "what would happen if we left" is crap. Look what's happening as we stay.

CPA Stan, Private Nelson, and Private Mantle (né Mandlebaum) return from a visit to the base hospital, where Private Holstein lies nursing a cyst on his coccyx. He went there, not knowing that he didn't have to stay, and they captured him. In three days his treatment was over, but they needed people to mop the place up. He has been there for a week, is not allowed to go to the PX--even *we* are--and gets no mail, as he is still assigned to our company. Mail may not be forwarded without orders, nor given to friends to deliver.

Private Barton Wasserman--"Big Martin's Baby Boy Barton"-- went down there with an infected foot, and when they said he'd have to stay he said, "The hell with you. I'll call my father and he'll call our congressman so fast you wont have time to answer the phone before they ship you out." He managed to escape, but Holstein remains a galley slave, and will have to go through basic training all over again.

You can stare them down by looking them in the eye and telling them, "You're nothing but a pack of cards." The Army fears a sense of integrity and nerve, which is why they spend so much energy trying to emasculate you.

The boys come back and tell about the hospital as they have seen it, a receiving center for wrecked and wounded Vietnam veterans. There are men with limbs and minds blown away haunting the place, creeping up on you like guilt--guilt at being free and whole, guilt at being homeward-bound in a few months --until you find yourself staring, and turn away, self-conscious or ill. The boys return from the hospital shaken and quiet.

CPA Stan reminds me that Walter Cronkite has already made the end of the war official by calling for our withdrawal. Across the plains Walter is truth, as in New York Huntley and Brinkley were once relief. The people stare into the face of Cronkite-- reliable as a dentist--and know they can trust it. Bless you, Walter.

GOD AND MAN AT ARMY

Enter Major Sheehy, the Catholic chaplain, as the lights snap on after a movie on teamwork. His stock has slipped somewhat lately, as he has been ratting on those who come to him for counseling.

He will speak to us today--or is it question, as he ends every sentence with a "hah?"--on, of all things, authority. Who else?

"Those who don't bow to authority," he screams in an angry crescendo, "are slaves to themselves. I'm going to let you in on a secret," he continues, about to share with us a religious confidence, a reverse confessional, "your NCOs aren't saints."

CPA Stan whispers, "He should know."

"But our people are winning in Vietnam," he decides, "and have been for the last ten years, because of the training efficiency of Army drill sergeants." Of course we have only *had* them since 1964, but no matter.

"You've got to have authority or else there is no law and order. When I was a boy there were no traffic lights or signs, and we had lots of accidents. Without authority there is no freedom, hah? The best thing about authority is, of course, Blessed Authority's reward, hah?" Hah?

"Look what happens when you have no authority. They have no Food and Drug Agency [sic] or American Medical Association [sic] in Vietnam. You can't drink the water. So we have to fight there so that they can." Sick.

"Now, men, what was the first example of man's exercising authority over man?"

I volunteer, facetiously, "Cain teaching Abel about the uses of power."

"No, I mean man making laws." No response. "Well," he informs us, "the answer is the Ten Commandments." Is he an agnostic or just stupid?

"What came next, after the Ten Commandments?" Private Nelson answers, "The Deuteronomic codes?" "Oh, well, I guess. You see, men, there was this nation Is-ray-el, and they had these laws . . .But I don't mean that, I mean civil laws."

Private Warsaw leaps up. "Hammurabi's Code?" "No." Others answer: "Roman law?" "No." "Solon and Justinian's codifications?" "No."

A law student rises, exasperated: "Magna Charta, Mayflower Compact, House of Burgesses, English Bill of Rights, Tennis Court Oath, Arabian Law?" "No." "For the love of God, what do you want?"

"The answer, men," intones Chaplain Sheehy, after the best of us have bitten the dust, beaten back by simple "noes," "is that after the Ten Commandments comes the U. S. Constitution."

Scattered applause greets the pronouncement, and CPA Stan and I rise to cheer the victorious American Forces, beating back all those old dusty foreigners. "It's not easy being first when you arrive on the scene so late," admits CPA Stan in awe.

It is apparent that the chaplain can step outside of history and logic as he chooses. By virtue of his captain's bars, he is entitled to teach anything that comes into his head, and that, I suggest, is the best lesson he could have taught us about authority.

"Exactly where in the chain of command is the Pope?" whispers a Texan sitting next to me.

"Men," the chaplain says, his exit imminent, "I want to leave you with this thought. Satan said, '1 will not serve.' "

There is more to this chaplain than benign banality; he is part of a quilt work. All of the subtle, minor, barely perceptible evils in the country, from Daisy Air Rifles to authoritarian chaplains, converge to form the monstrous distortion of our promise that now lays waste babies in an Asian jungle. Like a whirlpool, as the current speeds up in the center, faster and deeper, the evil increases in intensity as the people become more convinced of their Americanness and mission. It is suddenly stunningly clear after four weeks in the Army what Allen Ginsberg is getting at in "Wichita Vortex Sutra."

> Carry Nation began the war on Vietnam here
> with an angry smashing axe
> attacking Wine-
> Here fifty years ago, by her violence
> began a vortex of hatred that defoliated the Mekong Delta—
> Proud Wichita! vain Wichita
> cast the first stone!—
>
> • • • • • •
>
> The war is over now—
> Except for the souls
> held prisoner in Niggertown
> still pining for love of your tender white bodies 0 children of
> Wichita!

Nickel-and-dime stuff from the chaplain, maybe. But it adds up.

Private Peyser, angry over being sent to KP for being a nuisance, threatens to call his senator, but can't remember the name of either one. Plus ça change . . .

THE ARMY

During moments of work or exercise you begin to steal seconds of freedom. What you need is two hours of sleep, but being able to relax your grip on a weapon for half a moment--two seconds, perhaps--is enough. You take what you can get in the underground.

It is apparent that the Army and I are not the best of lovers, nor the worst of enemies. Like Outward Bound, or VISTA, or even summer camp, it is of value mainly for the personal challenge.

Haven't people endured worse? What is so precious about one's ego, comfort, pleasure and existence that they shouldn't be subject to some jolts and bruises? Is this any worse than waking up to face cracked and freezing windows and an arbitrary fate in Harlem every morning? Too many of my liberal friends, and I, will not work and walk with the people they're trying to help or reach or preach to. Maybe knowing that a sergeant's boot controls your life can teach you a little about humility and compassion. Maybe a little rigor wouldn't hurt.

ME: I BEG YOU, LISTEN

The memories have begun to rule me, like insects or bacteria, which, though small, are too numerous and swift to fight off. They own my body.

When I was a civilian my mind would flash forward, constructing plans, staging adventures, setting up psychic holidays.

But now I live as a prisoner and find furtive release only in the past. It haunts me and frees me. The future seems too implausible.

I am at Hobart College, in Geneva, New York, playing with power, feeling confident, living fearlessly.

I am driving in upstate New York with a girl from Wells, bound by nothing but a gas gauge. To worry about running out of gas!

I am traveling by train, or even plane, boundless.

I am in Boston, or dashing to and from it. I am adopted by a Vermont family for a night after an auto accident.

I am driving from San Diego to Vancouver, and almost Alaska, up the British Columbian coast; all stops between and back to Baja, in Mexico.

I am lying by a pool in Connecticut.

I am going somewhere through small towns at night, freely and effortlessly, into French Canada in an all-night dash to go skiing.

I am working, struggling, arguing, worrying, thinking, playing, teasing, laughing, talking, writing. I am going. I am living.

The memories slide in and out of focus, more captivating than any pot-soaked voyage: childhood, adolescence, college, summers, winters. It is past, and it is promised. It keeps me going.

THE FOURTH WEEK

What I Did on My Summer Vacation

Sunday

Private Stevens finds his bed filled with shaving cream, squeals to Drill Sergeant Wilson, and is given KP for not being able to take a joke. When he returns to his bed he finds that vigilantes have ripped it up.

The Pogy Truck, a soda, sandwich and ptomaine enterprise that cruises around selling fizzled soda and indigestibly cold food to mess-weary trainees--many of us don't even eat dinner any more, subsisting on bologna and cheese from the Pogy Truck--is declared off limits because its owner has cut off the sergeants' freebie cops' privileges. So much for the closest thing we have to a whorehouse.

Monday

Like a fighter pilot's risqué inscription on the nose of his plane, or a tank commander's cartoon on the side of his tin can, Private Upper, who cannot keep his fly up, has added a little motto to his steel pot helmet to give some flair to battle: "We Kill Gooks:"

THE ARROGANCE OF POWER

The weekly rainstorm on the desert lashes the rifle range and beats down targets. The sand remains dry as the rain turns to steam nearly a foot above the desert floor, and we all walk around soaked down to the bootstraps, like Achilles after being dipped in the river Styx.

A Battalion formation is called at the rifle range, and Alpha Company, which, rumor has it, has suffered two more suicide attempts--one trainee allegedly jumping through a barracks window and another swallowing a can of Brasso, a brass polish--is in evident high spirits as it belts out its cheer, a cross between a high school football chant and a summer-camp color-war fight song. They are kept "motivated" by harassment and punishment. Charlie Company doesn't even know it has a cheer. CPA Stan rises, alone, to the defense of Charlie: "Rah, rah, Charlie. Rah." Wild applause. Fuming officers.

A second lieutenant, full of his rank--as captains and lieutenants tend to be until they get bored enough to act humanly--attempts to impress us with his authority by demonstrating that his writ runs above the standing regulations of the rifle range. "My commands take precedence." He demonstrates his awesome power by permitting smoking in the vicinity of the ammunition tables. I am awed by the fact that no one gets blown up. He next commands us, still demonstrating his power, to fill our helmets with sand and move a sand dune fifty feet to the northwest. I spend the rest of the day observing his commands from the shade behind the field latrine--my first demonstration to the Army of the limits of power.

Private Peyser, unable after three days' efforts to "zero" his weapon--shooting rounds that hit close together, so that the rifle's sights may be adjusted to compensate for individual mechanical variations--is "administratively zeroed." This is a way of telling the Pentagon that, yes, the instruction has worked, and, yes, he can hit the beam side of a battleship when in truth, no, he can't. Presumably the enemy would "administratively eliminate" anyone he should come up against.

One almost forgets, in the hypnotic demi-fun of rifle practice, that we are shooting at targets in order to be able to shoot at people. Each bull's-eye is a beating heart. Lost also, in the efficiency of Army training, is the minor matter of values. Efficiency may be a misleading word. Rather, every parcel of necessary knowledge is broken down, like computer bits, or teaching-machine "minicepts"; we are trained, not taught.

Nowhere, ever, is there any hint that bombs and guns may not be the best or only way of doing things. Nowhere is there any hint that peace is ever desirable, even as an unavoidable consequence of victory. Nowhere is there any suggestion that we are anything but volunteers; as if we are all careerists, without homes or jobs or friends. As if we have no lives and thoughts but the Army. Nowhere is there any sense of softness, compassion or humanity, or any sense that lives, or any one life in particular, have any value. And civilians? At home they are an anchor around the neck, as abroad they are herds who get underfoot.

THE MODERN ACTION ARMY

We are lectured by an unfrocked Special Forces jock, who alleges, and appears to be telling the truth, that he is presently high on grass. He raps aimlessly for an hour, telling jokes on the Army--the best lecture we've had yet.

Yesterday a retired sergeant, overhearing me talk about my lack of interest in killing and dying, inquired, "what's this Army coming to?" I just don't know.

Another instructor tells us what we've heard in different ways for four weeks: If we pay as little attention to him as our performance indicates, then, well, we deserve the fact that we will most certainly die in Vietnam. "It'll serve you right." The U.S. Army is lucky to have Nam around to serve us right. I wonder whether Charlie listens to his lectures, or whether we serve him

right too. Why don't we both go home and go back to bed?
The signs on the outhouse wall, MacGregor Range branch:

"If you die in Vietnam, who cares?"
"Drop acid, not bombs. Shoot smack, not people. Blow grass, not cities."
"Gary of Chicago was here--will he come back?"
"Who cares if I kill my brother in Vietnam?"
And of course the simple, traditional "FTA"--which the Army thinks, in its illusions of belovedness, stands for its recruiting poster come-on of "Fun, Travel and Adventure," but which is more universally accepted as "Fuck The Army."

CPA Stan is still taunting Private Lawson, who did his homework and looked up "popinjay," "prig" and "martinet," and refuses to talk to me. CPA Stan asks him whether he gets down on beating up strangers during riot control. "Gee, Lawson," I hear him say, "I hope you get the chance every now and then to at least crack some heads of friends of yours."

A column of ants marches and swirls in a pattern that looks like the Major Deegan Highway's approach to the George Washington Bridge on a Friday night. I am very much impressed by their traffic patterns: no ant crashes, no stalled ants, no blocked access, no ant jams. Like Godzilla playing with skyscrapers, I lower a size 10-C government-issue boot and wipe out a million commuters on their way home.

LIBERTY, FRATERNITY, AND REALITY

Exploited classes continue to be exploited, mostly by liberal easterners. Minority types offer to sell their labors and take KP in place of grease-shy dudes at a rate that comes to fifty cents an hour. Imperialism begins at home.

Tuesday

Privates Wasserman and Warsaw, on wake-up detail, show no shyness about parading their geo-ethnic background as they wake us up. The two New York Reservists rouse us with "All right, campers, rise and shine, it's a beautiful day. Long pants and boots. Everybody up-up-up-up." The Texans are not amused and promise violence if there is a repetition.

VARIETIES OF NORMAN PEYSER

Privates Nelson and CPA Stan are engaged in a serious debate as to what, in the animal kingdom, Private Peyser most clearly resembles. It had been accepted as truth that he was a bleached, beached sea lion, but Private Nelson is pushing for a shell-less turtle, while CPA Stan argues the merits of a newly hatched dinosaur. Drill Sergeant Conboy settles the issue forever.

"Pea-zer, come here, sweetheart," calls Bronk, finding Private Peyser (correctly pronounced Pie-zer, but universally mispronounced Pea-zer) in the middle of picking his nose.

"You know what you look like, Pea-zer, stupid? You look like a monkey trying to fuck a football." This, in the scatological pithiness of military language, is but another way of saying, "Pea-zer, your shit is flaky. Unless you get your shit straight, I'm gonna jump in your shit."

TWINKLE, TWINKLE

I continue to wonder, in a literary rather than an astrological way, as I gaze skyward, whether the morning star is Venus or Mars. I decide that I will do no more war chores if it is Mars, because it will be final proof that the deck is stacked. "It's Venus, baby. Love is all around you, truly," says Drill Sergeant Wilson gently.

FORMATION

We have been called to a formation so that Field First Drill Sergeant Rawlins can find out if the men who sent their marriage certificates to Finance, to get an allotment for their wives, have gotten them back. "All right, listen up," he shouts, half blowing the words through his whistle. 'Did all of you mens receive your marriage licenses except some of you?"

There is an answer to that question I suppose, but Private Rackles asks a question that seems to make more sense. "When are we getting our laundry back?" Last week's is still missing in action, and we are into the eighth day of our five-day supply-- something like the first Chanukah, except we smell.

"You can use Rios', if it really bothers you," answers Field First Drill Sergeant Rawlins, alluding to one of the seven AWOLs, three named Rios, who left their fatigues in a pile near the post gate. I picture them dancing down the highway, glee-fully naked. Or perhaps they were making Yossarian's statement: "I can't fight without my clothes on." Most likely the FBI will spot their baldies and haul them in. I consider the uniform-toss a move that I am philosophically in sympathy with, and cherish it as an anti-Nam, antimilitary act, which it was probably not. My fingers move toward my buttons, but cowardice holds me back. So I roll up my sleeves, like a human at last. "Tauber," screams Field First Drill Sergeant Rawlins, "you're out of uniform."

"Yes, field first drill sergeant," I answer meekly.

MEANWHILE, BACK AT THE RANGE

Out at the rifle range again, I notice how nobody really cares. All the instructors deliver their lectures in unintelligible mum-bles between bites of sandwiches and swigs of Coke as they swagger around. Most are Mexican, Puerto Rican, or some exotic Latin combo. The officers sit up in the safety tower, playing "high command," squinting out over their coffee mugs to imaginary troops in the distance, waiting for "the balloon to go up."

The ex-Green Beret pothead, still stoned apparently, talks about Nam, women, grass and liquor. I get homesick. My eyes begin to droop as he talks, and I see a clear vision in my mind as he tells us how a "V.C. was bound up with concertina wire and dragged behind a truck. He looked like Shredded Wheat." I see a tablespoon of Shredded Wheat terribly clearly, oozing forth milk, growing more and more vivid until the milk turns to blood and it bursts forth in a red explosion. I sit up with a start, sweating.

"If you think Orientals are cruel and beastly," he says cheerfully, "you wait until you see a pissed-off GI."

"I don't know how some of those guys do it. They separate themselves from the human race when they're in Nam. I wonder what the hell they're gonna do in civilian life," he muses thoughtfully "That stuff sticks with you, you know."

One of the boys on my right, impressed with the blood and guts, not at all tuned in to the sergeant's sense of horror, whispers, "Damn, I wish I was over there," smacking a tight fist into his palm.

AT HOME WITH PRIVATE DOBY

I am conversing with Private Doby, who, I remind you, is scheduled to die in Vietnam sometime next year.

"I spent some time in the Job Corps, near Austin, way out in nowhere, near Johnson City. I guess they put it there 'cause of The Man's ranch. Compared to this, the Job Corps is heaven. This is hell, man, first cousin to a dungeon. A dog'd get more respect round here than we do.

"They taught me three different skills in the Job Corps, mostly machinist and shop work. I want to be an insurance investigator, work with people. I'd hate to tell people they can't collect, but I'd like to sleuth around and look for what went wrong. Only they wouldn't teach me how to do it until I learned to read. You know there are 140,000 accidents every day? Insurance is the only trillion-dollar business in the world. I can't investigate half a case here, and I just have to wait to learn to read till I get out. I tell you, man, this is no place for a body to be."

YET ANOTHER REPORT ON THE
INEQUITIES OF THE UNIVERSE

The Eastern Dudes continue to fire the M-14 consistently better than the Western Gun-nuts.

Most of the trainees have picked up the drill sergeants' habit, lifted from street-corner hoods, and particularly ballplayers (cf. Roger Maris' Contributions to Western Television Culture, 1961), of tugging, or simply grasping for increasingly long periods of time, at the genitals. Is this a form of bragging?

Holding his testicles as if the very words he says are inspiring him to hare-like desires, Drill Sergeant Grbr calls out, "Okay, anyone got some mail for Jody, bring it out." "Jody" is an Army invention, used to keep the troops fired up. At this writing Jody is sleeping with every trainee's wife, mother or sister--whichever is the girl he left behind--drinking his liquor, watching his TV, driving his car, spending his money, and, in a few limited cases, wearing his ties. I wonder who is kissing her now? It is considered likely that "she" and Jody laugh over our letters home together, delighting in our misery. Yet we continue to write. CPA Stan tells me that he thinks that Jody's last name is Maggio, as in "Where have you gone, Jody Maggio? A nation turns its horny eyes to you."

The benefits of having an unusual last name present themselves, as officers and NCOs no longer look at a roster of names when they want a victim for a detail, relying on probability instead. "Garcia, Jackson, Smith and Davis, report," they call, and ten people step forward.

PCPT

Once again we are put through the five events of the Physical Combat Proficiency Test. We claw and squirm through the low crawl as if we were sneaking under enemy machine guns. We run around hurdles and leap over a pit, cutting and shifting, spinning and twisting, as if a torn-up battlefield stood between us and our objective--most likely a safe hiding place. We hang by our arms, hand-over-handing our way down the rows of the horizontal ladder; down and back until we cannot hold any longer, simulating either a rope-bridge river crossing or a game of tag with Tarzan. We run through the 150-yard man-carry, staggering up a gradient with a soldier on our backs, saving perhaps a wounded buddy from capture, tripping over a mine field maybe. ("Isn't this the way we came?" asks CPA Stan, on my back.) And finally, without even a minute to catch our breaths, we are clustered on the track and we begin the mile run. In the bleaching sun, slowed by sweat-soaked fatigues and heavy leather boots, we thunder around the track, aching and wanting to fall. But we keep going. We have all suffered through four weeks of painful physical training. It tore our muscles at first, broke them down before it would build them up. But now we begin to see the results. Virtually all of our scores have improved impressively. The low crawl, which took me nearly a minute the first time I tried, now takes me less than 30 seconds. The run, dodge and jump, which took me 30 seconds, I now polish off in 28. The horizontal bars are easy for lightweights like me, and I get the maximum point score, seventy-six bars in less than a minute. The man-carry, which took me a minute and cost me some flesh my first time out, takes only 50 seconds--the 10 seconds gained as refreshing as a good night's sleep. And the mile. It too comes easier. I manage to stand up all the way through, coughing up but a few contraband L&Ms toward the end.

We are all a little proud of ourselves, having made it through and having changed so dramatically. Only Private Peyser does not improve. Drill Sergeant Wilson makes a ten-minute plea for tolerance, imploring us to "help the man," accepting his own complicity in the group mocking of the Blob. He resolves to help Peyser, and asks our aid. "He's got to pass the big one at the end," says Wilson, shaking his head doubtfully, "or they'll recycle his ass."

You can fail the PCPTs right up until the eighth week, but if you fail that last one, no matter how many you've passed, you go around again. That, the Rifle Record Fire and the Individual Proficiency Test (G-3), a series of practical and inventory tests that tell whether you have mastered soldiering, determine whether you will "graduate" from Basic Combat Training or remain a trainee forever. The morning line on Peyser is that no one will take bets on his ever getting out of Basic Combat Training any way but a box.

The complexity and compassion of Drill Sergeant Wilson continues to confound us. He seems to be too thoughtful and human for this line of work. His tolerance speech is definitely not "your standard drill sergeant-type speech."

Private Ricardo changes the subject as Peyser returns from God-only-knows-where. Ricardo asks why we can't rotate jobs during clean-up for the daily inspection. We've had the same jobs for three weeks now, and Ricardo is getting tired of cleaning commodes with Private Teddy Leonotto. "I'm Mr. Inside, he's Mr. Outside," says "Commo" Leonotto, laughing at his assigned task. He thinks it's a riot. Ricardo thinks it's a crime. Drill Sergeant Wilson suggests that we have won too many latrine inspections to break up a great team like Mr. Inside and Mr. Outside. "Don't you realize that you guys are the nucleus of the team? Our whole effort revolves around you. You're the stars of the show,"

"Yeah," replies Ricardo, unimpressed, "but what am I gonna tell my wife, when she asks me why I smell of shit?"

"How can she tell the difference?" blurts out CPA Stan. Ricardo leaps at him.

"If she won't have you, I will," injects Private Todd, who continues to add the expected gag line to every mildly suggestive hanging phrase--any phrase with even the slightest overtones of flittyness--fouling off some, knocking ones like this out of the park, and stopping all action as everyone stares, amazed.

RIN TIN TIN PAN ALLEY

At the end of every day loudspeakers blast retreat, and all movement is supposed to stop. If you are outdoors, you must face the anonymous source of music, if you can't figure out where a flag might be, and salute. So at five minutes to five, men rush frantically indoors as if they have just seen Japanese planes on the horizon, desperate to avoid having to stand outside and salute for three minutes. As the final strains are heard today, and we wait for the order to stand at ease, the silence of the beat after the last two bars is broken by a hearty "Yo, Rinny." Somewhere, I expect, an officer in charge of "respect for the flag" has just blown apart.

Wednesday

BOYS' LIB

A flood tide of obscene magazines engulfs the barracks. Having nearly forgotten what girls are like, most of us cluster around the porny and stare at the overly made-up prostitypes in their unattractive, blatantly sexual poses. The sex seems masochistic, like being beaten over the head with a woman. I think back to the bra and girdle ads of *The New York Times Magazine* and am mellowed somewhat.

PSYWAR

The Army has discovered the secret fear of Private Norman Peyser and is acting on it. (Mine, for future reference, is pain.)

He is being denied his mail by being assigned to details that co-incide with mail call. Drill Sergeant Wilson has realized that Peyser is dragging a 3,000-mile blanket, and needs to be made to stand up by himself. So, just as he seems beyond all redemption, a last attempt at motivation is being made. At first he whines and whimpers. He received fifteen letters yesterday and knows that there are more today. Then he threatens and sputters. Finally he begins to wail and howl, like Benjy in *The Sound and the Fury,* the order of his universe disturbed, his guideposts switched and mixed. He cries and weeps, like a wounded sheep, bleating a dirge of self-pity. Someone teases him and he acts enraged, like a blinded animal. He swings an ineffectual paw at his tormentor, a ludicrous, limp-wristed wave. Yet it is the first sign of emotion or intense reaction we have seen. It may be a hopeful sign. Maybe he will fight back. But for now he remains, weeping and trembling, helpless in a world that demands at least minimal competence.

We are beginning to get on each other's nerves. I continue to be pugnacious, taking so much nonsense from the Army each day that I am unwilling to absorb any noninstitutional crap. Private Watts and Private Terry have a rock fight and hit a passing lieutenant with rocks by mistake. They escape, but I nearly get nailed for laughing.

FIGHT OR FIFTY-FOUR-FORTY

They have us shooting at targets again, and Private Nelson asks me whether I've noticed that the targets are like the ones at the pistol range at the FBI building, shaped like a silhouette of a man. I have, but I'm trying to forget.

The loveliness of Canada keeps tripping through my mind. It's a lovely place even when you are not in the Army, captivated by its elsewherehood. But I am, and all the more reason that its forests and mountains should arrest my thoughts from the project at hand: learning to kill on my summer vacation. What I Did on

My Summer Vacation: I learned to think of Canada when being taught to kill.

BUM TRIP

While listening to instructors tell us about how to shoot straight I've been reading a collection of essays by scientist Isaac Asimov on the origins of the universe, cosmological problems, and other giggly stuff. He asserts rather blandly that the universe will collapse into an egg of protons and energy in only a few billion years. Very discouraging. I mean, why get out of bed? Nothing will survive. Nothing. No monuments, memories or theories will make it to a safe shore. No libraries, life or dynasties. And here we are, in green suits, wasting our time, when we could be out wasting the universe's. What a down it is to see oneself as future protons. Energy can have fun at least. (Oh, to be an Orgone!) Maybe we can move to a different universe.

Thursday

Private Todd is still displaying signs of yielding to the pressure. He hung his underwear out to dry on his bed today like an advertisement. He still makes sly jokes, waxing physical, but shows guts by hanging in there during training. "I don't know what you are, boy," Texan Wintergreen Waters tells him as they both come out of the latrine, "but you ever try to grab my ass when I'm in the shower again and I'll turn you into toothpaste."

Private Woodling, a deerlike Negro who is a spit-and-polish pro as a result of a glut of high school ROTC drum-and-bugle nonsense, assumes personal charge of the "Peyser case." Like the Army hierarchy, he is convinced that what's wrong with Peyser, or any of us, has to do with an inability to master the manual of arms and simple marching junk. They are comfortable in the notion that there is but one way to skin a cat, one set of American skills that demonstrate manhood, and one way to "grow a person up." All the way Ar-my. I used to think you became an American by necking in a back seat with a girl who had a name like an astronaut--having America lay its hands on you. I guess I was wrong.

CALLED BLUFFS

In a continuing series of discipline breakdowns bordering on martial disaster, the entire company fails to wake on time, straggles out of the barracks and wanders to the mess hall without a formation, an hour late. The drill sergeants stand in awe of our gall. We enjoy the extra hour's sleep.

At breakfast Captain Marshall, called "Asshole," the King of Alpha Company, challenges sleepy trainees, threatens others, instructs some to rearrange their trays. He tells me to switch my cereal and my eggs, and I arch an eyebrow and look him in the eye, backing him off by an expression that says, "What are you, Captain Marvel?"

Such impertinence is not my province alone. In a ballsy all-or-none maneuver bordering on mutiny, our entire company calls the Army's bluff and lives to tell the tale. Instructed by an uncaring corporal at the Rifle Range Tactical Training site to practice the low crawl in the hot New Mexican sand, we practice, instead, as a unit, the great Army art of avoidance. Two hundred men look at the sand and simply turn on their heels and walk off.

The corporal doesn't seem to care, and no one seems to realize that this single act may have been the opening shot in the great GI Revolution. CPA Stan and I observe the whole sorry episode from behind the field latrine, where we are resting.

NORMAN'S RIFLE LESSON

Drill Sergeant Wilson, impressed by the vigor with which I thrust my rifle butt at Private Peyser at the range last week, orders me to be Norman's rifle-range coach, and concomitantly to risk my life. "I joined the Reserves because I didn't want to die, drill sergeant," I plead.

"Your country calls," he answers sternly.

I give Peyser an empty magazine and watch him flinch from a phantom kick when he pulls the trigger. I finally make some headway, and by lunchtime he has actually re-zeroed his weapon.

YOU ARE WHAT YOU EAT

The final solution to the mess question is offered for lunch: C Rations. A word is in order about the surprisingly good meal this represents.

We are issued a box, "card-board, grey-type," stamped "meat, combat-type," which I interpret to mean "extra tough." My package also reads "Ham and Lima Beans," which, it turns out, is simply a lie.

Within the package are several attractive tuna-fish-size cans, Army green, with tasty labels: C-3, B-6, and A-2. One contains beefsteak, but it tastes like Spam or cat food. Another tin contains crackers and cheese. ("What," asks CPA Stan, "no wine?") A mini loaf of bread, called *panacha* in Mexican, meaning "little loaf"--and in Texan meaning pudenda--is in the other, and peaches are in the third. Other people's tins have peanut butter, pound cake, chicken and noodles (without the soup) and jam. Private Nelson gets tins with crunchy peanut butter, pound cake and a *panacha*. "Mmmurffnmf," says Private Nelson, trying to complain about the absence of liquids. "Dem's da breaks," says the mess sergeant.

Tiny can openers the size of a fingernail are supplied. "They're all right," says CPA Stan, "if you like the taste of blood."

A dessert accessory pack is issued with each box, containing three cigarettes and two sheets of toilet paper. And one Chiclet, the closest thing in the temporal world to "one hand clapping." World War II pilots, I am told, got a Hershey bar and a prophylactic.

OPTION TIME

Private Holstein is still among the missing, an unperson, captured by the hospital and not allowed back into the company. Were he here in a wheelchair, he could make out all right, because today is the day the reins came down. From now on, we are told by Drill Sergeant Wilson, we don't have to do anything we don't want to do. "If you don't want to go to bayonet or physical training, that's all right." The decision seems to have come because of the abnormally large number of walking wounded, trainees who continue to train in fear of a drill sergeant's boot, running on bad feet, pushing exhaustion, landing in the hospital. Fair enough, I say. The only catch is that we still have to pass all the final tests or be recycled.

UNMARKED ANNIVERSARIES

It is now, though no one in the Army seems aware of it, one year since Robert Kennedy was murdered. What would have been John Kennedy's fifty-second birthday, May 29, passed similarly unnoticed; there are no days and dates in the Army, no significant anniversaries. The twenty-fifth anniversary of D-day went by without a word.

Friday

NORMAN PEYSER REVISITED

Private Peyser continues to receive and accept phenomenal abuse, excessive KP and constant ridicule, and continues to earn them like an accomplished pro. You can't get something for nothing in this world.

And he continues to stand in Harm's Way, interposing his incompetence between hostile authority and the rest of us. If we are hiding or malingering, out of uniform or screwing up, we can count on Private Peyser to wander in a daze across the scene, pre-empting the drill instructor's charge. All official wrath is attracted to the Great Green Jellyfish because of the artistry of his ineptitude. He has become, thus, perversely beloved. Yet he is no longer funny--growing pathetic and melancholy. In our exhilaration at winning in the Army's game, we have forgotten that we know who Peyser is.

At my loneliest and most scared, I have shared his fears. I too have wondered whether they have all agreed on the rules in my absence; puzzled over when they made the secret understandings that enable everyone else to move in the American maze without bumping into the walls.

We have forgotten, as a psychologist friend of mine wrote me, when I described Norman to him, that "we may all be Peysers."

SIMPLE SONGS OF FREEDOM

After three days of effort CPA Stan and I finally recall all the words to "The Eve of Destruction," assuring us the largest repertory of antiwar songs of any duet in the company. The rules of the game are that anyone who remembers any antiwar songs must share them with the others. We Vietniks, being but a handful, need all the ammunition we can get. Years ago, I recall, we used to laugh at the kids who held hootenannies, singing songs to each other about the revolution, labor, and sweating alongside your fellow man, convincing no one but themselves, but reinforcing their commitment in a cynical world.

Other songs, as well, have their uses. To psych up the troops during the morning run, Field First Drill Sergeant Rawlins runs along ahead of us, singing and chanting, clapping as he runs, until we are all singing along:

> I wanna be a Airborne Ranger
> I wanna live a life of danger
> I wanna be a fighting man

> I wanna go to Vietnam
> I wanna jump out of the sky
> I wanna make the V.C. die.

And from the rear of the column, where the third platoon and the last third of the alphabet are running--the names that begin with the R-S-T-W Semitic quadrad--comes a counterpoint chant, moving to the front of the column, overtaking the Airborne Rangers, who will chant anything they hear without thinking. It creeps up row by row, slowly, because we are running away from this new chant and into the strains of the first, but moving row to row still: "Hell, no, we won't go!"

And now everyone chants it, Field First Drill Sergeant Rawlins, followed by two hundred trainees, smashing forward, a freight train of muscle, steadily pounding around the base, frightful in our boots and tee-shirts, running in step, mighty and martial, getting looks of approval from officers and sergeants we pass. Charlie Company! Ass-kicking Charlie! Thud, thud, thud. Chargin' Charlie! Singing as we go:

> "Hell, no, we won't go,
> Hell, no, we won't go.
> HELL! NO! WE WON'T GO!!"

Laughing and exhausted, we move back to the platoon billets, and Private Santiago Ramirez is whistling the "Eve of Destruction." "Aha, a convert," says Private Nelson.

"Hey," says Santiago, "that's a great song. Do you guys know all the words to 'The Green Berets'?"

WHY ARE WE IN VIETNAM?

As part of the great experiment in self-service training, several of us plan to say that we are not up to killing this morning, but back down. Only Peyser misses formation. His absence is noticed and he is sent to KP above his protestations.

Kid McDonald, the seventeen-year-old boy who has enlisted for three years, growing less and less happy with his seventeen-year-old assuredness, asks me whether I think we'll get off for Christmas. My mind wanders and, perhaps too vividly, I describe my plans for a Christmas party, skiing in Vermont, friends and freedom. Kid McDonald starts to cry.

There are other sources of tension between the weekend warriors and the hired guns. Not *just* the ethnic thing, and not just the fact that we'll be out soon enough and they are bound for uncertainty. During formations the Reservists and some Guardsmen fool around, talk, shove, smoke, read, and begin to feel their oats and get rambunctious. The draftees and Regular Army enlistees are tense and nervous, believing perhaps that unseen eyes observe every part of their anatomy and will kill them for a twitch. I wonder how long they've felt this way. Or there is the matter of jokes. The easterners prefer to ease their burdens with humor and let a laugh invade and conquer their misery. But the westerners, purists maybe, puritans, will brook no interference with their suffering. It must not be mocked and is theirs alone to wallow in. Anguish is an exclusive thing, not to be contaminated with levity. They act offended and assaulted by any attempt to cheer them up, lashing out at him who dares. Why are we in Vietnam? Go back a step and look.

At bayonet practice we are taught the butt stroke, preparatory, CPA Stan insists, to our first off-post passes. We are next taught the nullifying movement of how to ward off the very same butt stroke, and I sign an armistice with myself.

"What if you're up against someone and you butt-stroke him and he wards it off?" asks Private Wasserman.

"Ask him to enlist on your side," answers Drill Sergeant Grbr. "All together now," shouts Drill Sergeant Welch, "finger jab, finger jab, foot stomp, foot stomp," as we jab and stomp like the June Taylor Dancers, on cue, in unison. "Finger jab, finger jab, foot stomp, foot stomp," until we are all sucked into the mass and are jabbing and stomping on cue, unaware that the little dance we are doing is made up of two deadly parts. "Finger jab, finger jab, foot stomp, foot stomp."

FRIDAY AFTERNOON AT THE MOVIES

"When The Truth Is Found to Be Lies, You Know the Joy Within You Dies. Don't You Want Somebody to Love? Don't You Need Somebody to Love? Wouldn't You Love Somebody to Love? You'd Better Find Somebody to Love," Part I.

"This is the most important movie you are going to see, so watch and take notes," Lieutenant Beep-Beep tells us. "You'll be sorry," whispers CPA Stan. Symbolically, the film, on counterinsurgency warfare, begins out of focus, and starts to skip. It is officially titled, "The Third Challenge: Unconventional Warfare," significantly subtitled Armed Forces Information Film 1-2-3, and is apparently on the Army's Ten Best list, prompting the following notes:

It is narrated by Alexander Scourby, the voice of Eastern Airlines and a thousand documentaries, not to be confused with Westbrook von Voorhees, who narrated most of World War II. Scourby's Brooklyn-Oxford-Boston intonation lends the entire project a sort of instant legitimacy despite the pap that passes for content; sort of like Nixon standing behind the presidential seal.

His lines are typically pompous: "In remote comers of the world, where the heartbeat of freedom is threatened by a sinister shadow. . ." A few credits: Metaphors by Mixmaster; clichés by DeCarload.

The local Commie type in Insurgentelvania looks like a *Reichsjugend.*

Scourby tells us that, "it is the Communists who have unleashed the dogs of war." Cry havoc! Did he ever let slip the correct quotation! "We have not," we are gratuitously told, "seen their like in our time." Huh? (C+/B- . . . See me.)

Commie leader harangues local villagers in a manner much like Adolph's, and quite inappropriate to the scene of thirty people listening to him. The grass-hut scenery and Nordic villagers' faces place the action somewhere in tenth-century Lapland, and I expect a character from *Njal's* Saga to appear at any moment and set things to rights. Our sneaky American camera comes in tight on the Confederate in the crowd, who helps the leader recruit for the insurgent army. The director of this film, ambivalent and equivocal, has the crowd giving no support to the haranguer, but somehow he raises some recruits-- nearly all of the villagers. His final words are something about "imperialist lackey troops," by which I think he means me. Just another one of those days.

"Remember Fiddle Castro?" Sourby asks us, putting us on the spot. Whatever did become of him? "Remember how everyone thought he was the Robin Hood of Cuba?" Okay, let's get it straight. George Wallace made that line famous, attacking *The New York Times* and editorialist Herbert L. Matthews for their pre-revolution reporting on Castro's mountain movement. "They thought he was good," says Sourby, "because he promised a better life, talked about food, land and hope. Well, he turned out to be a Communist."

Okay, Alex, let me try it once: All people who promise food, land and hope are Communists. QED. Or, just to be on the safe side...

More: "Cuba's Che Guevara said 'no revolution can succeed without the firm support of the people.' " Caveat populi. "The Masters of Communist Aggression have a great stake in popular uprisings."

An old villager is shot, from nowhere, by no one. For the hell of it, I guess. You can't sell a film these days without sex and violence. I await the sex.

The Leaders of the Country, "beleaguered by Communist Insurgency" (and I hear it's even worse at the polls), white, bedecked in pinstriped tropicals, address the American ambassador, who looks American and ambassadorial. "This is the decision we have reluctantly been forced to make," they say, "and we hope that the U. S. will view it similarly. We need much U.S. military aid." Gimme, gimme, gimme.

Flash to the home front: A bogus TV news interviewer with a bogus General--both old TV-serial characters--asks, "Why are we going to be involved?"--As if such things happen all at once. A screen behind them flashes "Situation Now Critical." Any old situation. And in the last ten minutes. Maybe the country is wearing an electric pacemaker. The General flashes slides on the screen at will, as if he were one of the "news" show's producers, which he may well be.

Scenes of Special Forces fighting the Red Menace flash by. Lots of Laplanders bite the dust.

Communist terror is displayed. We see a random shot of children running. Maybe in terror. Maybe from Communists.

Item: "The Cold War is what passes for Peace in Our Day." American troops free the villagers and are greeted with a Cabin-in-the-Sky, All-God's-Chillun celebration.

"And where do you get the training and talent for civic action?" asks a voice. "Why, from the U.S. Armed Services themselves." Teach you a little about democracy? Have some candy, little boy? "It is the responsibility of you men," says an American officer to the host country's officers, "to show your country the way, because *only you* have the training in the political and social factors. You must direct your country's future."

Pacification: A U.S. officer shows some Orientals, who appear from out of nowhere, how to make a crude projector for "teaching," using a box, mirrors and sunlight. They nod and grin. Wily Americans. Ten thousand mirrors, boxes and $50 million in arms later...

Scourby chats a little about holding off the Masters of Communist Aggression, and we see some nukes going off. "The U. S. Army is busy training forces of all free governments who ask. Air Commandos instruct the country's Air Force--which is equipped with American planes." Makes you feel all warm inside.

Quoting for the fifth time a speech by Nikita Khrushchev given in 1961, Scourby catches the Soviet Union admitting that "there is support in the Soviet Union for wars of National Liberation."

But the Americans are winning. The Commie leader lies in the bottom of a boat to escape American fire--to escape and cause more trouble elsewhere, like Dr. Moriarty (cowardly sort). Concluding this Cinematic Kitchen Debate, Scourby, the Voice of America, says that "we have prevented the Communists from grinding their heels on mankind's face, in lands already bleeding from the Red effort to establish their dark dreams." Whew.

Two and a half stars.

LOSING BATTLES

We are bumped from the hand-to-hand-combat field by Echo Company without firing a shot. Some Army.

Private Warsaw asks a question on the physics of a particular move, and the Texans make a joint noise indicating, "Boy, what a stupid question." But a Texan asks, about the heel stomp, "You, uh, do it with the, uh, foot?" and he is deemed to have asked an important question, as heads nod in thoughtful approval of his asking. "If I hit it with it, when I should do it with the other, will I be doing it wrong?" asks Private Martinez. "No, that's all right," answers a drill sergeant after a moment's thought.

We are introduced to a new drill sergeant, who is replacing Drill Sergeant Welch. Welch left because he couldn't seem to cut it after someone poured sugar in the gas tank of his motor-cycle. The new man, Drill Sergeant Pyle, begins to threaten us with heavy physical training, but soon catches on when no one responds and the other drill sergeants don't seem to care. He arrives smelling and acting drunk for morning formation his second day, and falls asleep, snoring loudly, in a lecture class.

Saturday

THE GREAT DEBATE

Field First Drill Sergeant Rawlins of the jovial mien, the chipmunk cheeks, and the easy con, engages Private Peyser in debate. He advises Private Peyser to change into fatigues and report to the Special Training Company instead of going to chapel.

Private Peyser: "I don't see why I, out of all the company, should be singled out."

Field First Drill Sergeant Rawlins: "There are obvious reasons."

Private Peyser: "Besides, I have a friend back home who was a clerk in an STC. And he told me what it is like. So I'm not going to learn anything. I've talked with many people about it, and I've concluded that I don't need it."

Private Nelson whispers to me, "You recognize that last line?" I nod. It is the standard son-father line, used by sons when discussing their college choices, or their careers, or getting married at sixteen, or sailing the Arctic Ocean in a kayak: "Well, I've talked with many people about it, and they say . . ." You never really do talk with anyone about it anyway.

Field First Drill Sergeant Rawlins: "It's for motivation, and twenty others who failed the PCPT are going also."

Private Peyser: "I don't need the motivation."

The debate swings to and fro until Field First Drill Sergeant Rawlins orders him to change and see the CO to receive a direct order.

Peyser reports to STC for training, only to discover that there is no one there. Field First Sergeant Rawlins forgot to tell them Norman was coming. Field First Sergeant Rawlins has a nine-minute retention span, which is at least better than Private Peyser's, which is nothing at all.

When Norman returns, triumphant, Field First Drill Sergeant

Rawlins appoints me "owner and trainer," as Rudd Weatherwax was for Lassie, and sends Peyser to "the Pits," the grease traps of KP, out of habit.

SATURDAY FREDDY THE RABBI SLEPT LATE

The chaplain arrives two hours late for services as I sit beneath what must be the only tree in El Paso, smelling memories. I have mastered the trick of recreating the tilt of the middle ear, the feeling of a rush of blood in the stomach, the fragrances and tastes, all the feelings of memories, until I am kinesthetically borne away into the past.

The services drone on indefinitely, and no one even bothers to chant the same words. We feel a little apologetic to our guests, who have come to sample the much-touted food. The chaplain feels called upon to give a direct order to the congregation to shut up during the reading of The Law. He is ignored. His aides-de-cloth scurry about trying to find volunteers for the various functions in the service, but no mad rush to the ark ensues, and the chaplain is forced, like Alec Guinness, to play seven different parts.

Back at the company we find that the promised passes have been withdrawn to teach us some lesson about the arbitrariness of war. The company morale is shot. I go up to see Drill Sergeant Conboy, who is on Charge Quarters, when I am told that we will have a foot- and wall-locker inspection this afternoon.

A blast of rock music emanates from an elaborate hi-fi Conboy has rigged. When he is on CO he brings his drums and his tapes and plays along with the music.

I can't find him anywhere, but I notice that the door to the CO's office is closed. I open it and find another drill sergeant, nearly naked, on the floor, with Tama, a girl from El Paso Senior High, who hangs around our company headquarters. She is giggling and laughing beneath him. "Sorry," I say as I close the door. He comes bursting out, in his boots and a shirt, to usher me out. "Don't you realize," he says, "you could embarrass the poor child? Why didn't you knock? Come back later, Okay?"

"WHEN I WAS YOUNGER, SO MUCH YOUNGER
THAN TODAY . . ."

Private Thomas, who is having problems with his wife despite the pictures he sends home, is bent all out of shape. His wife is flying out to El Paso, expecting him to meet her. But now the passes have been canceled, and he is up a tree. "Why don't you use the CO's office when Tama is through?" suggests Private Wintergreen Waters.

On the wall of the barracks is a sign: "Need HELP? Going AWOL? Down in the dumps? Have a problem? Confused? Angry? Frustrated? Need some place to turn? Need some action on a problem? Call HELP! Chaplains will answer your call 24 hours a day to HELP you!!"

He calls HELP and tells the chaplain his problem. The wrong chaplain--Chaplain Sheehy, the stoolie, the company fink Chaplain Sheehy calls the CO and tells him that Thomas is annoyed with his decision to lift the passes, and that, by the way, he has broken the chain of command by calling HELP, since Sheehy is a major and the CO is a captain. Thomas receives no HELP, but is told to report to the CO Monday morning, and is given a dressing down over the phone. Sucker. HELP.

PATTERNS OF CULTURE

The lobby of the base movie theater gives you the immediate impression that Richard Nixon would feel comfortable here. A giant picture of Connie Francis looms over us.

A cartoon about two lynxes and a bear is well received by the audience.

The crowd sits, in free association, each to his own kind. Areas are eastern, southern, Texan, and "other." Subsections of New

York, New Jersey, Long Island, North and South Carolina, Georgia, eastern and western Texas give added definition to the arrangement. But lines run the other way as well, linking all the Reservists, regardless of state, all of the Guardsmen, the enlistees and draftees. After a while I become aware of the patterns in the network. "You know what this is?" Private Nelson asks me. "Yup," I reply, "it's a Mendeleevian chart."

"That's right," he says, "a periodic table of the elements. Look at the inerts. All Texan. My God. Peyser is lead!"

"And you and I are transuranic."

"I want to be Berkelium."

Private Stein, who was, as I recall, Protactinium, or maybe Molybdenum, returns to the company area drunk as well as stupid, skipping through Alpha Company singing something about "ass-kicking Charlie," and is set upon and beaten by hostile Alphavillians.

He tells his tale to Charlie Company and receives no sympathy until the same fate befalls a Texan, and half of Charlie rushes out with entrenching tools to do battle, drunk and disorderly on 3.2 beer.

Sunday

THE TEXAS TRIP

I have been getting into fights with increasing frequency this week over the New York business. I tried to separate myself when it was associated with the Brooklyn-Queens crowd alone. But now it's "Yankees and easterners." I've dropped my pretense of being a Californian, and yesterday reminded three Georgians of the final score of the Civil War. But they are right. This is their Army, and maybe their country. And I am getting into fights to show them that we're just as tough as they are; that we can out-Texan them. And I guess that means they've already won.

So Texans continue to be among my least favorite people. That goes especially, as Gabby Hayes used to say, "for the Whole United States aaaaand Texas!"

THE OPEN DOOR

They came right out and gave us our option this week: to train or not to train. That was the question. The only catch was that we will still have to pass all of the tests at the end; still have to run a mile in fatigues and boots in under 8 minutes, after swinging down 76 overhead bars of a horizontal ladder in under a minute, after running 150 yards in 45 seconds carrying a man on our backs, after running around hurdles and leaping back and forth over a pit in 25 seconds and crawling 40 yards in a sand trough in half a minute. That's all. Only three more weeks to get in shape, and one of them will be spent exhausting ourselves on a desert bivouac a week from Monday morning. Thus we all resign ourselves to actually going to physical training voluntarily, which has to stand as the sucker play of the year.

But there is another reason to *train,* shared by only a few of us who still retain some memory traces of the world beyond the Army. Something about discipline, the kind we never knew in our privileged lives, and pointlessness; arbitrary hardship makes it all a challenge. There is no reason to get up at four in the morning or have eight-inch rolled underwear or look like a poster soldier, with shiny shoes and gleaming brass--or do half of the inane things we are called upon to do in the name of soldierhood. But for those of us who will mercifully never see war these tasks are rewarding because they are so humbling.

Certainly it is not mental hardship that presents the challenge to us in the Army, and the physical hardship can be borne. What does present a test is the challenge of self-discipline, in or out of the Army, and the rigor of accepting arbitrary and irrational fate.

To those of us for whom the struggle for existence is easy, by virtue of nature and birth, those of us with gifts of talent and brains, to whom survival is no hardship, earning a living no problem, this, then, is the strenuous life. Living in a classless, egoless and consciousnessless cell, divorced from the manipulative logic we triumph by, separated from luck, we are isolated from reason and argument. We are trapped--as I realized the first time I was forced to punitive push-ups for another trainee's mistakes, days after an order had outlawed physical punishments--beyond logic and the law, on the far side of the looking glass. Could I cut it in the world if I hadn't been born lucky? Could I pioneer, or could I even face a Harlem winter's morning? I may never know, so here is where I test myself, fighting the personal corruptions that make the hard life harder: laziness, self-indulgence, self-pity and self-worship.

So the open door is open for but a few, as some of us stay inside the Army's cage, looking for elusive discipline. It's what--among other things--I came for. To leave without it would mean that I have lost the game in the locker room. What the hell, it's only six months--then the backsliding. The worst is halfway done.

Sunday ends for me softly, behind a closed door. My thoughts go back to the essay on the life-span of the universe. The Cosmic Joke continues.

Only a few billion years left before a universe determined to remind us how small we really are sweeps even the Army away. I'm enjoying the ride.

THE FIFTH WEEK:

The War Is Over

Monday

L a guerre est finie. "I declare," said Phil Ochs, Allen Ginsberg, and now me, "The War Is Over."
    We've toyed with ourselves long enough. The Army was great sport and grand fun for a few weeks, a fine test of physical and psychological hardiness and social adaptability. But now it's time to move on to something new, something real, something important. It has become an overlong party, a stale and sick joke. There's nothing magical about surviving eight weeks of bullshit as opposed to, say, four. The questions are answered, the challenges over. What's holding up my discharge?

> Why don't we stop fooling ourselves?
> The game is over, over,
> Over,
> Over.
> No good times, no bad times.
> There's no times at all,
> Just *The New York Times*. *

* From "Overs" by Paul Simon, © 1967 by Charing Cross Music, Inc. Used with permission of the publisher.

We *do* define the events and the universe we act in. Our semantic creations become our reality. And just as umpteen politicos can make us "win" in Vietnam by the simple assertion of that condition, one can, I suppose, simply decide that the War is over. "Why don't we declare we've won in Vietnam and get out?" suggested Senator Aiken. And *my* war too. "I am a soldier." There. Now let me go home, I say.

Not the best of attitudes to begin the week with.

I am not the only one who feels this way. Drill Sergeant Conboy completes the act of rebellion that we have been heading toward all week. Ever since we lost a week's inspection trophy to the second platoon because Field First Drill Sergeant Rawlins overheard Drill Sergeant Wilson describe him as "stupid," we have been at open war with the company.

"The jerk has it in for me, and he's punishing my platoon for it," says Drill Sergeant Conboy. "That's why he gave me Norman Peyser."

"But Peyser's name is alphabetically right for your platoon," corrects Private Thurmond.

"Even if it wasn't, he would have given me Peyser."

Drill Sergeant Conboy, effectively seceding from the company, leads us to the shade of a barracks wall, where we sit and shoot the shit for two hours while the rest of the company does chores.

"Shit," he says. "If he can decide that we're not the best when we are, just 'cause he doesn't like me, I can decide we're working when we're not, just 'cause he's stupid."

THE NOUN-VERB AS A WEAPON OF WAR

We are trained in the art of the pugil stick, which is not a descriptive verb, like 'heel stomp," but a noun, like rifle butt (which may also be used as a verb). Isn't it interesting that the Army has passive nouns that are also violent verbs?

Pugil sticks, which are dangerous nouns, are simply six-foot poles with wadding at the ends, and are used to teach bayonet fighting with a greater simulation of movement and pain than a dry-run bayonet class can.

Two opponents square off, each with a pugil stick (like Robin Hood and Little John), a football helmet, lacrosse gloves and a catcher's cup, to protect the "family jewels" (the Army's most artful euphemism). They begin to flail at each other, looking for an opening for the kill. It looks like an enjoyable game, testing your reflexes and your fighting skill, risking little.

Private Doby, in earnest innocence, not having had the surrogate nature of the pugil battle explained to him, asks Drill Sergeant Pyle, "What use are pugil sticks in Vietnam?"

Pyle tells him to steal the VC's football helmet and catcher's cup.

Time was when fighting with padded sticks was something we did while straddling the gunwales of a canoe as an event in an aquatic carnival at summer camp. Time was when pugil sticks were used in an exotic form of training I knew West Pointers underwent, having seen at least ten documentaries about the Point, knowing that pugil sticks was but another good reason why I would never go there. But time was also when I played a game called punchball, where, if you were halfway home, you were considered safe at home, a run scored, all the way home. And I am halfway home today, no safer and no closer than yesterday.

BOYS AND BOYS TOGETHER

The Clubhouse at empty Barracks #4 becomes the place where it happens, finally, and all at once. We knew it would happen, but it was a matter of where and when. Today. In empty Barracks #4.

It starts as wrestling and horseplay. Some of the guys are dozing on the bare mattresses; others, on bed springs, are making creaking noises. Peyser is lying on a mattress that rests on a partially disassembled bed, its foot support lying flat on the floor. Private Ellis, an energetic and playful Negro, with tight skin and wiry muscles, picks up a mattress and tosses it on top of Peyser. He leaps on it, holding the two mattresses around Norman by gripping the bed springs, lying on top of the "Peyser sandwich." He starts to twist and grind, as if he is humping the mattress. With a heave, Norman tosses Ellis and his mattress off onto the floor. But Ellis leaps up and jumps on Norman again. He pins Peyser to a mattress and yells "Rape" as he mounts him and starts to go wild with his pelvis. A dozen others all pile on, turning the pantomime rape into a free-for-all, a massive gang rape. Trainees slip off the pile, and two begin to rape Private Young from the front and back. Now there are twenty small clusters and pairs of humping, laughing, screaming, kissing trainees, bumping and sliding in orgiastic glee. Faces are buried in necks, arms interlocked, chests pound together, hands jump around, there is an occasional flash of flesh, fantastic noises. Two-thirds of the platoon are going sexually mad with one another while the other third watch. Panting and groaning noises--no counterpoint noises from the watchers break the mood--giggling and caressing, shouting and petting, kissing, kissing. A whistle blows, and everyone leaps up as silence washes over the scene. The screams and laughter subside and everyone scrambles for the door to make formation. Shirts are tucked, canteen belts fixed while running, buttons fastened and gig lines adjusted as the entire platoon runs silently, sweatily out of the door.

For the rest of the week no one mentions the scene or enters the empty barracks, which we once used as a clubhouse.

THE SKINNER BOX

Commanding Officer First Lieutenant Mott castigates the entire company for its lassitude and apathy, and declares the always-closed Day Room off-limits, as an incentive to hard work. Private Nelson, a graduate student in systems analysis, explains it: "His mind is limited, by military construction, in the alternatives for influencing behavior that it presents him with. Open a lock, close a lock. That's all he knows. Always on one plane." I agree with him completely.

PRIVATE SCHOOL

Second Lieutenant Tanner is on the "critical list," as is our young commanding officer, First Lieutenant Mott, and will lose his commission unless he takes the equivalent of two years of college courses. He enlists Private Holstein--who has nothing better to do while he waits for his new company assignment than write letters of protest to Allard Lowenstein--as his tutor in math. "Tutor" may be the wrong word. He enlists him as only an officer can enlist a private, and Holstein dutifully does Lieutenant Tanner's homework for him, sharing his time equally between Tanner and Drill Sergeant Conboy, who needs his help learning math, so that he can, in turn, tutor his girl friend in algebra.

EL EXIGENTE PERPLEX

We police up the weeds in the desert behind the barracks, in anticipation of The Colonel's Visit. They never tell you a General is going to visit, because it is too easy to imagine him getting sidetracked elsewhere. Why would he want to see us? But a Colonel! What better use has a Colonel for his time than to harass trainees and make minute inspections of the sand, looking for elusive weeds? He never comes, of course. It is just another Army hoax to keep you motivated. He may not even exist. I never knew a soldier who ever really saw The Colonel. Oh, Colonel Thorne and Lieutenant Colonel Treandley might sweep through perfunctorily once every two months on an inspection, but never The Colonel, whose name is spoken breathlessly, like *El Shaddai*, the holiest of holies. He doesn't reveal himself to man. But lest He whom we await should arrive, with a keen interest in our sand, we will be ready.

Most of us fulfill our military obligation this afternoon by standing on the edge of a highway hollering and whistling at passing girls in racy cars.

RECHERCHE DU TEMPS PERDU

I receive a letter from a female of strictly intellectual friendship replying to a request I had made. She had written me about her laundry problems at great length, and I replied that I had my own laundry problems and didn't need hers. What I did not have, I replied, but did need to read about, was sex. "Maybe you can send me a little in the mail, hey?" This evening's mail brings her reply, an explication of each and every one of her sexual liaisons for the last three years, with a flair for detail and variety that would make Rabelais blush. I read and reread it. I even turn down an offer to smoke some of Acapulco's Goldest-- on the grounds that the company area is a bummer--to keep reading the letter.

Tuesday

CUBBY FROM ALBUQUERQUE

When you're born clean and fresh, when your parents know that you'll grow up playing forward for Brigham Young University, they don't have to bother giving you a self-justifying grown-up name If they want you to be Cubby, it's Cubby. Cubby Worthington, an all-American National Guardsman from Albuquerque, New Mexico, has been chosen to be the trainee in charge of our platoon. In the middle of a crowd of anonymous volunteers the drill sergeant found him, looking like a giant-sized Cub Scout, his face shining like plastic, his teeth glistening like an advertisement for a fluoridated water supply, and anointed him. Out of service, Cubby Worthington is working as an assistant to a dean at the state university. No doubt in the admissions office; he's that clean. He says that he is doing a

Ph.D. dissertation on "legal impediments to business." I ask him for an example. "Well, there's licensing and registration of doctors, for one." He is a free-market man.

He continues to be an unearned blessing. It is a blessing when you find someone in authority who is touched by reasonableness. It is unearned because you can count the reasonable people on one thumb, and count on the fact that your efforts or character will not make the incidence any higher. Cubby must, as a consequence of his off-season job, be well practiced in the art of unnatural reasonableness. Fair, intelligent, humanistic, seemingly unawed by the Army, he is also one of the few people I have encountered with a sense of humor.

He is the only person around that I am really impressed by. Up each day at 4 A.M. with the rest of us, leading the platoon in every area of training, always the fastest to learn, he is always the best, getting everything done, consistently retaining his poise. And every night when I tiptoe out of the latrine, my letters or scurrilous essays having been completed, I find Private Cubby Worthington sitting in an empty drill sergeant's room, rocking gently in a chair, writing to his girl friend or reading a much-folded letter, with no urgency, no haste, no rush to get to bed. Maybe these westerners have something. He seems so sanguine and mellow, as if he has the peace and slow pace we seek with drugs. He has been raised far from the insistent east, and is content to let the earth do its spinning and never fight the flow. Why the hell doesn't he get tired?

We continue to luck out in other ways as well, and are beginning to believe that we are an experimental group. Our drill sergeants are widely acknowledged to be the friendliest and most humane around. Our field first drill sergeant is so hopelessly lost that his authority is nil. Our officers are indifferent and cajolable.

We lucked out when we got here by having only three days at the Reception Center instead of ten, one day of "orientation" when we got to Logan Heights instead of seven days of details. The men in my platoon will have no weekend KP, because the

KP list is alphabetical, and it will only be up to M when we leave. We will have a daily KP once, but we will not have a second daily KP, because that is another alphabetical list, and it will only be up to a second round for the L's when we ship out. My day for my only KP falls on the first day of bivouac, and if I stay at the mess hall, there will be only one company there instead of five, or if they have me do KP in the field, where everything is self-service and disposable, I will miss the poison-gas obstacle course. We have been, by all measures, the most fortunate group ever to coast through here. Thinking on it all, I hear CPA Stan singing, "When the moon is in the Seventh House, and Jupiter aligns with Mars . . ."

POSITION FIX

The Mets have won ten in a row and are inching up from second on the league-leading Cubs. Nixon is withdrawing troops from Nam, oiling his way toward the disguised defeat he doesn't want, and maybe peace too. I am in green fatigues. Two out of three ain't bad, so it's good to be alive.

"DO WE NEED TO KNOW THIS FOR THE FINAL?"

Drill Sergeant Conboy tries to give me directions to a class-room in Land Navigation, and discovers that he can't. So he takes me there himself.

The navigation class uses two maps: a detail map of Fort Knox and one of Loi Tan, Nam. We are quizzed on the maps, with junior high school test questions, such as "What is the box at the bottom of a map called?" Oh for a college question:

"What is the significance for man of the black lines on a map? Limit your answer to two blue books." (The answer is "Some of the above.")

The instructor tells us of a method of direction-finding that uses two sticks, the sun, and fifteen minutes. Private Nelson offers a method whereby fifteen minutes can be saved, but is told that the method shown is "the Army Way, used ever since the Civil War." The quizzes are not collected.

FIRST AID

We are given our first exposure to the tricky concept of preventing deaths and saving lives. Some of my platoon-mates seem disappointed, as if they had thought that when they ran out of enemy they could train their sights on their comrades and speed up the Darwinian selection process until they become King of the Whole Shooting Match.

We are shown treatment procedures for "sucking chest wounds" and "explosions in the abdomen." The synthetic, strapped-on abdomen is grisly in its realism. The guts hang out and ooze plastic infected pus. I become more peacenik.

The first-aid instructor is the first sergeant I have yet seen with a constant smile and friendly eyes. He looks as if he knows what he is doing, and can do it under combat conditions, and is very sure of himself, with no guilt to make him less earnest in his teaching. His friendly eyes have several nervous twitches and betray his utter lack of hostility He swallows, or jerks his Adam's apple every four or five words, making his sentences all locals and no expresses. CPA Stan whispers to me that he is in love with the instructor.

LOVE IN BLOOM

Private Worthington gathers us all together and lays it on the line in a way that inspires greater awe. He has the respect of the Texans and the easterners. They respect his size, and we his competence. It's like all those cowboy movies. The tall, quiet, clean man is also the fastest draw around. He keeps them honest.

"Look," he says in a way that none of us could put across, "Wilson's kid is being operated on tomorrow. I think we should take up a collection and buy her a big toy or something. Or maybe just give him a wad of cash to take the kid to an amuse-

ment park or take his wife to dinner. He's under a lot of stress."
And it is done, without a grumble, each according to his means.

Sergeant Wilson, who was scheduled to "give us a beating" for
the poor showing we made on inspection, thanks us instead for
the card and the money. It is the third time his daughter has
undergone surgery in the past six months. Twice at Army hospi-
tals the doctors fouled it up, and now, despite the cost, he is
taking her to a private hospital. Touched, he tells us that "it's the
first time any trainees showed me shit," which is a drill
sergeant's way of crying.

He promises us off-post passes this weekend "if I have to steal
them myself." "Look, Dave," I object, "don't read this wrong.
You don't have to do that. That's not why we did it." "I know,"
he says, "and that's why I want to do it."

Wednesday

RECORD FIRE

Several of us are plucked from our trundle beds and carted off
to the rifle range before dawn to set up targets for today's rifle
practice. We ride in the back of a flatbed truck, observing the
gravel, and repair some targets 350 yards away from the firing-
line foxholes, a very long way off to kill a man so easily.

When we were little we knew, just as we knew that illness was
the all-purpose excuse, and the world's concern for our health
transcended all other interests, that if we volunteered to do some
detail or clean up some mess, we would not be "forgotten."
Special food would be held for us if we missed a feeding. A late
snack would be set aside, accommodations made. In the Army,
however, if you are on a detail you go to the end of the line when
you are through, and if you miss a meal, well, you've missed it.
In fact you're lucky if your clothing and valuables are still there
when you get back. Back to work. The buses arrive with the rest
of the company, and we regroup, munching some candy bars,
smuggled through by friends in the underground, in place of the

breakfast we missed.

Rumor spreads that anyone who does remarkably well on today's rifle test--we are firing for the record today--will be Nam-bound forthwith. Of course, if you fail the test you've got to take Basic all over again, so you've got to at least aim. But Drill Sergeant Wilson kills the rumor by explaining that the Army's travel bureau neither knows nor cares if you can hit your own foot.

When the shooting is over and the smoke clears, I have hit only 20 out of 96 targets. But a kindly scorer credits me with 50. Others note a similar casualness on the part of the scorers. By the Army's lights I am now something called a "sharp-shooter," which sounds great--except so was Lee Harvey Oswald. "I'm a real straight shooter, if you know what I mean," says one of the scorers, stoned out of all connection with reality. I am now entitled to wear a snazzy medal to advertise my new skill. An Iron Cross.

Private Peyser fails to qualify, disappointing no one. He breaks into tears at the prospect, previously not believed, of his being recycled. "I'll lay 3-1 odds that he graduates with the rest of us," says CPA Stan. "If he never touches a rifle again, and sleeps for the next three weeks, they'd still pass him. If he were a watermelon they'd graduate him. You watch." I can't quite believe Stan, and most of us hope he is wrong. We *want* to see Peyser crushed because we have sweated and he has not. But sneaking up on us is the sense that CPA Stan is right, that at the last second, like the mythical Colonel's putative visits, they will let you know it is all a hoax--when it no longer matters. After they've gotten 95 percent of you to do what they want they can reveal themselves as a paper tiger, because you've been too scared to call their bluff.

DOWN FROM LIBERALISM

I am becoming race conscious. I came in here with tidy liberal beliefs about the basic goodness of people and the equality of "races."

But here's how it goes these days as we each slip into defensive racist patterns:

Mexicans continue to be unaware that they are living in a world with other inhabitants. They push, shove, sprawl and grab. And when you apply gentle counter pressure, they don't move.

Three times in the last twenty-four hours I have had to drop my guise of ethnic neutrality and come down hard against personal aggression.

Private Santayana, on the breakfast line, points to me and says: "There's another one. He's a Jew. I hate Jews. Hey, Jew--you know, I hate you."

Just as war erases the doubts of the man in the foxhole and rekindles his patriotism out of necessity, all doubts and inner conflict about ethnic identity and its relevance flee me. I must speak his language. "I'll tell you once, buddy, and only once," I hear myself saying to him, "if you don't learn some manners I'll teach you some. So keep your ugly face out of my sight or I'll smash your teeth in." I think I meant it, but speaking from my necessarily nonviolent muscular structure, I confess that I'm not sure. Santayana, however, recognizing his own idiom, is convinced and desists. Is that all they want, to see that we're just as bestial as they? Have we offended them by being less physical and more verbal?

In a fight between strapping Private Stein and porky Private Rackles, Rackles taunts and prods Private Stein, in the apparent knowledge that Stein will not strike back. Stein has told me that he is afraid of killing Rackles with a punch, and he might be able to do it. At any rate, we all encourage Stein. "Hit the jerk. I'd give my left nut to have a crack at him. Smash him, Stein." To no avail. "He won't hit him," says Hector Rodriguez to me, "because Jews are afraid to fight." Too much. In a move I have seen John Wayne do a hundred times, I keep my eyes riveted on the fight, raise my right hand in a fist and point a finger into the face of Private Rodriguez, who stands at my side. Without looking at him, but sticking the finger like a cue stick right under his nose, I say to him slowly and grimly, "Open your mouth once more, and I'll show you how wrong you are."

Private Santiago Ramirez, a five-foot-one-inch, 100-pound gerbil, whom I myself carried up to the Orderly Room when he was felled with a reaction to penicillin, gets into an argument with me about Vietnam. He says that he "just wants to kill people, and gooks are as good to kill as anyone." When I disagree, he says that he had a similar argument today with Peyser. I already promised to kill one Jew today. I won't mind making it two." "Anytime you're ready, buddy," I reply, "you just come on over and try it. I don't care if you have to wake me up, you just let me know, because it'll be a pleasure to split your stinking head." And I am thinking, paradoxically, about his prejudice, "Where does a wetback come off like that . . . ."

There isn't any tension with the blacks, who are to a man, whether college graduate or illiterate, all playing a role that reflects more the desperate need for black solidarity than our present situation. They have all adopted a posture of detachment, doing their jobs and betraying no overt feelings about the Army but resignation. And they are all affecting the mannerisms of the least educated, in a closing of ranks, to protect them all from our assertiveness. But their talk, even old graduate student Reisterton's, has become a mixture of back-on-the-block Harlemese and down-on-the-bayou Louisianan. Everything is punctuated with a "sheyit, yeah."

The Army has brought out the worst in us, made us go for each other's throats, made us look to animal-level criteria for judging each other, stripped all subtlety from our lives and set us against each other.

On one front, however, some progress can be seen. People now say "please" and "thank you" when they grub cigarettes from me. "You're welcome" still startles them, though, and "excuse me" leaves 'em gasping.

SING FOR YOUR SUCCOR

Usually I have a song in my mind wherever I go, like an over orchestrated melodrama, and every new experience stimulates the memory of some aimless lyric. A line from a tune will stay for a few days, relevant to nothing but the initial moment when it was born, passing only when some new impulse brings a replacement song to the front. In college, at exam time, I could never concentrate for the viral ditty that used my lobes as an echo chamber. Now, sometimes acting as a metaphor for events, sometimes as a simple distraction, the tunes keep me alive. I remember reading that Linus Pauling, or Glenn Sea-borg, or someone like that, once fell into a ravine in California, and had to busy his mind through a fearful night. So he recited the periodic table of elements to himself over and over, dwelling on each element and everything he knew about it. My mind does the same thing with the songs.

Some of them, like "To Susan on the West Coast Waiting from Randy in Viet Nam Fighting," or "Save the Life of My Child," are specific comments on the ravine I find myself in. Some, like "Will you still need me, will you still feed me, when I'm sixty-four," bear no relation to anything. They have a low position in the pecking order and can be bumped by a biggie. The biggest biggie of them all, the General of mind-songs is:

There's a young man that I know
Just turned twenty-one
Comes from down in southern Colorado
Just out of the Service, and looking for his fun
Some day soon, going with him, someday soon.

Singing and stooping, we devote an hour to policing the desert. It is a very clean desert.

DISPLACED PERSONS

I continue to haunt the PX and post library at night, like a refugee outside an overseas U. S. mission, hoping perhaps to be adopted. Inside I discover a copy of *The Graduate,* with a waiting list of eight people who all want a crack at it. One guy just reads the last ten pages over and over, reveling in how Ben makes up his mind what he wants and goes and gets it with all the passionate intensity he can muster, swinging a cross, driving, punching and running, until he is safe with his prize, far from the cloying grasp of "them."

When I was in college, I used to make a nightly run to a local drugstore to inspect the magazine rack, hoping to find some new messages from the Real World. Even after a blizzard, when it seemed impossible that any deliveries might be made, I made my trek. The Army is the only other place where I have heard the phrase "the Real World" used widely, referring to everything beyond.

Private Wasserman goes to sleep at 9 P.M. anticipating a 3 A.M. awakening for KP. He is awakened at 10 P.M. and told that it is four in the morning. He leaps into his clothing and bursts forth into the night, racing up to the mess hall, where he begins to pound on the locked door. He gives up after five minutes, and only then takes the time to look at his watch. When he returns he is greeted with a blanket party. A blanket is tossed over his head, and he is beaten by an anonymous mob. I observe the scene from my bed, as CPA Stan, hanging from the edge of his, calls the play-by-play.

THE WORLD AND NORMAN PEYSER

Private Peyser kicks over a soda bottle, breaking it. He picks up the broken hulk and takes two steps toward the trash can before accidentally gashing Private Young on the arm with it. Young begins to bleed profusely, dripping blood onto Peyser's toes, as Peyser stands transfixed, born between the temptations of cleaning up the broken glass, helping Young, cleaning up the blood, mopping up the soda, throwing away the bottle, running away, fainting, or handing the bottle to Young and ignoring the whole situation.

"I'm very poor at decisions," he says needlessly.

Finally he is given explicit instructions on how to proceed as Young resists the temptation to emulsify Peyser and decides instead to tend to his wounds himself. Norman begins to sweep the glass away, sweeping it under someone's bed, and is booted in the rear by the person under whose bed he's sweeping it.

"Sweep it *up,* stupid," he is told.

He leaves the larger share of glass slivers on the floor for lack of skill with a broom and dustpan, and rises from his final, futile effort to say something defensively explanatory. As he stands and begins to speak he drops his hands and lets all of the glass in the dustpan cascade back onto the floor.

Thursday

POWs

At a class in camouflage an instructor tells us how to treat prisoners of war and, incidentally, what the Geneva Convention has to say on the matter. The gist of his talk is that we are to suspect every orifice of every prisoner's body as being a weapon carrier, every prisoner as being wired to detonate at any moment, and the only good prisoner a talkative one. A mute one is better off dead.

Incidental information: According to our instructor, we pay the Viet Cong silver certificates to surrender themselves and their weapons if they agree to submit to a six-month Americanization course. Just like the Reserves, eh?

HOW I WON THE WAR AND THE WEST

SCENE I: *The Battle of Garbage Pit Hill*

For the first time we are called upon to integrate all of our combat skills in a sustained assault exercise. Crawling on our bellies, creeping on our knees, under barbed wire, over trip wires, hopping through stumble-foot traps, through an obstacle course, over log bridges, across a single-strand rope bridge, falling behind logs, bushes and trees, firing blanks, being fired upon, up a hill through blinding, choking gas--just like Berkeley, so far--we advance. We press on, up the steep hill, to overrun the defenders in the foxholes at the summit.

The presumption is that each wave of assaulters has captured the hill. But gazing down from the peak, I realize that we have been exposed all the way. Drill Sergeant Brown sits atop a bunker languorously lobbing imaginary grenades at bunches of charging troops, firing a few blanks at strays, wiping out everyone he sees like a gruesome quality controller.

We have captured the hill, panting and coughing, and at an undeniably great cost. Even with blanks, several of us suffer powder burns. We all would have been wiped out with real ammo. On top of the hill we have captured a classroom area already set up for our next class, Field Sanitation. In front of instruction bleachers stands a large diagram labeled "Garbage Pit." Thus ends the charge of Garbage Pit Hill, to be remembered as long as Pork Chop and Hamburger, no doubt. It was exciting, I must admit, and great fun besides. No different from the games of Cowboys and Indians I used to play willingly.

SCENE II: *Norman at the Bridge*

"Point man, move out," shouts team captain Waters, and point man Peyser jangles from his bunker to a rope bridge moat-crossing. He looks at it and turns to a sergeant on his left, gesturing in a resigned, offhand way. We can see it through a mist of choke gas that blows to and fro across the range: the palms are up, the hands make little circles from the front to the side with wrist motions. His shoulders shrug, his head shakes. He stands with his feet apart, one knee bent, as if he has no intention of ever moving, only of explaining why "I can't do it." The usual speech. Twenty minutes of this while the rest of his squad, the other riflemen and point men, having overtaken him, now sit in the middle of a gas cloud, waiting and choking, screaming "Come on, damn it."

Finally the sergeant orders him to go. He reaches up and grasps the rope bridge with his hands, and makes several futile attempts to swing his legs up. Finally he gets his legs up and grabs on, his helmet slipping from his head and hanging by the chin strap from his neck. He begins to make some progress out over the moat, and is halfway across when his feet give out. He lets go with one hand, as if to catch his feet as they slip off, and just manages to grab back on with that hand, almost falling off entirely in the effort. He hangs by his hands for a few moments, making no move to remount the rope with his feet, just hanging limply, sighing, as if accepting his fate, like Atlas. He hangs for nearly a minute, silently.

Slowly, inexorably, we watch his hands lose their grip until, with a short, resigned scream, he plummets to the sand and rubber pungi stakes fifteen feet below. The shriek is followed by a soft thud and a rattle. Private Teddy Leonetto falls out of his observation post in a fit of crying laughter.

Several minutes later Private Peyser emerges from the pit--on the wrong side. He is back where he started from, and a sergeant leads him to the rope again. He simply turns around and goes back into the pit, tripping and sliding down the side. He stops to take a quick leak at the bottom, and emerges again on the far side, stumbling up the slope, his rifle still slung down his back, its sling choking him at the neck, his helmet cockeyed and sideways, his glasses dangling off one ear. He trips, staggers and careens up the hill, coughing every few steps, sand pouring off him, looking for all the world like a drunken cartoon character. Lurching toward his squad, he collapses into an already occupied bunker. He is greeted with sustained laughter and applause.

Leonotto is still immobilized with laughter. Another trainee runs down the hill and surrenders. Others lie all about, rolling on the ground in stitches, neutralized by Norman's Conquest.

In fact the entire pseudowar ceases, to observe Private Peyser's travail for nearly a half hour. He is a Jewish Tet Lunar Holiday, bringing peace through his very special talents, the selective application of ineptitude.

Later, running to mail call as his name is called off, he charges up a hill like a rampant camel, his mouth open, a smile ruling the right side of his face, his tongue hanging out, loping like a great Newfoundland dog. A package is tossed at him and he reaches over his shoulder to grab it without breaking stride. He breaks into a smile at his good catch and spittle dribbles down his chin.

THE WAYWARD BUS

We are loaded up into buses for the ride back to Fort Bliss. As we get on the buses we pass the woman who runs the Pogy Truck at the rifle range. She is old, but solid. She wears men's socks, sneakers, a torn dress and a man's gray cardigan of many holes and many years. She has been selling sandwiches to soldiers, I am told, for twenty years, and I wonder what she is like.

The ride back becomes the occasion for a mass demonstration against the military brainwashing. From the back of the bus, Privates Romini and Warsaw begin singing "Down by the river side," and soon the entire platoon is singing "I ain't gonna study war no more." As we were taught to do as children when the flag passed us by, all action stops when an "important song" fills the air. Some salute by joining in, others stand stiff by ceasing their contrapuntal chatter. All pay their respects to musical royalty. The spirit is with the lyrics. Soon "We Shall Overcome" overcomes us, even Texans and southerners, as a favor to the

Negroes. A few blacks begin a song called "Soul Is Sweeping the Country"--a bit Uncle Tomish, but Negro nonetheless. They could have done "I'm Black and I'm Proud," but what the hell, you can't have everything. A meek black fist splits the air, asserting itself by inches, soon joined by others, black and white. "All power to the civilians," yells CPA Stan. A sea of V's waves about. The wayward bus rolls on.

Friday

MIDTERMS

We are paraded to the Army's Testing Area G-3. If G-3 is testing, and G-2 is intelligence, G-1 must be unanswered questions, and G-4 answers without questions. We are about to be put through a series of tests on all the skills and junk we have allegedly learned.

The place is a flat field dotted by eight shacks connected by little walkways outlined with rocks. Each shack is a testing point for a different skill; first aid, bayonet, hand-to-hand combat, drill and ceremony, military justice, field infiltration, guard duty, and general bullshit. It looks like the world's largest miniature golf course.

In the first-aid shack is a wounded dummy that is chillingly lifelike. Its wounds are so realistically gory that one boy loses his breakfast, and another, frustrated by the speed of the questions, jumps on the dummy's table and lies down with the body. The other tests are similarly successful.

After four hours of this we are informed that we have all flunked, with the exception of Private Worthington as usual.

Commanding Officer First Lieutenant Mott, called "Punk" and "Applesauce," wearing his captain's bars while he awaits his official promotion papers--consequently called "Lieutenant-cum-Captain"--tells us that we will all lose our passes as a result of our abominable showing unless we score phenomenally well on the afternoon Physical Combat Proficiency Test, which we had all planned to coast through. "Open a lock, close a lock," says Private Nelson. The tests are "like striking a match to see if it works," says CPA Stan. "The G-3 test will melt your mind if you really know that junk," he says, "and the PCPT destroys healthy bodies five ways."

Our characters are counseled before the PCPT for an hour by the Protestant chaplain, who, as usual, talks interminably and irrelevantly as we sit in a sweaty, stuffy room. Several of us get up and walk out, complaining that we will soon faint "if we have to sit in the middle of all that hot air:' He shows his ace film, on duty. "Most of us have been in trouble with the law at some point or other," says the narrator--which I suppose is true if we're talking about the same laws, which I suppose is not true.

Terrible scenes of terribly scared soldiers boarding landing craft for D-day are shown. The faces are pale and expressionless. No gung-ho here, just drawn looks of fatalism and a sense of "this is it."

The voice introduces Colonel Jack Treadwell, who has won every medal in the Army catalogues. Colonel Jack lights a cigarette, draws deeply, turns profile and, silhouetted in front of pictures of JFK and FDR, exhales slowly. And is never seen again. "I wonder if he does anything for the Army," whispers CPA Stan, "other than smoke for movies."

The film closes with FDR's Day of Infamy speech amid whoops and gleeful shouts from congressmen. Why whoops and shouts?

The afternoon Physical Combat Proficiency Test is conducted in the blazing heat, and despite our fears, we do much better than imagined.

Most of the trainees have friends who shout encouragement about the El Paso women waiting for them if they pass. I shout to Peyser, "This one's for your mother." CPA Stan shouts to me, "This one's for legalized grass. . . This'll get us out of Nam."

Peyser, despite his efforts in the name of his mother, does no better than he did on the first PCPT. "You know, Pisser," says

Drill Sergeant Conboy, "it's incredible. You did worse than the cripples on the PCPT, and worse than the Mexicans on the mental tests. If you were a horse they'd shoot you, dummy."

Private Nelson and I manage, for the fourth week running, to find a valid excuse not to parade ourselves before Colonel Thorne at Friday retreat, and fall into phone booths instead.

All mail is now subject to search as a result of a six-pack that was sent to a Texan, who, in his eagerness, drank it near its boiling point and landed in the hospital. Half of us are afraid that the CARE packages we expect full of hash brownies will be searched, seized and surrendered to the FBI. Before a malevolent inspector's eyes I rip open a package from home and discover. *The Complete Works of William Shakespeare.* Heady stuff.

RUMORS

Rumors, however preposterous, continue to spread like venereal disease at an orgy: casually, quickly and in a geometric progression.

Two very good reasons exist for this promiscuity of false information: We desperately want to believe good rumors, and so we cling to, and spread, improbable myths that relieve our fears, and we are too familiar with the likelihood of bad news dropping out of the sky. Credulity sits like a mousetrap awaiting the nibble of a rumor.

A nonrandom list of enlisted men and draftees is posted, ordering all of "the below-named personnel," all of them draftees or enlistees, to go to the rifle range and learn to shoot the M-16. The very same M and the very same 16 that are used in Vietnam. Many on the list hide, thinking ahead to the reasons for the exercise. Drill Sergeant Grbr consoles them by saying, "It's just an administrative procedure. We have to have a certain percentage trained in the M-16. It doesn't mean that you'll be going to Vietnam. Not many of our men will be going. Don't worry." It's a little too early to panic them, after all. "What will you bet me that he's lying and he knows it?" asks Private Nelson. Nearly all of the "below-named personnel," are black or Latin.

MARTIAL ORDER

A minor scandal has arisen from our casual regard for our officers. Private Holstein, with nothing to lose, calls them all by their first names or our nicknames for them. Lieutenant-cum-Captain Punk walks through a barracks and observes the strangest collection of salutes since the filming of *The Men*. Private Teddy Leonotto salutes from a seat on the front stoop, a cigarette dangling from his lips undisturbed. Lieutenant-cum-Captain Punk has to climb over him to get through the door. One private, on his knees shooting craps or something, salutes without rising or stopping the game. One private on the back steps smoking a joint in a cigarette wrapper, giving off a purple-brown odoriferous smoke, looks up and says, "Hi, Cap'n," and passes the joint to another private. "Hello," says the CO. He is offered a drag on the semidisguised joint and says, "Uh, no." Then, as he begins to walk away, he turns and says, "But thank you anyway."

TWO-WAY STRETCH

The heads and niks are trapped by their own competitiveness. We want to have it all ways. Despite our anti-Army, anti-war feelings, we want to get better scores on the tests than the Texans and Regular Army boys, because we have been brought up to believe that one must get good grades. And so we laugh at those who, like Peyser, cannot make the grade.

IN THE SERVICES OF THE LORD

Looking all around him at Friday services, Peyser tells me, "I've seen all these faces before. Yes. On sick call."

The chaplain delivers a presermon lecture on the evils of lingering around the coffee shop and coming forty-five minutes late to services. "We should have come an hour late and arrived just in time for the food," whispers Private Nelson.

"No chance," I reply. "This is the best part of the service, his sermon." Actually the sermon is pretty routine this week, with the exception that the chaplain manages a rhetorical miracle by working "go down" and Grandma Moses into the same sentence.

Saturday

THE WAR

Chastened by our experience of the previous evening, we venture no closer than a mile from the chapel, listening to tunes on a jukebox in a cafeteria for the first forty-five minutes of services, All of the songs are antiwar in some way, but all are too subtle for the Army to catch and eject.

"Every song is antiwar," says CPA Stan, "if someone who's alive sings it."

I discover myself on my way to the chapel, alone, walking by the Fort Bliss stockade, a group of squat, gray buildings surrounded by high guard towers and rolls of barbed wire.

Inside this cage sits a handsome young man--too handsome by our standards to be a killer or a rapist--playing forlornly with some pebbles between his feet.

"What are you in for?" I ask through the fence.

"Eight months," he replies without looking up.

"I mean, what did you do?" I ask hesitantly.

"Drugs. Grass."

I gulp. "How'd they get you?"

"A buddy turned me in." A buddy. Anyone is "'a buddy" in the Army if he is the same rank. Turned him in "for his own good," no doubt.

I flash him the V sign, and he shakes his head and returns it limply. I suddenly feel very foolish. It's easy for me to flash off V's and play subversive as I walk around cooperating and co-opted. The boy behind the wire is a casualty of one battle of the war, a sergeant to my John Wayneish buck private. He, and the boys who left for Canada or those who fill the federal jails, are fighting and getting hit so that I can make wisecracks in safety. I feel terribly sad for him, thinking that maybe he has no political thoughts and simply wanted a smoke and was caught. I have nothing to say to him of any sense, and feel a nagging shame for myself. So I walk on, and away, and that I guess is part of my problem.

And I remember an old fear. I used to have a great fear of dying in the electric chair, and crying down the last mile as well, as if the judgment of my executioners was as important as the judgment of my peers who sentenced me. Got to be a man about it, I would tell myself.

My present whimsical soul contends that this fear was simply an aversion to unhappy endings. But more probably it had to do with a fear of an official, state-sponsored, popularly-decreed disposal of me, as if I would someday be judged so "different" as to be a general menace, worthy of elimination by acclamation.

Much can be made of this, I suppose. Maybe it is a simple fear of a real, imminent death, or a repressed death wish or instinct (let Norman 0. Brown make what he will of it, I'm happy avoiding my death instinct).

1 always thought that I would avoid earning the chair by my seeming inability to murder. But now they've taught me how. And the situation I dwell in adds to the scenery: constantly on trial, being judged by arbitrary and unreasonable forces, ready to be whisked by fiat or caprice into the legal star-chamber of a court-martial or the symbolic one of a stacked-deck battlefield-- the potential recipient of a state-sponsored end at last.

And now, walking past a boy who might be me, an old fear, long defeated, returns.

STIFF-NECKED HEBREWS

Services become a shambles, as Peyser is called upon to carry the scrolls with the Word of the Law around the chapel. Like a group of twelve-year-olds, the rest of us sit in the back, dissolving in giggles, awaiting the Great Dropping which is sure to come. Right on schedule. It begins to slip from his grasp, but the chaplain snatches the scrolls away at the last moment. I am called upon to play some part, and fall asleep on my feet, listening to the drone of mumbles. Another sleeper is grabbed and made to hold the Torah scrolls, seated in a throne like chair. Looking sullenly at the chaplain, he sits, and the Law is laid in his lap mere seconds before he falls into a loud, snoring sleep again.

PORNOGRAPH RECORD

The Company Commander pulls a surprise inspection, looking for pornography and contraband. Private Santiago Ramirez loses 37-count 'em, 37-magazines for lack of redeeming social importance. Lieutenant-cum-Captain Mott suggests that with pictures as obscene as these, it may be possible to get syphilis of the eyeballs. I lose a breakfast-sized box of cornflakes and a lot of antiwar GI newspapers.

It is interesting that they search us *before* we get El Paso passes, but don't after we return. As if they want to snare anyone who is clever enough to have contraband mailed in, but not the good, dull American boys who buy their liquor in El Paso and take it back to the barracks. Reminds me of how in college they geared things to only one kind of bum. If you got a townie pregnant or raped her, or spent a semester drinking in a frattie lodge, you were a boys-will-be-boys boy, but if you sat and thought all semester, you were lazy, until you sat in at the ROTC building. Then you were a Commie.

LIBERTY PASSES

Passes to El Paso are handed out, and three of us take a few pre-El Paso moments to wander about the athletic field smoking the remains of some nondiscovered contraband. They'd never think of searching in, say, the liner of a "Class-A dress cap, saucer-type, 1 each." It makes the hour-long bus ride to El Paso a bit more enjoyable.

In El Paso we have some trouble making ourselves understood. We ask ten people where "the *best* restaurant in town is," and all of them direct us to cafeteriae. CPA Stan figures it out. "It's the uniform. They figure all a serviceman, straight off the farm, wants is a good, cheap meal." We try another tack. We ask the next ten people, "Where would the President of the United States eat if he came to town?" and they all agree "the Paso del Norte Hotel." We go there, only to discover that there are no tablecloths on the tables until 6 P.M. So we break out our bottles, Texas being a state where they do not sell liquor by the drink, and drink all afternoon. By dinner we are lying all over the tables, laughing and shouting. Private Mantle has passed out, his face in a bowl of soup, and CPA Stan, "as the executor of his will," refuses the waitress permission to remove it. "Maybe," says CPA Stan, eyeing the waitress sternly, 'he's not finished." Private Nelson and I try to get everyone to quiet down, on the grounds that we might all get thrown out. But Private Mantle lifts his head out of the soup and declares solemnly, as if he had been waiting all evening to speak up, "It's eight o'clock on a Saturday night, and we are the only people here in the best restaurant in town. You really think they'll throw us out?"--and falls back into the soup.

Able to stand it no longer, CPA Stan asks the waitress, "Tell me the truth. If the President of the United States came to El Paso, where would he eat?"

"Why, that's just amazing you asked," she drawls. "President Johnson did come to town last ye-ah and sat right over there"-- pointing to my lap.

We stagger home, swearing never to tell the secret of where the best restaurant in El Paso is.

The War is Over : 161

Sunday

IT AIN'T ME, BABE

All of my friends and I agree that "the Army" was what we thought of when we imagined natural disasters-floods, earth-quakes, and sewer breaks. If the job was too massive, menial, or inhuman, we always thought, Let the Army do it.

But when we charged up Garbage Pit Hill I realized that "I'm it," and I realized that there are other aspects to the "not me" illusion. "I won't be drafted. They won't train me in infantry. I won't be killed." No one firing down my throat on Garbage Pit Hill could see the browns of my eyes and know that it is me, that I'm somehow special and to be spared. And for seemingly disconnected reasons, I realized that "I'll get to this next year is not good enough. It may be never. When *will* I read all those books I swore I'd read "later"?

Clearly the game is over. It is just a matter of time. Long ago I vowed never to wish that time would fly quickly. There is never enough in a lifetime. But the Army has made a liar out of me.

BIVOUAC WEEK:

Beat Army!

THE MEN IN THE GREEN
FLANNEL SUITS

You'd know why they call our green suits "fatigues" if you ever tried living in the same pair of pants for a week.
For a week we camp in the heat and dust of the New Mexican desert, and we are bone-weary at the trail's end, though lifted a bit by the euphoria of completion. Time does not surge this week, nor does it flow. The events that for weeks presented themselves like surprise messages from exploding balloons this week seem to be like the sagebrush on the desert floor: random, disconnected lumps, relating to each other through no pattern but their common existence in a cruelly viscous environment. The time and distance between each event swell unnaturally as we spend great energy plodding through the sand from here to somewhere else, for seemingly pointless reasons, dogged down by mooring lines of sleeplessness and pain.

"After bivouac," said a weary trainee to me four weeks ago, who had already been through it, "if you survive, it's all over but the shooting." "As they say in Vietnam," added CPA Stan.

BIVOUAC EVE

The night before we leave for bivouac nearly everyone in my platoon sits around the barracks looking at everyone else blankly, as if we are about to embark upon an invasion in the predawn hours, I watch Texan Private Wintergreen Waters shift his eyes around the room, cocking his head one way, then shifting his eyes on some secret cue to somewhere else, watching the noiseless air like a bird in a nest.

Two rainbows stretch improbably across the Texas sky, from Fort Bliss to our bivouac site in New Mexico. CPA Stan tells me that he thinks there's a pot of Acapulco gold at the other end, while Private Warsaw reminds me that "The Lord put his sign in the heavens. No more water. The fire next time."

Inside the barracks what talk there is is whispered, and bivouacian. Lots are drawn to see who will share tents with Peyser and Rackles. The winners attempt to sell their unlucky assignments for ten dollars, the going rate for weekend KP, but find no takers. Money has become valueless, it seems. Even Private Peyser refuses the challenge of an offer of ten dollars for showing enough nerve to hit the offerer in the mouth, or to take ten dollars for letting the guy hit *him* in the mouth.

KITCHEN POLICE

Mess Sergeant Jimmy B. Long is fat from his food, and knows that if an Army travels on its stomach, he is the traffic controller. He is absolute monarch of the only fixed star in the Army's constellation. No one fucks with chow. You eat when you are supposed to, and if you don't feed the troops, you'll have Congress and a million angry mothers to answer to. He stood up at dinner one night and screamed, "All right, youse mothers, I wanna get out of here for a beer tonight, so shaddup and eat." A trainee yelled back, "So go home already." A lone voice in the filled mess hall. A lonely voice in the intimidated and silent crowd. An easily located voice. But, hurling Jovian vengeance,

Mess Sergeant Long missed and nailed an innocent victim with two days of KP, plus another day, like a technical foul, for protesting his innocence.

The entire company is trucked to the bivouac site, but CPA Stan and I stay behind to do morning KP for the quarter-filled mess hall. By showing up late we miss the really important assignments of scrubbing pots and cleaning grease traps, and are ordered instead to direct traffic in the dining room. Seven out of the nine companies that eat at our consolidated mess are in the field, so CPA Stan and I have an assignment that in difficulty is to regular KP what a game of catch is to a World Series.

"Good morning, sir, we've been expecting you. Table for two? Right this way please. Mister . . . Jackson? Ah, yes, reservations for four, correct? I think you'll like what we have on the menu this morning," chirps CPA Stan as each trainee enters, greeting him by name. *"Do* try our Rice Krispies. A truly superior box. Your gracious host has picked up the check. There will be no charge except for those on the American Plan." A chuckle or two breaks the bonds of Army-Green blues, but "asshole," "Shut up, creep," and "shithead" are more frequent responses. Alas.

For a CPA, CPA Stan is not, as they say in CPA circles, "your standard CPA." For one thing he is always saying outrageous things to people, insulting them with a straight and nonhostile face. They usually don't believe he has said what he has just said in the way they think it's meant. His face--mellow and mild--belies it. But when confronted with the ferocious physical types we live with, he sometimes gets fiery and aggressive. Last week he told a giant red-necked southerner to fuck himself, without getting hit. But I got pounced upon by the behemoth for saying nothing more than "You take your-self too seriously." He shirks with the royalty of Shirkdom, but looks, CPA-ishly, conscientious. I am always caught when I shirk, because I look as if I'm enjoying myself or getting away with something.

Like Private Lorenz, a Howdy-Doody-faced Italian-Mexican, who manages to remain anonymous and thereby unnoticed when he disappears from work details, CPA Stan can be forgettable when he slips away from sweat and toil. Better, like Privates Briss and Barrett, the Tweedledum and Tweedledee of gold-bricking ("Goldbrick," I have often heard Private Briss say, "is a Jewish name,"), he brazens out the tough stuff by turning his back and purposefully walking away.

Briss, out of the University of Nebraska, seems to know what's up in the middle-American Army, and plays it for all its worth. He discovered an empty drill sergeant's room in one of the barracks and posted an outrageously fictitious name on the door --Mess Sergeant Perry Stalsis. No one ever bothered to knock on it, figuring that a mess sergeant, up at any old hour of the night, needs his sleep, and would kill to defend his ZZZ's. Inside, Briss plays records and gets stoned. Barrett, his sidekick, follows, does what he is told, and gets his share of the goodies. They have both escaped and evaded 23 out of 23 injections, all dirty details, all clean details and virtually all work. Yet they have scored well on marksmanship, Individual Tactical Proficiency and Physical Combat Proficiency Tests.

CPA Stan, worshiping at their shrine, does all right too. But he is, in one giant way, marked as a CPA. At twenty-two he is hairless, bald, smooth as a businessman from the top of his head to the top of his head. Below his eyes he is hairy as a raccoon. "Man," said a stranger walking through our latrine one day as CPA Stan stepped from the shower, "did anyone ever tell you you were *hairy?* Man, you look like an *animal"*

Outside of the latrine, in clothing, it is his dome that attracts attention, though. "Hey," called a Specialist 4 on KP, "How old are you?"

"Forty-six. I've re-enlisted."

BIVOUAC

Halfway into our KP we are picked up and taken to the desert to join our company on bivouac. The limitlessness of the desert is oppressive, confining as any jail. Back at Logan Heights we still had a foot on dry land, access to civilization. But now, as we approach the bivouac site, a sea of scattered pup tents, half blown down, looking like Resurrection City without the mud, we feel adrift in the Army's sea and futureless, now marooned on their island as well.

Our KP is continued in the form of slavery to a burly black mess sergeant who growls and mumbles ceaseless orders while he smokes and plays cards, not even looking up to give the orders. At the end of each assignment he tells us still without looking up, that we didn't do it correctly and that we should do it again. His speech is unintelligible and his orders difficult to understand and follow. So I tell him. It is that or hit him with a meat cleaver. Now I know how Nat Turner felt.

CLASSICAL GAS

CPA Stan and I grope around in the dark for an hour trying to locate our duffle bags in a pile of two hundred. Finally I find mine. I won't have time to read it, but for finding your duffle in a pitch-black desert, there's nothing like the *Complete Works of William Shakespeare* bulging out from one side. From the little I know about the Avon laddie I can assert that he has nothing to say about bivouac in any sense that can help us out here in the desert this week. On the other hand, the Bible gives us another use for the common tent peg. In the Book of Judges, it seems, Jael stuck one through Sisera's head to prove a point.

CPA Stan and I are safe in our trundle bags when the company returns from a night of shooting BBs at each other to simulate close combat, and of firing in the dark to simulate firing in the dark.

Private Nelson knocks on our tent "Gas," he whispers hoarsely. Yes indeed, gas. This is what we learn we have missed:

The whole company was taken to a tin shack even farther into nowhere and given a lecture on chemical, bacteriological and radiological warfare. "What should you do in a direct hit?" asked a sergeant. "Sergeant," answered Private Wasserman, "I believe you should place your head between your knees, look up and kiss your ass goodbye." "No," replied the sergeant seriously, you should fall on the ground, with your head away from the center of the blast, and your rifle under you to protect it."

"To be disintegrated neatly," whispered Private Nelson.

"Sergeant," asked Private Mantle, "when I fall on the rifle, should the operating rod handle be skyward or earthward?"

"I don't know," answered the sergeant.

"Well, sergeant," asserted Private Mantle, "I just want to do it right if it ever happens."

Only the Reservists were amused.

Led into a room, the trainees were instructed to remove their gas masks and one by one, in alphabetical order, recite their name, rank, service number and a few other irrelevancies while sitting in the middle of choking, tear-making gas. If they got everything correct, they could don their masks; if they made a mistake, they had to try again. The Y's and Z's were on the floor throwing up, near collapse, from the nausea-and-tear-producing CN and CS gas, the favorites of the Army in Nam and the National Guard at home. "How about an orgone gas," suggested Private Teddy Leonotto later, "where everyone who fell under it would have continual orgasms and lose all his will to fight? Why do they have to make people throw up?"

"Men," shouted a sergeant when the last man finished crawling out of the room, "I'm not gonna tell you my name because you're not gonna like me when we're through, and I don't need to get shot at" Below him Peyser, who was held in the room longest, coughed and wiped his eyes, rubbing the gas into his skin, worsening his plight. "Don't rub your skin, men," said the sergeant, as Norman continued anyway. "Just let the air clean the gas away.

"All right. Now. You're gonna crawl under this barbed wire until you see the white cloud of gas. when you see it you will call out 'GAS' and mask up. You will continue crawling until you have finished the course. Anyone who stands up will have to crawl the course over again."

Privates Nelson, Barrett and Briss calmly got up and walked

away, looking purposeful.

Two hundred trainees were on their bellies under barbed wire, waiting for the cloud of white gas, which did not come--only a colorless, odorless, choking gas that settled in all at once.

"Gas," yelled Private Warsaw, gagging in mid-word, unable to complete even that small syllable. "The first breath I took," he said later, "was the last. I thought I was really going to die." He got up, in violation of the rules, and began to run. Two-thirds of the company were up, tripping over barbed wire, screaming, shoving and pushing. Drill Sergeant Wilson tried to grab onto Private Wasserman, who looked as if he was going to run into some concertina wire, his face twisted with torment, his eyes half closed, tears streaming down his cheeks. Charging at full speed, Wasserman straight-armed Drill Sergeant Wilson in the throat and shoved him backward into the barbed wire and gas cloud. "We were ready to kill each other," said Private Wasserman later, "especially those who were getting in the way."

Mass panic set in as the disorienting gas began to sear un-suspecting lungs. "I can't breathe," screamed Private Peyser through his mask as he dropped his rifle and began to run. He was tossed to the ground by Drill Sergeant Robinson as others ran in every direction, screaming and wailing, weeping and shrieking. Peyser attempted to bolt, but Drill Sergeant Robinson held him to the ground and yelled at him to crawl, while Drill Sergeant Conboy toyed with the filter valve he had removed from Norman's mask, rendering it useless. Peyser lay on the ground quivering and howling. Drill Sergeants Robinson and Brown attempted to drag him back over the course, but he refused to move, moaning that he had already done the course. The inside of his lungs, like everyone else's, was burning and aching. He lay on his belly, shaking and twitching, twisting his head from side to side, pounding the ground. He cried for nearly thirty minutes, hysterically, weakly, pathetically. He was finally dragged off the course, through the stinking cloud. His pants loosened at the waist and slid to his knees, the burning gas and rocky sand rubbing all over his lower abdomen and groin. Off the course, he collapsed in a heap, sobbing, choking, retching, his clothing half off, curled up in a ball. He was moaning beyond pain and torment, filthy and bleeding, victimized inside and out.

Private Smith, a massive football-playing black, leaped from the cloud and ran shrieking off the course, like others, white and black, hollering, "Mamma, mamma!" Some others later claimed, with little pride, that they were terribly afraid and thought they were dying. "It was the worst experience of my life," said Private Worthington. "I don't know how I got the hell off that course. If I ever find the bastard who runs this place, I swear I'll kill him. If I were Peyser I'd kill everyone."

An hour later, trainees were permitted to drink from their canteens, but found that the water had been spoiled by the gas and had a taste of the chlorine, now no longer a benign reminder of swimming pools.

Thinking about how much we missed by having KP while everyone else went through the gas, CPA Stan asks me what I would do in a gas attack. I tell him of the recommended SDS procedure: cigarette filters up the nose, a hanky in the mouth and Vaseline on the eyes.

"I was sort of thinking," he says, "of two Rolaids."

Many traumatized trainees sleep tonight with their gas masks on, or at the ready, in case of a surprise attack.

FORCE MARCH

Walking five miles in full gear, we finally arrive at a point somewhere, where we take off our packs.

"Where the hell are we, lieutenant?" asks Private Nelson.

"We're *here,*" answers Beep-Beep. "Okay, packs on, let's go."

"Lieutenant," suggests CPA Stan, "that's quite a stiff pace you're keeping."

"Thank you, private," he answers. "I'm just in good shape, that's all."

"I bet you could really show the men what good shape you're in if you had to carry a rifle and a pack like the rest of us, eh?"

The gauntlet flung, Beep-Beep dons a pack and a rifle, and leads a more leisurely stroll back to the tents at a rate of two miles an hour. He stumbles and reels the last mile under the weight of the pack and rifle.

On the way back my dog tags dangle outside of my shirt, and I realize that I am still wearing the peace medal that I bought along with the FTA stickers at the Greenwich Village Poster Shop in downtown El Paso.

Later an instructor tells us about a friend who let his dog tags dangle onto a power line and was electrocuted. "Really straightened his ass up, though," he concludes.

SUPER-NATION AND ALTER-NATION

"Range *three-five-zero-zero;'* calls an instructor as I daydream about Canada.

Looking out at the range, I see what he has us focusing on. No longer do the targets masquerade in silhouette. Now, in great, undiscriminating bursts, we blow down targets painted with slanted eyes and Vietnamese faces. Some are women, some are old men, and--pray for our souls--they now have us doing an exercise called a "fire field," in which we fire through a bed sheet that blocks our view of the targets, hoping to kill something, anything; sweeping across a horizon because we have been told by an authority that there is an "enemy behind the sheet." And we kill anything that stands more than two feet tall in a hemisphere in front of us for a range of 450 yards out. I await a lapse of consciousness that will permit me to do this, but it does not come. I hand a full clip back to the ammunition officer, having fired not a round. "My rifle jammed," I tell him.

But I would now tell him and any other light in the Pentagon that, no, I will *not* fire again at people I do not know, symbolic or real, unless I know that they have fired at me. And, yes, you'd better get the court-martial papers ready for next time, because if anyone ever ordered me to fire on those faces without discrimination I'd mutiny and remove him of his command at the point of my gun.

Sweating with anger, I move out with the rest of the company to police the desert, and join, instead, three Reservists who are getting stoned behind a dune. We return a little later to rap and nap with Lieutenant Tanner, in joyful disregard of rank, while the company continues to police.

SEX AND THE SINGLE SOLDIER

Shaking out the sand from our pants, several of us drop our trousers and shorts, and Private Todd, like a hound smelling blood, zeros in. Goosing, pinching, tugging at shorts, he moves with lightning speed and great professionalism, but with the enthusiasm of an amateur. Last night we spotted him taking a shower while another trainee, naked as well, held a spotlight on him. All day long we have been trying to find out who the other trainee was.

"Do you realize," asks CPA Stan in astonishment, "that we haven't heard 'Barnacle Bill the Sailor,' or '100 Bottles of Beer on the Wall' yet?" Two Reservists leap at him and cover his mouth to prevent the word from spreading. "You want to ruin a good thing?" asks Private Mantle.

We haven't heard "Barnacle Bill," but we have heard its equivalent, as every sergeant feels it is his duty to spin elaborate and involved sex stories as we approach our monastic seventh week.

"And there she was," says one, "begging for it, and I'm just teasing her, trying to get her really hot, so's she'll explode when I do put it to her. Course, I'm kinda big, so it's gonna be a hell of a party for her anyway, but what the hell, I'm eating 'er and just driving her crazy. Those of you men what's never gone down on a bitch, you ain't got no idea what you're missing. Anyway, she's really screaming and writhing, and she pulls me up as if she's gonna bite it off herself, only it's too big. She can't get huh mouff round it. She ain't no cock-sucker for me, I guess. So's not to drive herself total loco, she directs old junior to where she wants it, and starts to ride up on me. Weeell, I'm not sure I wanna do it jest yet. I think we can work the old girl up a little more, so I just re-lax, you know, and now she's jest going ber-serk, cause all the while I'm still playing with her with my fingers, and so I twist around down and really go at it with my old tongue, and damned if she doesn't spin me around, swivel me right on my old tongue, and just pull me up by my armpits, so's I just gotta give her the hose where she wants it-Hey, where you going, boy?" he yells at Private War-saw, who is climbing down from the bleachers over the hypnotized trainees.

"Going to the latrine, sergeant."

"Takin' off the hat, boss," yells Crazy Willie Buck in the manner he learned on a Louisiana road gang.

"What you gonna do in the latrine? I ain't give you no permission to go."

'I'm gonna pull my pud, sergeant," he answers.

"You wisin' me off, troop? I'll bust your ass."

"No, sergeant. I am going to jerk off."

"Well, get the hell out of here, then, troop."

"Yes, sergeant."

"All right men, now where was I? Oh yes, this bitch is beggingforit".

SOMEWHERE ELSE

The Protestant and Catholic chaplains are holding forth to let the men see what combat services in the field are like. The rabbi has failed to show up, so we are free to nap and talk to Lieutenant Tanner.

Lieutenant Tanner begins to tell me, compulsively it seems, about his boyhood in a town near Ithaca, New York, that I once stumbled on, lost at three in the morning. I thought I had stepped through time as I walked into the Weatly Saloon, No one knew how to get me home, and I had to get lost again before I did. I couldn't tell you how to get there. You have to be lost to do it.

There was a time when I never imagined I'd ever think fondly of the Finger Lakes, after years of doing battle with the locals over campus issues. But I think about wandering the back roads and highways, the mornings spent camping on Lake Cayuga's western shore, afternoons passed in post adolescent play and frenzied put-on, and evenings spent attempting to civilize the farmers' daughters. The tug of memories, cool nights, trees and streams, contrasted against the unpleasantness of the instant scene--even the desert air smells sulfurous from gunfire--makes me look for a home in *my* mind. I plan travelogs and memories-to-be: canoe trips, horseback pack trips, a catamaran voyage; wine, cheese, crackers and a girl and to hell with Army Green.

"What's the matter," asks Lieutenant Tanner solicitously, 'haven't you ever been camping before, you old city slicker? You look like you're really uncomfortable."

Here we are, camping in the desert amid sand flies, rattlers and ceaseless Solar Rays, and my mind turns to other times, as if to answer Lieutenant Tanner's question. I think of nights at Big Sur in California, in moist forests of giant pines, and on the beach at Carrillos or down at Punta Bandera in Baja, hearing the slap and roar of the Pacific as it stroked and washed the beach; or at Cape Cod, or in upstate New York.

I remember taking children on summer-camp overnight trips, playing pranks all night, keeping them up; horrified when one awoke the next day with a reaction to ant bites--a face that looked like a jack-o'-lantern. I remember the nights spent in a garbage dump in Fort Lauderdale and on the restricted front lawn of a West Palm Beach manse. And the nights in a bag on the side of the road in Indiana and Ohio, off to join the McCarthy crusade; on a living room floor in Milwaukee; in strange college dorms; and at the sufferance of a fraternity, fibbing about membership on my own campus. And the times I slept in my back seat, pulled off the Jersey Turnpike; and coming through Georgia or Florida; and in a sleeping bag in a freezing apartment, having forgotten to pay the heating bill and pick up fresh linen. I remember adventures, discomforts, disasters. They were all worse than what we have to do here, but they were all better for lack of Army Green.

BLOOD TIES

A desert rat bolts into a gathering of troops, and a mass of laughing, running soldiers give chase, first this way then that, all over, until they have him surrounded. He cuts for an escape, but is blocked, then back another way, and is blocked again. The ring closes and he is stomped to death, lying bleeding on the sand, spilling his blood and gore, panting, until a self-appointed matador applies a coup de grace: a left heel stomp, on the shouted order of someone else, and the rat is obliterated.

A mourning relative arrives, and again heady, nervous laughter reigns as the sense of painless combat sweeps over the scene, *Lord of the Flies* grown up, and the relative is killed. Blood unites the troops as they stare at the vanquished and walk away, laughing.

We march off, and now we are at familiar Garbage Pit Hill. "It ain't so tough," says Peyser, who should know.

Once again we are going to the top, this time in darkness with booby traps and other surprises along the way. We have been trained to search for booby traps at a forward speed of about two miles a week, but with waves of trainees coming in behind you, the best way to discover the booby traps is to let everyone else go first, or else to trip over them yourself. The surest way, for example, to find barbed wire is to taste the blood on your face when you run into it. Bloody but unbowed, we retake Garbage Pit Hill.

Drill Sergeant Wilson, skunk-drunk, as many of us are getting sky-high, calls the whole company together to ask who the 'bastard was who stole my Scotch and replaced it with Kool-Aid." Worthington grins guiltily, unseen, as he is already in his tent, half-finished with the Scotch, ready for a good three hours' sleep.

HAND GRENADES

CPA Stan and I, having hopped onto an equipment truck as it pulled away, hearing drill sergeants yell for us to get off and walk with the rest of the company (one-tenth of which was clinging to the truck with us), find ourselves at the grenade range, loading grenades. We assume that a mistake will kill us, and so we make none despite the distraction of contrapuntal tunes that rattle through my mind, occasionally bursting forth in a disconnected line here and there:

> My thoughts are scattered and they're cloudy.
> They have no borders, no boundaries.
> They echo and they swell.
> From Tolstoy to Tinker Bell.
> Down from Berkeley to Carmel.
> Got some pictures in my pocket
> And a lot of time to kill...*

At the pregrenade-tossing instruction period an instructor demonstrates the various types of grenades, including one that gives forth a billowing purple cloud that looks like hash smoke or kif. Private Garth is called on to demonstrate the proper grenade technique and drops a live one in front of the bleachers we are sitting in. I in turn demonstrate a perfect backward swan dive from a sitting start, 20 feet up on the top row of stands, hitting the sand face down, my hands covering my head. I roll under the stands for cover as Private Wasserman shouts: "Six points for execution, on a two-point-three degree of difficulty." The grenade is a dud, the fumble a hoax. Drill Sergeant Wilson says,

---

* From "Cloudy," © 1966 by Paul Simon. Used with permission of the publisher.

"This is just one good reason why Nor-mun--his new, condescending way of referring to Private Peyser--will not be allowed near the grenade range.

"Hear, hear," yells one of the Reservists.

At the grenade range, set up like a golf-driving range with concrete walls, we each get to toss one grenade to get the feel of it. No big deal, except that it can waste you if you do it wrong.

We are lined up against a concrete and Plexiglas wall to watch Private Peyser and a brave range safety officer tempt fate. Peyser hurls the grenade fifteen feet out of his foxhole, and he and his coach are covered with dirt as they dive for the ground to keep themselves intact, bumping heads along the way. The range safety officer explains that Peyser has made what would be a good offensive move had this been actual combat: "He would have helped his men immeasurably by the more than likely suicide he would have just committed."

Several of us hop a truck again and avoid walking. When we awake from a short nap for lunch we find that the officers and NCOs have the only table and chairs within a mile, while the troops must eat on the hot sand. Twenty of us sneak up and depose them, carrying them off and depositing each in a monster-sized trash can.

MILITARY BEARING

Drill Sergeant Wilson is riding Peyser pretty hard for picking his nose. "You know, Nor-mun, I ought to let you go on burial detail, so that you can explain to some poor girl why you've got your finger in your nose while you bury her boyfriend. But I can't, because it wouldn't be fair to her. So I'm going to send Tauber, Nelson, Mantle and Thurmond instead. Which probably won't be fair to her either."

"Actually," says Private Nelson, "when you think about it, in the Army picking your nose is definitely the thing. It really makes a lot of sense." Understanding heads nod in agreement.

THE MACHINE-GUN INFILTRATION COURSE

A surly lieutenant addresses us for an hour, making no sense at all, but intimating that we shouldn't believe any of this talk about "wit-drawin' men from Veet nam. . . . Sure, they'll take out a few tousand. And they'll also send over a few tousand. Don't you worry about that. That's the catch." (Catch-22?)

Beep-Beep tells us--unleashing boundless, and unreasonable, doomed hope--that we will get out of Bliss on the third of July and not have to report to our next post till the thirteenth, free for ten days to wander the earth like kings or snails. But Beep-Beep, we learn, gets his information from the same trustworthy sources as we do: rumors.

We spend the rest of the afternoon crawling on our bellies over rocks, gravel, chopped concrete and stones, so that we can get oriented for the night infiltration course.

As night falls we listen to a stentorian voice from the darkness—"God," suggests CPA Stan--explaining the added hazards of nighttime. We will have to march through a trench 10 feet deep, in total darkness, until we reach a point 100 yards away. There we will turn into another transverse trench and line up behind log ladders. We will have to climb up the ladders, roll over a horizontal log and crawl the distance of the course on our bellies, with rifles and full packs, while explosions surround us. Every few moments a flare will be fired, at which point we must all lie still. In our way will be several obstacles: barbed wire, logs, bunkers, shallow trenches, poles, booby traps and smoke bombs. The bunkers will rock with the detonation of half-pound sticks of TNT, the barbed wire will be impossible to slide under without setting off booby traps or getting cut and bloody, and all the while, two and one-half feet off the ground, 50-caliber machine-gun bullets and rockets will whiz overhead in the darkness, an occasional tracer lighting the paths of the rounds.

Private Masterson reports to a medic, who is standing by with an ambulance, that his back is acting up. The medic assures him that everyone's spine is feeling a little weak. CPA Stan, Privates Nelson, Barrett and Briss simply walk away, for a change, telling a sergeant who challenges them that they are going to direct traffic, in the desert.

The option of walking away is compelling, but something about the challenge is more so. I will never know if I have the guts, I guess, to participate in the fraudulent bravado of war. But I at least have to try this surrogate. The medical officer reminds us that a trainee stood up last year to see if the machine guns were real, and learned that they were by being blown apart. "If you doubt me," he says, "hold your rifle up and see what happens to the stock--if you're ready to pay for it and get hit by shrapnel. Another trainee tried that one." And another reason for daring myself is creeping up on me. Private Worthington comes over to me and says, "Look, I hate to do this, but one of us is going to have to crawl alongside Norman. I'll do it if I can, but we might get separated, so will you do it too? We've gotta make sure he doesn't kill himself." The prospect of sublimating my fear into heroism causes me to grit my teeth and nod my head in agreement.

"Are you ready to take the challenge?" calls the voice in the blackness.

"Yes," we scream, resounding through the desert.

"Can't hear you," he taunts.

"Yes"--like bloody murder, shaking the bleachers.

"Are you sure?" he teases, playing us like a matador his bull. "Yes!" with all our might, causing the dust to rise and helmets to fall off "Yes! Yes!"--hoarsely and thunderously.

"Are . . .you . . . ," he screams at us as loudly as we have answered, but casually, as if he *knows* what is ahead, "certain?"

"YES!"--obliterating all other sound, until even the hurricane of our "Yes!" is made but a whisper by a blast of flares and TNT explosions, rockets sweeping flatly across the horizon, zinging over the barbed wire, exposing the vulnerability of the plain we will cross. Three machine guns sweep the course with a deafening racket, spitting red tracer rounds and thousands of bullets on low, flat arcs. Bursting machine guns, TNT, flares, noise beyond all measure. Fear and panic crash about, dust flies and even above the freight-train-loud apocalypse before us can be heard our unitary cry: "Noooo!!!"

But here we are, four abreast, with Worthington and me around Peyser at the end of the trench, now in front of the ladders. An immobilizing, crushing silence settles in, and we are all scared beneath our blank faces, aware for perhaps the first time that we cannot turn around and we cannot quit in the middle. "You can't talk your way through this, Norman," says Private Worthington. I vow that I will hit him in the skull or stomach with my rifle butt before I will let him stand up. Tending to him has taken my mind off my fear, which has grown prodigiously since the demonstration. I had previously tried to imagine the machine-gun bullets as just so much noise. Even though the word is that the machine guns are bolted in place and fire down alleys where no one crawls, the visual evidence is to the contrary. I saw them strike sandbags directly behind where we stood, sweeping across the horizon, leaving not enough room, it seemed, for even a turtle to survive.

Peyser tries to mount the log ladder, and after one rung, hangs his head down, quivering, sobbing quietly. I jab him twice with my rifle muzzle and he squirts over the top and lies flat on the ground, hugging it, shaking. I crawl up next to him, as I hear Worthington call, "Where the hell are you?" "I'm over here," I answer in the strobing darkness as a loudspeaker voice calls, "Break it up in lane 23"--my lane. Worthington crawls away. "Bye, Cubby, you candy-ass," I call.

Coaxing, shoving, pulling at his shoulder straps, shouting and poking, I get Peyser moving. Slowly we make progress while machine-gun bullets and flares tear the night. Dozens of trainees crawl past us. In front of a bunker Peyser rolls over onto his back and says, "I can't go any further."

"Hurry up, lane 23," the voice calls. "What? . . . Oh . . .Move your *ass, Nor-mun"* it taunts. "Break it up and get moving." The bunker we are lying by shakes with a sudden explosion, and Norman is nearly on his knees by the time I get my helmet off my face. A quick, reflexive thrust of my rifle butt into his stomach sends him sprawling to earth.

"I can't go," he wails.

"Go, you son of a bitch," I shout, convinced that I am John Wayne. Painfully, achingly, under the wires and bullets, past the treacherous hazards, we finally approach the far edge of the course. The noise and danger are behind us, the pain and fright beaten. I give Norman a shove over the last log, and he falls into a trench to the sand, eight feet below, with a thud. We crawl up an exit ramp, and I pull away, getting distance between him and me and what are sure to be a coven of drill sergeants descending on him to taunt and tease. But the first to reach him are Drill Sergeants Wilson and Conboy, who hug him and carry him off. With some justice, he is proud of himself, as I in turn, tired, bloody and dusty, feel vaguely heroic. Drill Sergeants Wilson and Conboy come over to me and, lightly slapping me, then pinching my cheeks, say, "Good . . . work . . . shithead." My bruises feel like medals and I smile a little.

Weary and filthy, we march home, soaked with sweat but elated by our triumph. And as a reward we are treated to some Kool-Aid.

PRIVATE TODD

Private Todd, dancing again by the moonlight, with two partners this time--"It's spreading," says CPA Stan, looking at me as if I might "be one too"--is nearly caught by Colonel Thorne, who arrives by jeep, making his nightly check to inquire if we have enough toilet paper.

The close-combat exercise is staged, a running, jumping, crawling game with loaded rifles. Half of us simply walk away. "You can get killed in this one," says Worthington grimly. Privates Mantle, Nelson and CPA Stan get taken to the hospital to complain about splinters, which seem to disappear before they get there and I lie in the shade behind a latrine with four others until Private Todd comes along, and the others leave me at his mercy. "You're from New York," says Private Yates from Uvalde, Texas, as he leaves, "you're used to talking to queers. Me, I might just jump all over him." Todd tells me about his favorite calf and still denies that he is deviant. And the caissons go rolling along.

An air-raid siren sounds and we hit the dust, Todd on top of me, as I call out, "Get the fuck offa me, you fat fag." He rolls off and looks hurt, as I hope that a stray rocket will land nearby, perhaps even in our midst, and liven up an otherwise dull day.

TRAIL'S END

While everyone polices the desert, half a dozen of us chosen for future burial duty--we will inter fallen soldiers--practice our pirouettes and twirls with rifles, and I practice losing my mind burying the Vietnam dead.

After a march of three miles through the dunes in full warrior's regalia we arrive at our very last, utter, final stop on bivouac, the Land Navigation Course. Like a treasure hunt, we split up into teams and have to follow instructions to move from point to point, until we either do or do not get to a finishing point. Private Peyser is discovered lost in the desert, wandering around like a stunned animal. The very same Private Peyser who said to me, "I can live my life without challenges." Private Martinez and four others are found wandering near the New Mexico-Mexican borders, while two of the New York Reservists go off in search of peyote, knowing nothing more about it than that it is "buttonlike." They return authentically ripped off. "Peyote?" "No," one replies, "we couldn't find any, so we smoked some dope instead." "How did you get back?" I ask. "Well, we shot some real fine azimuths, and here we are. What are you doing out here, looking for a *New York Times?*"

"No," I reply to the two of them, freaked out of their compasses, "I'm John the Baptist, looking for Salome."

"I've got some tuna fish and bologna," answers one, falling down from the hysteria he has just loosed.

We board the waiting buses and the Desert Foxes are on their way home. The buses roll by the night fire, the record fire and hand-grenade ranges, night infiltration, Garbage Pit Hill, the machine-gun infiltration course, and all the other scenes of our travails. In the daylight, uninhabited, they look tame and conquered, like abandoned sets of old-home movies. As they slip silently past the window I remember my feeling as I entered Fort Bliss. Like a proton being shot at a nucleus, I thought I would stick in the center and never pass through. Entrance was eternity back then. But now, as time and trials roll by on the safe side of glass panes, I think, I beat you, you re not so tough, not so scary. And I'm almost through. Almost.

When we arrive back at our billets we are mustered into the latrine, and Drill Sergeant Wilson tells us that we're going to have "a de-briefing." Todd giggles, and CPA Stan tells me, "Todd probably thinks it means we are going to take off our shorts."

"Okay, everybody, take off your shorts," says Drill Sergeant Wilson, and we watch as tons of sand cascade onto the floor.

Later I toss my clothes into a washer, and it chokes to a halt on the weight of the sand and mud. It stops in mid-cycle and leaves my clothing in hot, boiling grime. I scald my hands removing the load, drip all over the barracks, break my glasses, get into the shower to wash off, and don't know where to begin. The soap falls down the drain and I give up. Things are back to normal, except for my pectoral muscles, which are swollen beyond all naturalness.

TRADITION

"Boy, am I gonna give the new recruits hell," says Private Williams as he sits on his bunk in his fresh underwear. There is a convention among soldiers that "veterans" must tell new recruits that "you'll die on bivouac. Wait 'til the DIs get ahold of you. You'll hate Basic." I resolve, as the best thing I can do to make the world safe for little boys and clean away some of the cobwebs of fear, that I will tell the truth: "Bring a lot of books or you'll be bored to death; and don't bring many principles."

A radio is playing "Piece of My Heart," sung by Janis Joplin of Big Brother and the Holding Company, which sounds like the organization I work for. I listen and find myself trying in vain to remember the feeling of hearing it, zonked in New York, among friends and free spirits, light-headed and deliciously evil.

Private Peyser is called outside as he prepares to take a nap and told to get ready to go to the rifle range. He is being given yet another chance to qualify with his rifle. The threat is that if he fails again he will face two years as a broom-pusher for Uncle Sam. He demands a new weapon, claiming that his is all messed up. Looking closely at it, one can see that, indeed, it is all messed up. Aside from the accumulated filth of the past five weeks, someone has jimmied the sights; perhaps the same drill sergeant who was playing with Peyser's gas-mask filter as Peyser writhed on the ground. Still, Norman never even noticed the broken sights and may just not have known that they were there in the first place.

LAZERUSIAN NOTES

"My God," calls Private Thurmond, "Eddie Fisher is getting divorced."
"Divorced?" calls Private Warsaw.
"Divorced," answers Thurmond. "It's terrible."
Thurmond has been collecting fan magazines and has his girl friend send him any really hot news about the stars. On the other hand, my copy of Rex Reed's *Do You Sleep in the Nude?* has been confiscated for its suggestive title; the CO later returns it to

me. "All talk and no action," is his comment.

"Divorced?" asks Private Williams. "Who's Eddie Fisher?"

"My God," says Warsaw, "divorced. I thought he was dead."

"Now that Nixon's been resurrected," said a friend of mine on Election Day, 1968, "I guess we're going to have to get used to talking about things like Virginity and Fallout Shelters and Eddie Fisher again."

Private Nelson and I duck another Friday parade and skip over to the Commanding Officer's shack, where we sit around and drink Cokes with Unperson Holstein and the officers, while the new First Sergeant McMannus, already renamed "Madmans," screams about the apparent state of trainee junta.

"He's crazy as hell," whispers Lieutenant Tanner to me on his way into his office to get tutored in math by Private-Unperson Holstein.

"What the hell is going on here?" demands the new first sergeant. "Have the trainees taken over?"

"It looks that way, doesn't it?" answers Lieutenant-cum-Captain Mott.

"What are we going to do about it?" demands the new first sergeant.

"I guess nothing," answers Beep-Beep, shoving some papers my way. "Don't worry, you'll get used to it. It just takes time, that's all. This is the new Army."

Madmans walks out as we remain sitting at the officers' desks, our feet up, drinking the proscribed soda, joking and laughing.

"Here, do these," says Beep-Beep. "Initial these PCPT results. Don't use your initials, though. Use any ones you want but your own.

"Any?"

"Uh huh."

Okay, Pentagon, search your files and see if you can find the Physical Combat Proficiency Tests that were graded by: H. H. Humphrey, R. M. Nixon, CIA, FBI, CPA, FTA, New York City, Young People's Socialist League, Front Liberation National, E. J.

McCarthy, St. Thomas Aquinas, League for Spiritual Discovery, S. Claus, W. S. Churchill, JFK, RFK, Martin Luther King, John V. Lindsay, McGeorge Bundy and IKE. Three points for any of you who knew that HQ stood for Henri Quatre.

'No mail tonight," calls the mailman, who, an hour later, after we have all scattered, delivers it to the four people who are still around.

HONOR

"When the world goes so far out of its way to make you un-happy," says CPA Stan as we are all-of-a-sudden informed that we will be having guard duty, "I think you have an obligation to be miserable." To show the "high command" what a bunch of go-getters we are under his enlightened tutelage, our new first sergeant has volunteered us for guard duty on Sunday. On Saturday many of us have burial detail, so both days of rest will be given "ver to these "honors."

"Guard duty is an honor," says the new first sergeant.

"He's fuckin' crazy," says Drill Sergeant Conboy, who will have to sit on guard duty with the rest of us.

"Burial duty is an honor, men, intones Colonel Thorne in a short lecture on the joys of burying the fallen. "Someday you'll have one yourself, so do it right."

"Now, are you sure," asks Lieutenant Tanner, "when we fold the flag and hand it to the boy's father, that we have to salute it?"

"Of course you salute it, lieutenant," replies Colonel Thorne. "What did you think? It's the goddamned flag, for God's sake!"

"Well, sir," Tanner answers, "I just want to make it clear. It might look like we're saluting some dizzy-assed civilians."

"Remind me not to die," whispers CPA Stan.

"Good thing we bury 'em with their boots on," says Private Nelson.

"We'll have to take our chances," answers Colonel Thorne after a moment's reflection, "but I admit it's a problem."

We are trucked to a small town by the Rio Grande several miles through the disconnected foothills of the San Andres Mountains northwest of El Paso, near Anthony, New Mexico. It is a modest green-and-white town tucked in the hills, a picture postcard of middle America: gentle lawns and awnings, white picket fences and bushes of flowers, a gazebo here, a cupola there, and a sense of timelessness and slowness.

In the middle is a tiny cemetery, with neat little grave markers all in a row, a cross or two, some roughhewn granite, but mostly slab tablets with efficient inscriptions.

It is a hot afternoon, with no breeze or clouds, and standing by an open grave are the remaining members of the family that has lost a son in Vietnam. An erect father in a blue business suit (he has taken off his jacket, the heat is too much) and a mother in a gray-and-white-print dress. Her age is showing, like her grief, more than the man's. She carries a handkerchief and keeps it close by her eyes, dabbing and blotting; another one, fresh, waits tucked in the arm of her short-sleeved dress. A young boy with close-clipped hair, perhaps fourteen and already six feet tall, stands by the mother's wing. Around them is a Second circle of relatives and young friends, the young people looking alike-- neat, well dressed, clean and in their early twenties.

The father turns to look at the others and walks over to a pretty girl in a yellow dress, wearing a black veil, and taking her by the arm, guides her over to the mother, where the two women embrace.

"Engagement ring," whispers Comer Thurmond.

She wears an engagement ring, and as she hugs the mother I can see her shudder as she stifles a sob. The others cup their hands in front of themselves. They relax their grips and break, holding hands. The girl seems peculiarly at attention, while the parents seem relaxed. She hasn't had the practice, I suppose. She looks terribly proud, her head back and shoulders square, a soldier in her own right, doing battle against a more universal foe.

A citation is read and I wince at its insufficiency. We fire our three volleys of blanks: twenty-one guns bark for the hero. "Died of his wounds while defending the Republic of Vietnam," says a major as the casket is lowered.

" . . . to dust. We commend him to God," says a priest.

There is silence as the casket settles easily onto its brace at the bottom of the grave. The coffin's flag is folded into a triangle, the blue field of truth wrapping it all so very tight, and it is presented to the boy's parents. The father drops his grasp of it, and now the mother clutches it to her breast, shaking her head and hugging it. The father puts his arm around her and whispers to her. Taking the flag from her, he hands it to the girl in yellow, who stands at her side. The mother kisses her on the cheek, touches her arm and nods, and the two parents step backward a pace. We are all still motionless and silent, but I am quaking.

The girl stands for maybe a minute looking at the flag, and then she looks up at the major who read the impersonal citation for that personal body. She is searching the major with her eyes, and one can see the first sign of emotion on her face. She looks and looks at him, and his left eye and the corner of his mouth twitch in betrayal of his lifeless masquerade. She looks again at the flag she is squeezing and then at the major, the flag and the hole, and again to the flag. And she looks up at us all. Drawing her breath--it seems as if she hasn't breathed in all this time--she holds the flag out in front of her and looks over it to the hole. With a motion of contempt rather than anger, shaking her head "no," she drops the flag on the ground, not hurling it, just letting it go, and turns on her heel and walks away. She is followed by the father and mother, the priest, and the circle of friends, and finally by the official United States Government funeral procession: seven privates, a drill sergeant, and one major carrying a soiled flag. We break ranks outside of the cemetery. The major gets in his car and drives away, and we seven privates board our truck for the silent ride home.

GUARD DUTY

As a result of a typical Army foul-up, we are sent to guard duty without breakfast, and begin bellyaching in several ways. The Guard House is a wooden shack with no air-conditioning, only a few ineffective fans. We are assigned cots, where we may cough ourselves to sleep when we are not guarding something that needs guarding. A few, like CPA Stan, who were recruited as "spares," will hold down a mattress all day. "It's my way of defending the free world," he says. "It's what you're best at," I reply.

"All right, you mens," the captain or corporal or sergeant of the guard tells us--I can't remember which is which--"you will not let anyone enter your post unless he is authorized. I don't care if he's the President of the United States. Shoot first. He should know the rules."

"Even," asks Private Masterson incredulously, "President Johnson himself?" Pssst.

"Yup, even President Johnson," answers the captain or corporal or sergeant of the guard. Pssst again.

"What'll we shoot with?" I ask. "You're certainly not going to trust us with live ammunition."

"Make them do a front leaning rest until help arrives. You'll have to just wait for your relief. And don't hassle the garbage men. Last week some dodo got orders not to let anyone leave his post with anything and arrested the garbage man. Made him lie face down for two hours until the MPs came. I catch any of you jockos pulling a wise-ass one like that, I'll have you in the Guard House."

"We *are* in the Guard House," suggests one of the more alert troopers.

I am assigned to guard the post commissary, and immediately locate a safe place to take a series of catnaps, gaining about two hours' sleep and risking twenty years in Leavenworth. Private Young is assigned to guard Toyland, the home of a thousand Teddy bears, plastic machine guns--like daddy's," and doll carriages. Private Nelson asks whether "Victor Herbert is authorized to enter Toyland," with only a snicker or two of response. Private O'Neill guards a Disneylandish replica of the original Fort Bliss, an Alamoesque old mission that seems outrageously small for real use. It was a bone of contention between us and all the Indians in the world for many years and gave us sufficient excuse to exterminate thousands of redskins. "Looks like we lost," says Private O'Neill after his assignment. "My major job was telling little boys where the bathroom and 'the lady who looked like my mommy' were." Private Miller guards the Combat Development Area, where new weapons and other toys of violence are the subjects of research, and where Russki spies are certain to be lurking. Actually, by percentage, the post commissary is more likely to be robbed, but as these things go, it is Miller who gets the live ammunition, because the Free World is depending on his steely nerve and hawk-eyed aim.

At five in the morning a little man arrives to open up the commissary, followed by the juice truck, the milk wagon and the cake man. We are all having a light continental breakfast, looking at the pictures the little man who opens up has of naked German girls. "I used to be a sergeant," he tells me. "Took these in Germany. Come back next Saturday and I'll take you up to my place and show you my whole collection. Oh, I've got boxes full of 'em." The truck arrives with my relief.

IN RE PEYSER

And Private Peyser, a voice cries. Why do we treat him so?

Perhaps because he represents the worst in all of us, what we might become if we surrendered to the demons of sloth and indifference. We are all capable of not speaking the secret tongue of code and symbol that guide the privileged through reality. That is Private Peyser's crime. He doesn't speak the language under the floorboards of communication. Someone hasn't let him in on the big secrets, the fundamental facts; he was somewhere else when we were all told, so he moves in jerky disrhythms; his is not the politically current idiom. He is tuned out, and can't understand, let alone hear. Is it his illusions, or our secrets, for many of us only lately shared, that make his world so far removed from ours?

And what is it about ourselves that makes us reject him and despair of his redemption? "What shall we do for our little sister who hath no breasts?" asks the singer of the Song of Solomon. And what, indeed, for the guy with no balls?

Perhaps it is because we perceive him as an anchor around us, tying us to other men's myths. He is like one of the Wise Men of Chelm, a middle-aged imbecile, ineffably sad as he is inordinately funny; yet always the fool, loudly abrasive by his excessive ethnicity in our homogenized culture. We hold him off and say, "He makes it harder for the rest of us." Harder to be what? Other than ourselves. Perhaps by dropping him like ballast, our buoyancy in the American Sea is increased. We say, "We are not him. We are willing to sacrifice him. Why hold onto him out of irrelevant, alleged kinship?"

The mob would love it were he alone. The only New York Jew and self-proclaimed intellectual, utterly incompetent; the perfect target for their prejudices, validating their vanities, protecting their blind spots.

But we fight and frustrate their intentions by winning at their game, keeping the hounds at bay. Do we then offer Private Peyser as a sacrifice to them, as the price of joining their club? Or to ourselves? For whose benefit do we join the lynch mob? Is *that* the Great American Social Event, the Country Club Party, the Church Social? By joining in the ritual slaying, do we gain entry into their bloodstream?

Is it his incompetence that riles us, or his illusions and fraud? We laugh at his inability to do Army tasks, because we say, "It is fine to be a sloppy soldier, but another thing not to be *able* to be good when you want to." And we play into the Army's hands by pretending, for our egos, that the Army's challenges are symbols of life-tasks, extensions of the coping game. We say.

Why do we worry that he has never been challenged, never

been called upon to carry himself, never been punished? Why do we lust for his punishment and torment him as we wait? Why do we hope that he will not be discharged until he is brutalized and broken, reconstructed in our new "American" image? Is it because he gets away with his illusions or because we cannot be as free of reality as he is? For whom must he be punished, by whose standards does he deserve it? For all of our "beat Army" games, who is the only one who has really survived and remained the same as when he came in? And who has become exactly as "they" wanted us to become?

THE SUGGESTION BLANK

"Look what I found," exclaims CPA Stan, waving a piece of paper. It is a copy of DA 1045, ref: CPPM 1, sec. 12, which lay hidden in a box at Battalion HQ. At the top, in Gothic letters, is its title: Suggestion Blank. "We've never lost a war, says Private Warsaw. "Maybe we hadn't oughtta fuck with a good system."

"How about just telling them to stuff it," suggests Private Wasserman.

"Look, they give you a cut of the take if you save them some money--like eliminating watch pockets or something," explains Private Nelson

"Let's see," says CPA Stan, "general disarmament would save about fifty billion. Ten percent of that is--"

"No, it's got to be something that they'll do. And if you save them too much they'll just steal the money from you anyway," corrects Worthington, who seems to know.

"Lookit all the boxes. Thirty-two spaces and impossible instructions. We'll never get anything of substance down," wails Private Warsaw.

"How about a real, thoughtful essay," I muse, "on how the Army's cover-your-ass command system robs its personnel of any faith in their abilities; how everyone becomes the lackey for the man a notch up the ladder; how everyone is afraid not to be a sycophant; how respect and efficiency are destroyed by men who are unable to cut it in the real world but are permitted by the Army to treat their subordinates thoughtlessly and callously; how there is no motivation but greed and sloth and fear; how a civil-service mentality robs the system of any vitality; how there is no justice or respect unless you have your hands in someone's pants; how the Army's training and psychology is geared for World War II and not for today; how the training reaches the lowest 1 percent, but turns off everyone else; how the arbitrary personnel system robs men of desire; how the entire system makes the men in it hate not the enemies of their country but the United States Army."

"Are you fuckin' crazy?" ask CPA Stan and Private Nelson. "They'll court-martial you."

"Exactly," I say.

"Exactly. They'll court-martial you."

"And how about the fact that all those anti-Army scare stories we always heard," suggests Private Wasserman, "were full of shit?"

"Must be about some other Army, eh?" replies Warsaw.

'Well, you gotta admit," says Private Nelson, "this one's a joke," and we all nod, as CPA Stan throws away the suggestion blank.

"And how about the fact that they seem to take more trouble making little boys like McDonald afraid of them than--" But they are all gone, on their way to the PX, making do.

SEVENTH WEEK:

"Why Would Anyone Want to Do Anything?"

Here we go again," we chanted in cadence early in May before the word "again" was really appropriate, "marching down the avenue. Eight more weeks and we'll be through."

"Am I right or wrong?"

"You're right!"

"Here we go again," we chant, "marching down the avenue. One more week and we'll be through!" we scream with a lustiness faintly embarrassing to the Army. Liberation, it once seemed, would never come. It might forever be part of a marching song, all promise and no feeling. We have learned to distrust hope. All we know is what is.

Monday

SLOW CHANGES

Private Peyser returns from the rifle range, having had yet another "last chance" to hit 30 out of 96 targets and qualify with his rifle. Private Stevens who also took the test again scores 61 (with an asterisk), but some things never change. Peyser scores six.

As my way of telling the Army that it gives me a severe pain in the ass, I trek to the doctor to complain of hemorrhoids. "I don't want to look at your hairy ass," he tells me. He recommends daily baths in the infirmary's hot tub. I lay in a stock of cigars in preparation for my treatment. While I wait for the doctor a sergeant finds me writing and starts to fight with me. The doctor interrupts and points out that, even though I may be right about needing something to do to keep me from falling asleep, the man with the stripes is always more right. End of discussion.

Lieutenant Beep-Beep, wanting to be one of the guys, looking up to the Reservists, waves cheerily at a group of us as we pass him. We are walking away from a detail and we wave back. We respect each other a little more these days.

Lieutenant Beep-Beep sends two trainees in to Field First Sergeant Rawlins to paint two signs, one for reenlistment and one for artillery school. The signs read: "Renlistment" and "Atilarry." When the misspellings are pointed out to Field First Drill Sergeant Rawlins he looks at them carefully and asks, "Which one is misspelled?"

In times of stress, snobbery surfaces. Crazy Willie Buck, a frantic and tense black who carries the company standard and beats up his platoon-mates at the drop of a hint, calls Privates Nelson and Mantle "motherfuckers" for fifteen uninterrupted minutes without a breath. The verbal assault complete, Crazy Willie would have left in peace had he not been provoked into a more physical form of aggression by Private Mantle, who replied coolly at the end of the harangue, "Spell it."

DRILL SERGEANTS I HAVE KNOWN

Some lines of class and privilege are crumbling, however. Three of us sit in our underwear at the company headquarters after curfew, talking with the officers and drill sergeants. Drill

Sergeant Wilson tells us that when he gets out of the Army after his sixth year he is going to become a cop for the Los Angeles Police Department. He may yet be the gentlest cop since the one in San Francisco who got canned for having his picture taken smoking a joint with some hippies. Despite the Army's anti-intellectualism, he remains sensitive and bright; having achieved those states without any formal schooling beyond high school. Most of all, he renews our faith in human elasticity. He retains his sense of humor and an essentially liberal nature. He is hip without being, like, say, Drill Sergeant Grbr, hip twenty years late.

Drill Sergeant Grbr has just latched onto "See you later, alligator." Dead hip styles, like greasy hair and pegged pants, eventually land in Army warehouses or in C&W circles, where they are picked up as the latest thing; or maybe it's that they are sure to be nothing like what's doing in the Gomorrahs of the two coasts.

Drill Sergeant Bill Robinson purges his frustrations as they present themselves, by expletive. "You dummy. You shit," he marvels as trainees fail to observe his lessons. "You must be stupid," he says, "because I *taught* it and you didn't *learn* it." He doesn't take the Army home in a briefcase each night. He solves all his problems by sundown.

Robinson treats the Army as his home. He doesn't get tense in his own living room, while Grbr, who may have been in since Henry Knox's day, acts as if his world would crumble if his men weren't the best. These two are contrasted against Lieutenant Tanner, who may be single-handedly responsible for the complete breakdown in discipline, and who, like Beep-Beep and Lieutenant-cum-Captain Applesauce, the twenty-year-old Old Man, wants to be liked, more than feared.

I should point out that all this is going on against a background of horror stories leaking from the ranks of Alpha, Bravo and Echo Companies--tales of abuse and terror.

AND THE SUNSHINE SOLDIERS

"Youse sons of bitches are no-good bastard shirkers, that's what you are," yells a sergeant to a gathering First Sergeant Madmans has called of Reservists and Guardsmen. Scattered applause greets the definition.

"How many of you bastards know what you're in for?"

"Six months and a bad time," whispers CPA Stan.

"You," he says, pointing to Private Roth from Wisconsin, a National Guardsman, who must be reckoned with, "what's the purpose of the National Guard?"

"Sergeant," Roth answers, "we stand ready to mobilize whenever the governor of our state needs us to help keep civil order, or when nationalized by the President of the United States."

"And in the meantime?"

"In the meantime, sergeant, we prepare for these eventualities through ceaseless drill and unending boredom."

"In the meantime, troop, you're weekend warriors, isn't that right?"

"Except in the summer, when we go to summer camp, sergeant."

"Then you're summer soldiers."

"These are the times that try men's souls," whispers CPA Stan. "The summer soldiers and the sunshine patriots will shrink from the service of their country and keep their asses out of Vietnam."

"What are you whispering there?"

"We were talking about the job of the Reserves, sergeant," says Private Nelson.

"What do you candy-asses in the Reserves do?"

"We stand ready to finish up what the Army can't get done."

"Sunshine patriots, aren't you? Ready to help in fair weather."

"No, sergeant," objects Private Leonotto, "sunshine *soldiers.* There's a distinction."

"I don't see it."

"It's a subtle distinction, sergeant, but it's there. It depends a lot on what you're fighting."

Whereas the Reservists, the Regular Army and draftees seem to coexist better than before, the National Guardsmen seem to be the most aggressively hawkish bunch around, as if to prove that they are something more than weekend warriors. Such guilt is unbecoming. Whenever we bad-mouth war, death, chauvinism and the new action army, the National Guardsmen, many of whom are southerners, shake their heads in disapproval. They keep a hawkish front, safe within the bowels of the weekend guard. "Chicken Colonels, that's what they are," grumbled one Reservist after a fight with a Guardsman. They all think of themselves as Regular Army, morally superior to all other strains of summer soldier. The Regular Army treats them kindly because they are mostly southern and at least violent. It seems that the state militias were all full up, and these rubber patriots had to have some kind of uniform to wear when they lynched the folks back home. Some of them actually brag that their units may be activated to go to Nam. They have seemingly not benefited from their stay here, while the Regular Army and draftees *have*. None of *them* wants to do anything but go home and burn his fatigues.

MIDNIGHT COWBOY

Wintergreen Waters returns from guard duty to tell his tale. In the dark of the bayonet assault course he stumbled upon a figure walking across the barbed-wire-strewn field carrying a strange implement. He accosted the man and detained him until the captain of the relief arrived. The man claimed to be a Colonel.

"Thought he was kind of ordinary-looking," says Waters, "not like a Colonel at all, I mean, he was wearing a sport shirt and Bermudas."

"Sounds like a Colonel to me," says Cubby Worthington.

When the relief arrived, the man established his identity as a genuine Colonel.

The implement, Waters learned, was a metal detector. He was

looking for loose change that may have fallen out of trainees' pockets as they crawled under the barbed wire. "To get enough money," the Colonel said, as Waters held back a tear, "to buy my little girl a pony." The captain of the relief apologized for the interruption and relieved the guard. "How about singing three verses of 'Scarlet Ribbons,'" suggests CPA Stan.

"That's okay," adds Waters. "Todd almost shot a major who was practicing on the putting green at the Officers' Club golf course at three AM."

"How could he shoot him if he didn't have ammunition?" asks Private Yates

"That's why he *almost* shot him. He tried."

"Woulda plugged him too," adds Todd, "but the damned gun wasn't loaded. Sorta thought of throwing rocks instead."

"I'd hate to be alone with you on a golf course at three in the morning, Todd," mumbles Worthington.

'Afraid you'd get shot?" asks Todd.

Worthington shakes his head, and replies with a long, slow "Nooope."

Tuesday

THE QUICK AND THE DEAD

An ambulance comes screaming into the company area at three in the morning, waking us up earlier than usual. The night fire guard has discovered a body on the top bunk of Private Muñez' double-decker, head between its legs, legs over the shoulders, a handkerchief over its eyes. The fire guard has noted that the body is not breathing and so has registered Private Muñez' death; hence the ambulance. It takes Private Muñez fifteen minutes to explain the difference between yoga and death to the ambulance driver.

In other medical developments, CPA Stan has noted the success of my complaint about hemorrhoids, which has won me three hours in a bathtub every morning.

Following in my footsteps, he tries a similar complaint, but is whisked to the hospital instead. The medics actually looked at his rear and have discovered some kind of cyst. Scheduled for immediate surgery, and seemingly doomed to recycling like Unperson Holstein, CPA Stan protests his good health.

"Look," he tells the admissions clerk--like Yossarian insisting that "I see everything once"--"I can jump." He jumps. "I can stand." He stands, hiding his pain. "I can walk." He walks.

"Sorry," says the medical specialist at the desk, "but you're scheduled for admission and surgery. There's nothing I can do. Now, what's your name and unit?"

Realization smirking all over CPA Stan's face, he says, "But look, I can run," and runs out of the door and back to the company, bleeding from the ass.

Back at the company, he faints rather dramatically in Field First Drill Sergeant Rawlins' office when Rawlins asks for his signed sick-call slip, which CPA Stan has left at the doctor's. Returning to the doctor's, he tells him that the hospital has decided not to operate.

"Where's their note to that effect?" demands the doctor.

"I left it at the hospital. I'll go back and get it," says CPA Stan, bluffing.

"Wait a minute," calls the doctor, as CPA Stan feints toward the door, "not so fast. I'm not going to let you goldbrick like that. Okay, get your bleeding ass back to the company, and come here for soakings every morning. I'm putting you on profile"--which means that CPA Stan won't have to do anything physical for as long as he can get away with it.

Rejoining us, with a large red spot covering the seat of his fatigues, CPA Stan listens as we hear a medical instructor at First Aid urge, in a voice filled with angry challenge, "Can you . . . save a *life?"*

"Last time I heard something like that, they started firing machine-guns bullets," says Private Nelson.

"What's that smell?" says Private Wasserman, sniffing the air, as CPA Stan sits serenely on top of a puddle of putrefying blood.

AMERICA AS A CIVILIZATION

"And what is it we're fighting for?" inquires a staff sergeant named Michaels. "Well, I'll tell you," he answers as rhetorically as he asked, and my mind flashes quickly to the possibilities: a short quote from Jefferson, perhaps, or the Constitution's preamble; maybe a word from the learned justices on freedom and liberty; maybe John Stuart Mill, or even the Federalist Papers; Rousseau would do, or Voltaire. Could be Locke, maybe the U.N. Charter; John Kennedy had some good phrases, or it even might be a short dialectic from William F. Buckley or Henry Luce. "The House I Live In" or other inspirational pieces might do; even some old World War II democratic propaganda would be sufficient; "Ballad for Americans" lends itself nicely; certainly there is a plenitude of essays on our way of life and justifications for its defense.

"We're fighting," he answers himself triumphantly, almost unbelievably, "for the malt stands, the hamburgers, the drive-ins, and the Coke machines."

"Maybe we can get that on a little card and send it to all the parents who've lost sons in Nam," whispers Private Cubby Worthington, shaking his head. "My God," he mutters.

"I never could figure out all that sea-to-shining-sea stuff, with its fruited plains and all," I whisper back.

THE WILSON COMMISSION

Private Peyser, just back from his absolutely last try at the firing range, reports that he has hit 56 targets as Drill Sergeant Wilson winks broadly. Wilson lets on that he guaranteed Peyser that score by a ten-dollar bribe to a scorer. Norman insists that he may conceivably have hit 30 of the 56 he is credited with. But Drill Sergeant Wilson, knowing that a score of 30 or 31 would look suspicious, opted for a whopper instead.

Wednesday

TEMPUS, VITA ET FORTUNA

Magazines: *Time* this week has its best cover since it showed CIA Director Helms with a top-secret paper exposed to the camera--GI Joe ready to withdraw from Vietnam. But *Life* hits the stands with a grainy cover photo of a boy's face. Inside are twelve pages of other boys' faces, many smiling, many enlarged out of focus. They are all dead. Vietnam. Last week. They might have lived, and there but for chance ...

> Whose was the right and the wrong?
> Sing it, 0 Funeral Song
> With a Voice that is full of tears
> And say that our broken faith
> Wrought all this ruin and scathe
> In the Year of the Hundred Years
> --Longfellow, "The Revenge of
> Rain-in-the-Face"

PINOCCHIO ON THE DONKEY TRAIN

CPA Stan and I are kidnapped by an outfit known as Committee Group. It should be noted that this is the first time the concept of volunteering even crossed my mind--fascinated as I was by the name "Committee Group"--and will be the last.

The name "Committee Group," the ultimate in redundant bureaucratic obfuscation, sounds like nothing so much as a radical campus insurgency that has seized control of the student body but can't de-anarchize itself long enough to agree on a name. This one, however, runs Basic Combat Training for the Army.

We are assigned an unending stream of menial tasks: mopping, buffing, sweeping, latrine-- and ashtray--cleaning.

We are in the care of a surly sergeant, who, when I inquire

where I can get some coffee, bellows back, "I'll tell you what to drink and when. You'll drink piss if I want you to." CPA Stan and I look at each other as if in amazement over the overwhelming absurdity of the man, the Army and ourselves. He tells CPA Stan to double-time to a barracks for some brooms. CPA Stan, having had his cyst lanced by a medic, sallies forth in the postoperative limp he uses for a walk. The sergeant screams, "Run, you son of a bitch. I said run!"

"He just had an operation," I interrupt as CPA Stan tries to trot and falls down,

"Shut up," the sergeant howls at me. "You don't talk unless I talk to you. When I tell him to run he'd better run. RUN!"

"Run!" I add.

"You open your mouth again and you'll be picking up rocks all afternoon. I'll burn your ass into the ground, wise guy."

I chuckle at his frothing depravity.

Later I overhear the sergeant give testimony to a hatred of the Army that quite equals our own, but that he takes out on us rather than the Army. "Because he can't cut it outside and has to stay in," explains CPA Stan. "He stays in because he's a bully and likes to operate like that," I add.

The other personnel are no more kind to their new janitors. A private with as much rank as CPA Stan and I, apparently having decided that, since this is his turf, we are his slaves as well, begins to get abusive. As he leaves for lunch CPA Stan and I, our shirts removed to keep our names secret, jump him. CPA Stan holds him bound in a half nelson, while I, through simply stated threats and finger pokes, advise him on how to survive until dinner.

We are cleaning the office of the Maximum Commander of Committee Group, a mighty Colonel he. It is dotted with pictures of him alternated with pictures of great battles in American History and a parchment copy of the Declaration of Independence. I am suddenly caught up by the feeling that the Army has stolen American History from me, that perhaps it was never mine in the first place, and does in truth belong to the Army; and I feel, all at once, very futile.

WHAT'S IT ALL ABOUT, ALFIE?

"Where is he?" we overhear the surly sergeant ask someone on the other end of a telephone. "Which stockade? Why can't you kick him out in a uniform? Well, I don't know if he's got civvies. Throw the bastard out in his birthday suit if you have to. Okay, give me some time, I'll get the sonofabitch some clothes. Call me back in ten minutes. What procedure? Hell, I don't know. Lemme ask the kid lieutenant. Hey, Lieutenant Gibson," he calls to a reedy officious-looking junior officer, "what's the exact procedure here?"

The young lieutenant describes a ritual whereby the person in question is supposed to walk down a corridor and through a door that empties onto a civilian street, without looking back. "Once he gets out," the lieutenant says, "he's a civilian and can look any damned way he pleases, but you have to find something that isn't an Army uniform--it can be a Navy uniform, for all we care--and make sure he doesn't look back until he's outside." He describes the rite with the full seriousness of a fraternity president delivering the initiation incantation. "And before he gets out, the CO wants to say a few words to him too."

"How the hell can we do that if he's not supposed to look back?"

"Blindfold him, for all I care," replies the lieutenant, not wanting to bother with actual consideration of the problem.

CPA Stan and I try to figure out what's going on, and conclude that some form of less-than-honorable discharge is about to be bestowed on the soldier who so far is but an object of a preposition.

Momentarily a Green Maria pulls up, and a shy-looking soldier is dragged from it. He has a shock of yellow hair and wears clear-rimmed glasses; a gentle and frightened look rules his face. He is wearing an ill-fitting set of stockade fatigues. The surly sergeant frisks him and then makes him strip. The arms and legs of his prison suit are squeezed to check for hidden instruments, as he is shoved, in his underwear, from one corner to another.

CPA Stan and I recede from the center of the action as the sergeant begins to work the soldier over verbally, physically maneuvering him from corner to corner, telling him that his future is ruined, and that he feels like "kicking the shit out of your puking ass." The sergeant continues to describe the tormented future the now-cowering soldier will have, and how he would like to kill him because of it--making no sense at all. The sergeant's rage grows as he describes how horrible the young soldier's life ahead will be, thanks in large measure, I imagine, to the Army, and he cracks a massive hand across the kid's mouth; the soldier doesn't react.

Neither CPA Stan nor I know the nature of his crime, and the scene we watch makes us wonder whether he does either.

WOODEN SHIPS AND IRON MEN

On yet another cleaning detail, CPA Stan discovers a literary magazine on an officer's desk, and guesses that the officer joined ROTC as a way of beating the draft. On the walls are photos of the Korean war with soldiers dressed in the last of the snazzy uniforms. Or so it seems, unless it is simply that we are trying to fulfill an image imprinted on us during the Korean war. But the leather-brimmed hats and the belted jackets seem to speak well for the wearers, as if those were the last of the shyly proud reluctant warriors, the boys who made the American military such a welcome novelty. But now the hats have plastic brims, and the dress uniforms lack the belted dash of the Korean-war coats or the improvised flair of the Eisenhower jacket, looking instead like the clothes of men straddling the line between the military and the bureaucracy--bland, anonymous suits, half soldierly, half insurance man. We are made plastic. Sycophantic and synthetic, the leather and wool give way to plastic and Dynel. There is no more pride or respect.

The peaceful citizen-soldier who breathed life into the New

Adam myth has been similarly phased out, it seems, replaced by the tough rabble and young fascists who believe that myth is theirs by birthright. They seek action in the Army, and fulfillment of, not the promise to liberate, but the right to conquer. We have solved the problems of juvenile delinquency by extending the draft.

Stoned as can be, several of us are overtaken by Lieutenant Tanner, who squeals with glee that he is being granted his request to be sent to Vietnam, as are Beep-Beep and Lieutenant-cum-Captain Applesauce. Tanner is overcome with Joy, and runs all around looking for us to tell us. "Isn't that great?" he pumps.

"Yeah," Nelson replies. "Just don't get your ass blown away. Have you told your wife? Bet she's just thrilled."

"No," he answers. "Haven't told her yet. I don't think she's gonna be too happy. Thought I'd tell you guys first. I'm gonna go over to Juarez and get some pussy now before I tell my wife."

SHOWDOWN AT THE OK LATRINE

Moments after lights out Private Garth is relaxing comfortably on the can. It is the only one we are allowed to use out of eight, so that we have only one pot to clean each morning: a sop to Misters Inside and Outside.

Sitting there in serene repose, he is unwinding, maybe playing with himself, maybe just daydreaming, when: the door bursts open and a thirty-gallon can of water is emptied on him as he sits still, dazed and unbelieving.

ON AGGRESSION

It is now midnight and I am alone in the bathroom, reading *Violence in America: The Official Report to the National Commission on the Causes and Prevention of Violence; Historical and Comparative Perspectives,* when suddenly an unknown lieutenant bursts in and orders some trash cans dumped. I look around the bathroom and reconfirm my solitude. Yet his order has been tossed impersonally in the air like a jump ball; the objective is not to catch it but to tap it off.

I pass the buck up a notch and awaken Platoon Sergeant Woodling--a trainee who gets out of details and KP in return for such vulnerability--who in turn wakes up Private Peyser. Norman is in charge of dumping the trash in the morning, as it is one of the few things that can not be irredeemably screwed up. Norman protests that he was sleeping. The whole platoon protests that until Peyser began to complain at the top of his lungs they were too. He argues that he has been singled out for this harassment, yelling and gesturing at Private Woodling, insisting that he will not empty the trash, no matter what anyone says, until morning.

Finally, though he argues and resists, he is out of bed, obviously leaning toward compliance. Woodling, as a last thrust, shoves Peyser toward the overflowing garbage can, and one can vicariously sense the heat under Peyser's skin, the rush of adrenaline, the *wetness* in his throat and the weakness in his knees; tears now well in his eyes. We will not even let him sleep in safety. He advances toward Woodling in mincing sideward steps, and is pushed again. This time he turns his head sideways, out of danger, and begins to paw and flail at Woodling with his leading arm. None of his strokes strike flesh, and when he turns to investigate why, Woodling slaps him lightly on the cheek.

As tears roll down his stung cheeks he cries out, looking about in his glassesless blindness, "What kind of people are you?" It is a pathetic wail, but so comically clichéd that it loses its pitifulness.

No one steps forward for Norman, although arguments awaken everyone in the barracks. "Shut up, Pisser, or I'll kill you," shout several previously uncommitted trainees.

Epithets and slander pour from the beds as Peyser stands in his underwear, squinting astigmatically, shaking, still faced-off against Woodling, looking like a blind potato sack. He turns his ear, not his eyes, toward each new sound, making him seem even more out of phase.

"I've never been in a place like this. I've never seen people like you. What kind of a world is this?" he sobs, heaving his chest and body in great waves as the words burst forth. "Why do you enjoy doing these things to me? What pleasure does it give you?" he screams. Ricardo looks at me. He is tough and sharp. There is panic in his feisty eyes, as if he senses that we have poked the elephant enough with our cattle prods, and now it may expire from the cumulative shocks.

As more angry words are hurled at the sad hulk from all around, he moves alongside Peyser, who cringes as Ricardo enters his periphery of awareness. Ricardo places a hand on Peyser's spine and says gently, "C'mon, I'll help you do it."

Peyser turns and looks me in the face with that unseeing yet demanding gaze, asking me the same rhetorical question he has asked the crowd: "Why do they do these things?" I am not there to answer questions, because I have thought about them before he even asked and have found no answers. So, instead, I whisper some advice, encouraging him to comply with the orders and accept Ricardo's help.

Into the pale, floodlighted outdoors waddles the sad figure, garbage can attached to one arm, the other held out for balance, gesturing plaintively.

I return to reading *Violence in America.*

Thursday

CLOSE SHAVES

As we are shaving, Peyser tells me, "I still can't move my jaw. I never saw Woodling's punches coming." He shaves in a most intriguing manner: a dab of cream here, shave it off, another dot there, shave it off--apply a little, remove a little, never more than a nickel's area covered with cream. He showers by standing outside the stream of falling water and merely washing his pits with a washcloth. Small wonder he smells like a horse, his two-hundred lipocytic pounds not having had a sponging in his tenure here. Being an unbaptized civilian, and a confessed non-swimmer, he may never have really bathed in his life. ("Why doesn't he get mildewed and moldy?" wondered CPA Stan once.) Norman stands before a mirror examining his wounded jaw.

"Punches?" I ask, incredulous. He nods.

"There were none," I tell him. "You didn't see them because he only slapped you lightly once on the cheek."

"Then, how come I can't move my jaw?"

"If he had hit you like that, you'd have been flat on your back?"

"Must have gotten me right in the mouth," he asserts, wiggling his jaw, examining the nonexistent damage.

CPA Stan and I, on our way back from our daily ass-soak at sick call, notice a group of twenty trainees from our company sitting in the shade of an old, abandoned infirmary. "When does sick call begin?" calls Private Leonotto from his siesta position.

"It's already been. You're at the wrong infirmary," yells back CPA Stan.

"Better wrong than pots," yells Leonotto.

Our puzzlement at what he meant is dispelled when we return to the company area and find out that Privates Leonotto and Lacey have escaped from KP. "You two go up and fill in until they get back," instructs First Sergeant Madmans.

"Now I know why none of the slaves liked Dred Scott," I mention to CPA Stan.

The mess sergeant tries to get us to do pots and pans. We argue that we have volunteered to help him out, and if this is the way he treats volunteers, we'll just quit and he'll never get anyone to help again. CPA Stan whispers to me, "Isn't that like arguing that only *draftees* and *no* volunteers should be sent to Nam?"

"Shut up," I whisper back.

When the fugitives return we split for the barracks and stumble over Private Smith in a dispute with the first sergeant. Smith has been wandering around the company area in a daze ever since he received orders to go to Fort Ord for pre-Vietnam infantry training. He has refused to take any more training or do any more work.

"Collect yourself, boy," commands the first sergeant. "You're gonna need this training and exercise in Vietnam. Get with the program, son.

"Get laid."

"You can't talk to a sergeant like that!"

"What can you do to me? Send me to Vietnam?"

"Start acting like a man and stop sniveling, boy."

"Fuck you. Out of my life, sergeant."

CPA Stan just shakes his head as we enter the barracks. Drill Sergeants Conboy and Wilson want our aid grading evaluation reports on the trainees in our platoon. "Where are you guys supposed to be?" asks Drill Sergeant Wilson.

"Taking naps," we reply.

Drill Sergeant Wilson, who takes himself, if not the Army, seriously, gives studied attention to each report, assessing each trainee's performance, grading each to the best of his judgment. Bronk Conboy, knowing full well that the reports will never be read by anyone, and will, as likely as not, be ignored entirely, grades everyone the same, from Worthington to Peyser.

"Who's this cat Lorenz?" asks Drill Sergeant Conboy.

"Who are you?" asks CPA Stan.

"No, I don't mean like that," explains Bronk. "I mean *who* is he?"

"The one with the freckles. Like her," I say, pointing to a picture on top of a pile of scraps cut out of obscene magazines. Drill Sergeant Conboy has made an entire scrapbook of obscene photographs, with riotously clever captions pasted below each. He is torn between the two, the pictures in their earthiness and the captions in their wit. "What do you want to be when you grow up?" asks CPA Stan.

"Oh, I guess a marriage counselor," replies Bronk. "Must be a hundred thousand guys as fucked up as me. Think of the bread you'd make. Gonna do it too. Don't need a license or anything. Just a sign. Soon as I get my divorce and get my girl friend off my back I'm goin' out straight-aways and start givin' out advice."

Private Todd enters the barracks and Drill Sergeant Wilson whispers hoarsely, "Hold onto your balls, men, here she comes."

"Drill sergeant," says Todd, "I'm supposed to report to you for holding."

"I wanna hold him, too," squeals Drill Sergeant Conboy.

"What the hell is holding?" asks Drill Sergeant Wilson.

"I think it means that the CO wants to see me and they want you to confine me to barracks," explains Todd.

"What for?" asks Drill Sergeant Wilson.

"For court-martial maybe," answers Private Todd lugubriously.

"Don't worry, Todd, unless you queered the mess sergeant, we'll get you out of it," says Dave.

"What if he queered--" asks CPA Stan, interrupted by a Wilson glare.

"What *did* you do, Todd?" asks Drill Sergeant Wilson.

"I, uh, slugged Rodriguez."

"That all?" remarks Conboy, amazed. "You didn't queer nobody?"

Todd shakes his head.

"What did you hit him for?" asks Drill Sergeant Wilson, knowing that he can, indeed, get Todd off the hook now, since no one was queered.

"You know the big green water bags we carry around, so's everyone can fill their canteens and take salt pills? Well, he's lookin' down into it, from the top. It's still half full up, and half a dozen of us is getting water out of it, like pigs at a sow."

"Finish the story, will you?" demands Drill Sergeant Wilson impatiently. "Skip the farm stories for once."

"Well, anyway, this old boy Rodriguez is lookin' into the water bag, and he spits into it. Just like that. He spits in it. So I cold-cocked him. I mean, why would anyone want to do a thing like that?" he asks plaintively.

We all look at each other in wonder. "Why would anyone," responds CPA Stan at last, with a fine insight into the existential absurdity of the Army, "want to do *anything?"* That is it. The word for all seasons, but particularly this parched one.

Friday

GOLDBRICK DAY

"It's Gentle Friday," says Private Wasserman as he and Briss and Barrett stroll away from a formation to take a bus to the central post. Privates Nelson and Mantle go to the rifle range on a detail to be scorers and spend the day in the desert, hiding and getting stoned. CPA Stan and I walk into company headquarters and sit down at the desks, fucking up the Army's paper work, typing an occasional list incorrectly, writing letters home. Private Masterson simply wilts. As soon as the order to snap to attention is given, he folds and hits the ground with an anguished cry and a devilish smile. He is soon on his way to the infirmary, on a stretcher carried by six cohorts, to complain of a bad back; a plot to spring seven men free. But Masterson is way ahead of the game. He has been falling down a lot since the machine-gun infiltration course, and since a bad back may show no other signs than pain, he is well on his way to a discharge. So every time he falls the smile gets broader.

CPA Stan and I linger at the infirmary, reading as we soak in the tub of warm Phisohex. A civilian employee attempts to grab my letter pad, saying, "I'll rip these up."

I wrest them from his grasp with "I'll kick your fuckin' ass." The Army has made a killer out of me, and I will defend with deadly force those things that are important to me.

I hate, but rarely object to, military orders. And, on the whole, I prefer civilians to soldiers. But when some civilian, who has forfeited his claim to that title by working on an Army base, thinks that I am his lackey as well as the Army's and that he is entitled to give me orders and have me take his crap, I'll maim to make my point that he is wrong. Some of these mutants seem to think that rank and pay grade are the same, which, alas, the government also believes. So if you make more than I do, you can abuse me. There are some fertilizer tasters in the recesses of the Department of Agriculture who can make me "drop for twenty."

THE WAR GAME

Drill Sergeant Conboy calls me out of a review class in germ, chemical and nuclear warfare to help him with something. He wants to play a hoax on the company--an Army tradition, he says--and together we create a message that begins the War of the Words.

When we finish writing it he types it out and I sneak back into the classroom. He enters soon after, looking worried. He shows the message to Drill Sergeant Wilson, who exhales a long, low, "Holy shit."

Drill Sergeant Conboy asks him, "Do you want to read it, or should I?" as everyone's attention is diverted from the lecture to this tense conversation.

"You do it."

Drill Sergeant Conboy walks purposefully to the front of the classroom, glancing occasionally at the message. He takes the microphone and starts to speak into it, but finds it annoying, so he tosses it away, and says, "I don't need this" He reads the message in a hurried, undramatic way, which lends it greater credibility, and without inflective clues, adds milliseconds to the time it takes to understand its import. It is such a silly and patently false message, but it plays on so many deep and immediate fears that it commands belief as it is spoken:

"0945 hours. Seven Regular Army divisions of North Korea--KorCom--today poured across the 38th parallel in a sudden surprise invasion of the Republic of South Korea, inflicting unacceptably heavy casualties on South Korean, United Nations and American forces stationed in the area.

"In light of this premeditated act of aggression against American troops, the President has declared a State of National Emergency and has called a special joint session of Congress, which he will address tonight on national television.

"By executive order, he has Federalized all National Guard units and ordered all Army, Navy and Air Force Reserve units to immediate full active duty to await orders. All members of training units are hereby mobilized to standby alert status until further orders."

A massive shock wave grasps the company, as most are caught with the breath in their lungs, unable to inhale or exhale--or knowing which to do. I, who know that it is a hoax, am caught in the silent panic as well. I see the world crumbling before me, as I have seen it so many times before in nightmares of mideastern confrontations gone mad, nuclear bluffs called, uncontrollable events ganging up on those of us who are hostages of terror diplomacy. My head shakes involuntarily. I am terribly tense in spite of being in on the plot, smelling blood in my nose as you do when you miss a step on a staircase and plummet into unknown space. I don't know what lies before me. The faces around me are grim and hollow. Eyes stare blankly ahead, and mouths open in silence. A National Guardsman calls out, "Anyone want some Christmas cards from Seoul?" A vast exhaling does for laughter. Gallows humor bounces from mouth to ear, but terror is in the heart of each joke and jokester.

Drill Sergeant Conboy comes back in with another message, and gives the paper on which the first one was written to Private Garth as a souvenir. Again he reads our fate, stumbling over the bigger words:

"Pursuant to Executive Order #3174985, 27 June 1969, a Declaration of National Emergency:

"From the First Sergeant:

"To all Personnel:

"Subject: the Korean Situation:

"All National Guard and Army Reserve troops will repair immediately to their respective billets. At 1300 hours they will form a column outside of Charge of Quarters with packed duffle and equipment bags. Army personnel carriers will convey said troops to Personnel and Finance Offices, where they will draw pay and travel allotments to rejoin their home units immediately, pending further orders from Department of the Army and CONARCUS. Goodbye and good luck, May the training you have been given here in Basic Combat Training help protect you and our way of life."

A brief abortive cheer arises from the Reservists and Guardsmen at the instant thought of going home. But it dies as it hits the air, like an anaerobic bacterium, dead as soon as we hear it, as the simultaneous realization of the implications of the journey strikes. Again the hall is plunged into silence. Suddenly, as Conboy leaves by the rear door, half the company leaps to its feet and bolts to the billets.

In my barracks Private Peyser is half-laughing, half-sobbing. He cries, "I'm through with Basic! I've passed!" Then, "I'm not ready for this. I haven't trained. You guys are ready. I'm not. What'll I do?"

Private Warsaw is near tears, holding his head in his hands. Private Wasserman is talking incoherently, saying that he just wants to call his parents. "My God, what would they do if I were killed? I'm all they've got!" Private Stein is stunned and stutters as he talks. Private Yarborough, an ascetic-looking Connecticut Yankee who thinks that pain is redemptive--for others--and sleeps with a Bible under his pillow, crashes about aimlessly, saying, "I'm not proud. I don't mind admitting it. I'm scared."

"Yarborough," I say, "I've wanted to tell you this for two months now. You're a son of a bitch."

"Thanks," he replies, missing my meaning altogether, smiling back, "you're a sonofagun too. Let's get together in Korea and have us some good times, hey?"

Private Reisterton, the only black Reservist, says, "I'm going to cry. For the first time I really believe I'm in the United States Army. I'm scared."

Several trainees attempt to call home but are stopped by drill sergeants "for security reasons."

Only a few trainees, acting more out of psychological denial than skepticism, claim that it can't be true.

Peyser turns on his radio and finds only music, which further fuels the fears. "Something's wrong," he blurts, "all I get is music."

"God, it must be serious," cries Rackles, "if even the radio stations are cooperating."

A newscast comes on, without a word about Korea, and this is instantly interpreted as another example of the deadliness of the Korean situation. "They aren't saying anything 'til the President speaks tonight, to avert panic. Just like Cuba," suggests a helpful Private Todd.

Private Sanders, a black from Amarillo, Texas, sits in a corner, pulling slowly on a corncob pipe. He looks very peaceful and tells me that he is going to get married as soon as he gets home. "I thought you were all busted up over some girl who ran out on you half a year ago. Who you gonna marry?" asks Private Yates.

"Same one," says Sanders. "Ain't got much of a choice. She'll just have to do it. Ain't goin' to die without a wife."

Draftees and Guardsmen, Reservists and enlistees, Texans and New Yorkers exchange handshakes and best wishes. We teasingly promise to send each other gifts from Wonsan. Brave talk fills the air. "Behind the brave words," says Private Wintergreen Waters, as we sit on the back steps drawing circles in the dirt, "little tears are in the back of every head." I look at Wintergreen Waters from Lubbock, Texas, and realize what a clean and honest face he has, the clarity in his eyes, the long, fine, almost girlish lashes. He is strong and popular, very good at everything he does, yet quiet and unaggressive. Very cool and thoughtful. I look at the desert, out beyond to the mountains, and below to the little box houses I've watched for eight weeks. They look different and distant again, as they looked the first time I saw them, before I was at home here.

Field First Sergeant Rawlins, who wasn't let in on the hoax, and didn't even hear the announcement, only hearing of it through secondhand rumor, immediately believes it, and breaks into laughter when he thinks of "you jerks going in to fight."

As other companies pass we tell them the news in our innocent and petrified way, spreading the panic beyond our borders. We all fall out of the barracks in simple-minded following of each other. Field First Drill Sergeant Rawlins sees the spontaneous formation that has just materialized, and not sure whether one was scheduled, reasoning *a posteriori,* believes that there is a cause for this effect, and marches us off to lunch a half hour early. Bolder jokes continue, and one trainee finally succumbs to his fright, passing out on the lunch line.

I am feeling fantastically shitty for my part in the hoax. I had no idea it would get so far out of hand and strike such terror. But I am now afraid that if I blow the whistle on it all and give away my part in its perpetration I'll be lynched by my barracks mates. The chain reaction has gotten out of hand and by its heat melted the only control rod--me. I remain silent.

Soon after lunch many doubts arise. The scared argue with the skeptical, and Private Peyser insists that "this is too serious a thing for them to fool around with. It must be true."

Drill Sergeants Wilson and Conboy call a formation as an heady battle-weary platoon falls in to hear the news--like the breaking of a children's camp color war. "We're not going to have to go to Korea. Bronk and I have called off the war and bought you guys a keg of real beer--not 3.2 Army suds--for a party tomorrow."

"Thanks, drill sergeants," says Private Yarborough, 'but you guys don't have to cheer us up. We've got the guts."

"Somebody wanna explain things to Audie Murphy here?" says Drill Sergeant Conboy.

Immediately after the formation Commanding Officer Lieutenant-cum-Captain Applesauce wanders into a group of moaning Reservists who haven't yet heard the good news.

Private Leonotto snaps to attention and flips off a salute. "Charlie Company, somewhere on the hill, sir."

"Who said that?" demands the CO, looking straight at

Leonotto.
"Uh, I did."
"I did, sir."
"Sir."
"I did, sir."
"I did, sir."
"Button your pockets."
"Button your pockets, sir."
"No, dammit, button your pockets on your damned uniform, troop. How long you been wearing that uniform?"
"I took the oath in January, sir, and I've been in eight weeks."
"I mean consecutively."
"Two days."
"Sir."
"Sir, two days, sir."
"Looks dirtier."
"Sir, maybe five days, sir."
"Let's see if we can find anything else, troop."
"I'm sure you can, sir, if you look, sir."
"What's your rank, troop E-2?"
"Yessir, sir.

"An Article Fifteen punishment would come to about, uh, one quarter of a month's pay--is about $25--and seven days confinement and seven days extra duty . . ."

"Sir," interrupts Private Stein, 'he's under great stress. He just learned with the rest of us that he's going to Korea because of the invasion."

"Korea? Invasion? Both of you report to my office at 1600 hours for Article Fifteen."

"Sir," asserts Leonotto, "don't you have to give me a choice?"

"Yes, but--" answers the young "Old Man."

"Well, I want a full court-martial with all the trimmings."

At 1600 hours the two report to the CO's office with a supporting cast of thirty.

"Privates Leonotto and Stein reporting, sir," they chirp, spic and span in neat dress uniforms.

"Get the fuck out of here, all of you," yells the CO, "Good-bye. Scram."

"Yes, sir," we all shout, and skip out.

Saturday

FINALS

With only seven days to go, we are taking our first final exam, the Physical Combat Proficiency Test. Sweating and straining, we push through the grueling series of events, simulating combat by forging on despite injury and pain--except CPA Stan, who is given a "pass," by virtue of a doctor's note.

"Fat lot of good that'd do you," snarls Drill Sergeant Grbr contemptuously, "if you were trapped behind enemy lines."

It is like a pentathlon, as each man knows his score going into the last event, the mile run. Each man knows how close to collapse he must push himself.

In the first event, the low crawl, we no longer crawl on gravel and sand, but on tarpaulins. Halfway down the 40-yard lane, making great time, I crawl right into a sergeant whom I have never seen before. He is standing over me, and slowly steps on my fingers. "Get up and do it again," he says without any inflection in his voice.

"What for?" I protest. "I was doing it the way I've always done it. I was doing it all right!"

"Just get to the end of the line, sonny."

The second time around, after about ten seconds of furious crawling and rigorous attention to the rules, he kicks me in the ass.

"What's that for?" I demand.

"Off the course, troop, no arguing. You're disqualified. You're getting no points on this event."

I carry my protest to Field First Drill Sergeant Rawlins, for whom a smile has always been the most effective form of bribery, as predicted, and tell him that I was on my way to a time that would have gotten me 75 out of the 100 possible points. He tells me not to worry.

"Here, put this on your hands," he says, dusting some stickum powder on my palms, "it'll help you on the horizontal bars."

"I'm okay on the bars--I should be able to get 100 points for 76 bars in less than a minute."

The powder helps rip the skin off your hands, and after seventy-six bars, closer together and thus easier, my hands are raw and bleeding.

The run-dodge-and-jump event, though shorter, and over a smaller pit is, as usual, just a pain in the neck, easy only for former halfbacks, one of whom, in his competitive fever, slips and cracks his head against a hurdle. Another runs right into one, and flips over it.

The 150-yard man-carry, downhill this time, finds me with a private on my back--who has gained at least thirty pounds since he last weighed himself--and an incipient hernia. Halfway down the track he knocks my glasses off, and I attempt to grab them as they fall. I twist my knee and we both hit the dust. But he gets back on me and we stagger across the finish line. Looking at my scorecard, I see that I am now nearly over the top, with one event to go. Field First Drill Sergeant Rawlins has seen to it that I got my 75 points for the low crawl.

The last event, the mile--no longer a mile-plus, now only a mile--finds me limping around the track. Knowing that I have only to finish without stopping to walk in order to pass, I hobble home in respectable time, collapse behind a latrine and learn that there is no water to be had.

There is a huge mob behind the latrine, as it gives the only sliver of shade around. Cigarettes, and the remains in canteens, boiling hot in the midday sun, are shared, as if we have all together defeated a common enemy.

Thirty trainees in the company fail--a high number--and twenty are from my platoon. Private Peyser's score is barely higher than the one he achieved when he first entered eight weeks ago--100 points out of 500 possible. 300 is passing, 400 average. But as a graduate student in psychology points out, after a quick flash of formulae, it is well within the bounds of probability that his gain is not a "significant" improvement. Private Rackles scores ten points higher than Peyser. "Pisser," grumbles Drill Sergeant Conboy, you piss me off. All my work with you, and you get 50 points less than a plant could."

Our awe and wonder at our remarkably bad performances are struck down by Private-Unperson Holstein, who brandishes a copy of an Army Training Center memorandum, which he says he swiped from the company clerk's clipboard. it tells of a company, in "the Valley," the other basic training site--other than Logan Heights--where 60 percent of the troops failed the final Physical Combat Proficiency Test. According to the memo, the entire cadre and all of the drill instructors were given Article Fifteen for "negligent training." "That's something to beat," says Unperson Holstein, impressed. "Maybe we can do worse than them on the G-3 finals." We take the G-3--Individual Tactical Proficiency Test--an eight-part practical inventory, early next week.

"I doubt it," says CPA Stan. 'We got too many guys who are serious about passing. I think even Peyser would pass if he could. Of course he can't. But they'll pass him anyway. The real problem is we have dishonest officers and DIs."

"The pussy platoon will please fall out," Drill Sergeant Wilson screams at us. "We're going to a show."

The whole sweaty lot of us are forced to watch a drill team competition, which our company accidentally wins, because Bravo Company keeps turning the wrong way, and someone from Alpha Company stabs someone else during a fancy bayonet movement, nearly slicing off his ear.

THE PARTY

Hours later, on the bayonet-assault field, in the shadow of a rubber practice dummy, which dangles from a beam like a hanged man, five of us are smoking dope, preparatory to intensive record listening, and as fortification for the beer party that Drill Sergeants Wilson and Conboy are hosting for us.

The party is held at the stark and fetid NCO club, and half a dozen mooching NCOs liven it up by falling down a lot. Three crepe-paper streamers break the dank atmosphere above us, and music from a jukebox in another room drifts flatly in on the heat. Former First Sergeant Theodore Bower, now sergeant major of the battalion, his chest heavy with ribbons, waddles over to a group of us and speaks a few drunken and lonely words. Out of compassion more than interest, we ask him what his battle ribbons stand for. He stumbles confusedly, repetitiously, and often erroneously, over their identifications, but he is obviously happier for being able to tell us.

A drunken sergeant whom we have never seen before corrals me to tell me, his arm draped over my shoulder, "Don't let anyone tell you the Army is a bad career. I've seen places, Europe, the East, the States, Asia, the Mid-East, that I'd never be able to afford to see as a civilian."

"The world is our suburb," says Private Warsaw. Everywhere else in the world is part of metropolitan America, and this massive Army of ours is just a vast social welfare project to enable even our lowest classes to do what no other country's highest classes can--tour the conquered provinces.

The party stagnates to death, and scattered drunks stagger home.

HOME STRETCH

Private Leonotto is lying on his back, staring at the moon, rolling onto his side from time to time to ease his beer-swollen stomach. "And what will we do when we get out?" he muses. "We've forgotten how to be people."

"We'll be like children," I tell him, "rediscovering the world. But we'll already know intellectually what it is we're exploring. We'll just have forgotten the tastes and sensations. We'll have the thrill of the 'first touch' again of things we already know. It's like we've all been dry-cleaned."

"You know what I want to discover first?" he asks, his mind far away.

"What?"

"Sex."

A sudden noise breaks up our discussion, and we both run to the barracks to see what's going on. "Must be a fight," says Leonotto.

"What are we running in for if it's a fight?" I say, screeching on the brakes. "All we're gonna do is get hurt."

"Let's take a look anyway," he implores.

Private Yarborough, the Connecticut Yankee, has just split Private Rodriguez' face open with punches in response to Rodriguez' having called him "gringo" with seven different, presumably derogatory, Spanish adjectives attached. Yarborough is upset that he had to punch him, and more upset that Rodriguez should have started up.

"Don't worry," Todd comforts him, "you just struck a blow for peace and civility. Next time he won't start and you won't have to use force. It's the only way to keep some folks honest. You gotta show 'em you're tough."

"Anyone ever tell you, Todd," asks CPA Stan, "that you sound just like LBJ used to?"

And, "here we go again, marchin' down the avenue, three more days and we'll be through."

> And the seasons, they go round and round,
> And the painted ponies go up and down
> We're captive on the carousel of times
> We can't return, we can only look
> Behind from where we came
> And go round and round and round
> In the circle game.

THE EIGHTH WEEK:

Pomp and Circumstance

REPENT! THE END IS NIGH: A DIGRESSION

I am, I suppose, a sentimentalist about some things, despite pretensions of cavalier cynicism.

It is a quality of adolescence to be blasé about important things, serious about trivial things and impious toward all things. While claiming my full measure of those traits, I must still reckon with a spirit that struggles against my technocratically bred pragmatic and analytic consciousness, which, for want of a better word and a surfeit of the liberal arts, I might call romanticism.

I should note that my generation was, in its infancy, weaned on Danny Thomas endings. The only dramatic rule on the old "Make Room for Daddy" television show was that any tendentious and solemn message had to be immediately followed by a tension-relieving impiety, moralizing by buffoonery; sort of like having Jesus tap dance through the Sermon on the Mount. In the same kind of taste, too.

Similarly, no one these days is allowed to say anything embarrassingly honest or revealing without covering himself with a joking disclaimer to preserve his neutrality and cool, lest that mobility and potential be lost through too sticky an association with some rooted concept; One's intellectual bachelorhood must not be sacrificed for light and transient civilizations. But I believe in celebrating the small markers and monuments that are strewn along life's way like so many asteroids on a ride to oblivion. They're not much to look at--Last Gas Before Forever--but they're all we've got.

We are entering the last four days of Basic Combat Training, about to seal the book on eight weeks in our lives. One New York Reservist chuckles, thinking that his first postgraduate degree is Infantryman. The Army seems to think that, having endured basic training we should feel somewhat sentimental about its passing, that it should represent a heart-warming and a rewarding moment in our lives--a time to stand proud and tall.

For many, to be sure, it is such a moment, a coming of age just as surely as I once saw it as a coming of citizenship. The Army expects us to regard it with the emotional commitment due a super-high school graduation: American High. For a vast number of men the title "veteran" will enfranchise them. They will be permitted to sit around the cracker barrel with "the men" back home, because they now have proof that they've "been there."

But for me--and many of the others--despite my philosophical attraction to such fetes, the entire concept is meaningless. The idea of dragging myself across a hot parade field in El Paso one week after the summer solstice looms as a large-scale pain in the ass. Some things I am not sentimental about.

Monday

SIC ARS TRANSIT

It is the last day of the fiscal year, which has something to do with the relationship of the sun to the House of Representatives, and we are consequently running out of everything. By law we should be out of supplies at midnight, but we're a week ahead of schedule--probably because our funds were lifted by the ABM or

Nam. We've had Kool-Aid with our Special K for breakfast three days in a row, and toilet paper is worth its weight in cigarettes.

My barracks has responded to the great toilet-paper crisis of 1969 with a great offering of comic books to the needy, which causes great John-lingering if you haven't read what you are about to render unreadable.

INCIDENT AT CHARLIE COMPANY

The last-week-jitters erupt into a battalion-wide pillow fight; all the entrenching tools and other sturdy weapons have already been collected, The street in front of Charlie Company is the scene of the hand-to-hand battle, as Echo, Alpha and Bravo take their revenge on us for having had such a seemingly easy time of things while they endured torture. As feathers fly and pillow cases shred, all sense of order breaks down, In the swirling chaos of the thumping, bashing brawl, the men lose sight of the reasons for the fight and begin to attack men on their own side. The pillows, nearly useless now, are largely abandoned in favor of fists. Since no one can, in the confusion, identify friend or foe, the fight turns into a free-for-all except for certain personal vendettas.

Yet lines of combat begin to emerge, and a pattern develops. Within minutes the picture has definition and resolution. Whites are fighting blacks and Mexicans. Some of the whites are waging regional and ethnic battles. In desperation we have retreated into classic racist patterns, blaming our misery on those who are easily perceived as alien rather than on the specific agent of our mistreatment, the Army--which is too big to be fought--or on the general cause, our human frailties.

The fists and blood fly, and what once was a toll of 6 men and 38 pillows now reads 56 men cut and bruised, 200 pillows destroyed. Down and linen are all over the place, as are the beaten-up bodies of dozens of troops. The war rages for forty-five minutes, black against white, Mexican against gringo, New Yorkers against Texans, southerners against everyone, CPA Stan and I against a wall, watching. Finally, strength and hatred at an ebb--only in strength do we divide into racial moieties, educational phratries, and regional clans; in weakness we bleed alike--the companies drift apart with their wounded, leaving only the battlefield carnage behind.

RACKETS

Private Barry is trying to get back at the Army. He is a Jewish New York Reservist, but he is freckled, cute and mild and looks like an Irish pixie, so he escapes much of the shit that gets thrown at the rest of us. But he has a thing about KP. Since his name is alphabetically high on the list, he has been stuck with daily KP twice and weekend KP once. The first time, he showed up nice and early, to get a good job, like sponging-off tables, but found that when you come early they give you an important job, like pots. The second time, he came late, and found that the guy doing pots had been taken to the infirmary--pot washers having a high incidence of hypochondria--and he was assigned to pots again. When the third time came he sold it to a Mexican for ten dollars. The Mexican took his ten dollars and went AWOL. When they woke up Barry to take him to KP, he was delirious, insisting that he didn't really have KP, that some imaginary Mexican did, and they had to drag him, screaming, out of bed. He got dressed but hid behind the physical training area, sleeping on the instruction stand until the sun came up and the infirmary opened. He reported to sick call with all the symptoms of appendicitis and the Seven Warning Signs of Cancer. When he was released that night, after observation, he was told that a mistake had been made. His name had been typed on the wrong list, and so he didn't have KP that day after all. He had it the next day. It took three people to pull him off the bearer of that news.

He leaves now, convinced that the way to get back at the Army is to waste its time. He is going to spend a day wandering around the post, on the pretext that he has to see the supply people, because after seven weeks he has just noticed that his boots don't fit.

Private Nelson journeys to the Finance Office to change his insurance-policy beneficiary back to what it originally was before he changed it last week. it seems that he's decided that the League for Spiritual Discovery and Santa Claus are not as worthy this week. Private Harrison goes to the foot doctor to see about eye glasses, which he doesn't need anyway. Privates Barrett and Briss simply leave.

After eight weeks of salutary neglect the AWOL racket is finally busted on the second from the last day by First Sergeant Madmans, who yells at the malingerers for a solid fifteen seconds. But stronger still than his wrath is the power of the "psych," and he is undone by a sea of stares that challenge his confidence--looks that probe deeper into his eyes than his assuredness and ask him whether he takes this silly stuff all that seriously. It is a cocky, bluffing mask that can land you in the stockade if the eyes you are looking into sense weakness. But the percentage is very, very good if you can let your opponent holler himself silly and still look at him with incredulity.

FATE AS A MIMEOGRAPH MACHINE

Indecipherably encoded, the new orders for the soon-to-be-graduated trainees arrive, sending all the New York Reservists to Fort Huachuca (watch-hookah) in Sierra Vista, Arizona, and most of the Regular Army troops to uncertain futures.

Attached to each set of orders, is the number of the MOS--Military Occupational Specialty--each man will be trained in. The Reservists from New York, all going to Supply School, will become skilled 76-Alpha-10s, and soon thereafter, A-1-A civilians. None of the numbers mean much except one, which reads like craps: 11-Bravo. Eleven-Bravo is what we have all been trained as in basic training, and everyone in the Army is considered an Eleven-Bravo if necessary. But some will go to learn more about Eleven-Bravo at Fort Ord and Fort Polk, and then all that can be known, in Vietnam. Eleven-Bravo is Infantry

Rifleman, small-weapons expert. It means you get paid to get shot at.

The New Yorkers, going to Fort Huachuca's Supply School, will be joined there by Privates Briss and Barrett, who will be studying at its Electronic Warfare Center. Private Stein will also go to Huachuca, to learn radio repair. Crazy Willie Buck will learn supplymanship with us. The National Guardsmen from New Mexico and Arizona, such as Cubby Worthington and Ronnie Woodling, will stay at Fort Bliss to learn missile repair. Privates Todd, Rackles and Beadleman will go to Fort Sam Houston to learn the arts of the suture and the plaster. But for the most part the men will be going to places where they teach warrior skills. Hardly a draftee or an enlisted man receives the assignment "promised him" by recruiters and Army personnel offices. Most get the very short end of the stick. Kid McDonald will get a stateside assignment until he turns nineteen and is old enough by the Army regulations to go to Vietnam. In the meantime he will train at Infantry School in a place called Tigerland, at Fort Polk.

Privates Doby and Martinez are ordered to MP school, a sidetrack on the road to Nam. Private Matéo Ascensiõn, called Gorilla, who looks like an aborigine, is ordered to Fort Ord, his only way station before Nam, with two dozen others. Another dozen go to Fort Polk's pre-Nam Infantry and Fort Lewis' pre-Nam Engineers. Fort Sill's Artillery, Knox's Armor, Benning's Airborne, Gordon's Communications and even Huachuca's Supply School will send their share of our men to Vietnam.

I wonder if there is a national policy at work here. One cannot tell because the Army does not justify its ways to Man. But from my impressionistic scorecard I am led to conclusions that brown the rosy glow of my *patriotismo.*

You could have picked out the boys who are going to Vietnam and won 90 percent of your bets. The faces are suspiciously and disproportionately Latin and black; and of the whites, the youngest. The dead men have become a type. You can spot the moribund children not by their pallor or their grave look but by their innocence.

We had been told, however, that very few of our men in Charlie Company would go to Vietnam." And when several dozen men were called upon to qualify with the M-16 weapon, the one used in Nam, they were told not to worry, that "it's just an Army administrative procedure. A certain percentage of trainees have to qualify. So we picked you out at random."

Sometimes--though rarely--if you listen very hard and watch very carefully, you can see and hear the earth move. And sometimes you can see the molecules of lies that make the fabric of deception.

Two more lies, and countless lives, in the names of Vietnam. Two fewer reasons (and countless lives) for loving your country blindly today.

PARANOIA

The heat is now so intense that it rises from the pavement in waves, as if concrete has a saturation point and gives off its stored-up heat in the same rhythmic pulses that it receives new radiation from the sun. It grabs you by the feet, then the ankles, the calves and legs, and finally the trunk and head, until you are beaten and leave its turf.

Sitting in a barber chair (again) for the Army's notorious 10-second haircut, I see David Brinkley giving the news from the tube. Can he hear me cry, "Help"? We've seen some hard times together and shared many a good joke, and now it is strange. He is alive and speaking. I am the one who is trapped inside a box.

WHEN THE WORD IS GIVEN

Marching raggedly back from a training session (Chargin' Charlie all the way), we are halted by Drill Sergeant Grbr, who tells us that our "shit is flaky." "If you don't get your shit straight and stop bullshitting I'm gonna jump in your shit. I'll walk you on your knees the whole way back. If you think I'm *bull-shitting,* just try me, because I COULD SHIT-CARE LESS."

I could shit-care less! It leaps from the lips as a melodic epigram of the Army's value to us all. It is immediately adopted by the troops as the word of the decade. I could shit-care less.

Optioning the opportunity to pose in sweaty fatigues for a group picture, ten New York Reservists fall into the empty Barracks #4 to shower, change and listen to Simon and Garfunkel albums on a borrowed phonograph.

> "Kathy, I'm lost," I said,
> Though I knew she was sleeping.
> "I'm empty and aching and
> I don't know why."
> Counting the cars
> On the New Jersey Turnpike,
> They've all come to look for America,
> All come to look for America.*

Assigned to instruct a class in the barracks reviewing all the things we have learned, Private Larkin jealously holds on to his authority despite being frequently wrong, because it is the first time in his life that he has ever been on the right side of a teacher's desk, the first time the instructor's authority was not used to oppress him. When it is pointed out to him that according to the training manual he is incorrect, he hurls the offending volume across the room at his challenger.

Tuesday

MORNING SONG...

Sunrise is an ordinary thing, I suppose, if you are the planet

---

* From "America," © 1968 by Paul Simon. Used with permission of the publisher.

Earth and see one every moment every day for three billion years. But to a mere human the pink-and-gold-light show, tardy by an hour (the result of eastern clouds), seems, in spite of its ordinariness, enough of a miracle for one day. Its drama brings an old melody with it:

Daylight came late, over high coastal mountains
The Renegade stood watchin' with his rifle by his side
Then he emptied his gun up into the pale yellow sunrise
And he ran down the hillside to the place where he died.

Klahowya Mother, I leave you with your White Man
I curse their Church that tells us that our fathers were wrong
And I'll hunt my own Mowich, and I'll drink my own whiskey
And I'll sing until morning the old-fashioned songs.

AND SWAN SONG

Drill Sergeant Wilson has seen us through our eight weeks and, we imagine, should be as elated by our coming triumphant graduation as we. But he betrays the meaninglessness of it all. He lets us know that although we think the world should stand still and take note of our victory, it is of little consequence to anyone but ourselves. Not even to him.

After sweating and straining for him sometimes, and fearing his wrath, we are about to say goodbye. We assume that we will leave our drill sergeant behind as one of the symbols of graduation. But we are told that his semiannual leave is beginning today and that he will not be hanging around to watch us graduate. "I can't think of anything that would bore me more," he says.

Like the ancient and honorable custom of laying it on school-teachers at Christmastide with gift certificii, we "tip" him with another wad of trainee cash. With a wave of his hand and a short farewell speech--"Watch out for your asses"--he is gone. Not even a hearty "Hi-yo Silver." Just like that he is out of our lives.

Private Peyser tells me that he was given a special goodbye.
"What did he say?" I ask.
Norman tells me, "He said 'So long, shithead.' "

THE LAST BATTLE

The last test of Basic Combat Training is administered to us:
The Individual Proficiency Test (IPT), or the Tactical Practical,
Q-3, examining our competence in eight areas of soldierly
ability.

We are marched over to a room where we take a 20-question
multiple-choice test on military courtesy and justice, and another
on general information.

At another station we are put through the movements of drill
and ceremony: facing, shouldering arms, inspecting arms,
opening and closing ranks. CPA Stan and I excel in "At ease."
Peyser consistently turns the wrong way. The best performances
are turned in by robots.

Then to a hand-to-hand-combat pit, where we strangle each
other for a while and kick a rubber dummy in the groin for a
moment or two, and on to a bayonet practice area, where we find
that try as you may, you can't stick a moving target without
getting hurt.

We move to an infiltration course and go through the motions
of pretending we remember what we have never been taught.
Twenty points for walking with your rifle out in front of you,
yelling "Bang, bang."

Then to First Aid and Other. Having avoided all training for
the past few weeks, and having lucked out of the gas-chamber
and chemical-warfare exercise, when called upon during this test
to react to a "spray attack," I do what I would do for an atomic
blast. I dig a foxhole, jump in and start to pray. The correct
procedure is something like: crouch under your poncho, then
take some atropine and gently rub it on your wrist or inject it or
something. I still prefer prayer.

At the Guard Duty station we are supposed to walk around a

little circuit and pretend we are on guard duty. A "stranger is supposed to be ignored, but I say "Hi." Another one is wearing a faded set of captain's bars, which means that I am supposed to present myself for inspection. I still say "Hi." I am supposed to notice a box of TNT lying carelessly on the ground. I see it all right, an empty cardboard carton with a crayon inscription: "A box of TNT." I am supposed to stop and call for the commander of the relief, who sits in a little hut ten feet away. But I walk over to the hut, lay my rifle down and stick my head in the door. "Excuse me," I say, "but there's an empty box of TNT sitting ten feet back there. Want me to pick it up and throw it away?"

Despite my martial fiasco at Guard Duty and the other stations, my score does not fall below the Army's incredibly low passing grade. Not until the scorer at the Drill and Ceremony station neglects to enter my score there altogether.

I am sent back in the afternoon to take the IPT again along with nearly every Mexican in the company, most of the blacks, a few Reservists who could shit-care less, and Private Peyser, who is admitted to these retests automatically.

Also with us are all of the fatties who had failed the physical training test--the PCPT--and again Private Peyser, who failed by such an incredibly low score that there is some question as to whether he really showed up for it in the first place. Our company led the brigade in failures on both the IPT and PCPT tests. Most companies had three or four failures in each. In ours 30 failed the former and 35 the latter; my platoon had 20 failures alone, on each.

All I really have to do is show the Drill and Ceremony tester the blank space where he failed to fill in a score, but they put me through the entire test again. At the Guard Duty test site, an "interloper" approaches me. He does not heed my command to halt because it is incorrectly phrased. He marches relentlessly toward me as I yell at him three times to halt. Finally I point my empty rifle at his head and tell him, "Take another step and I'll blow your motherfucking head off." He takes another step. I shrug my shoulders, hand my rifle to him and tell him, "OK, I'm your prisoner."

Private Peyser has to take the Physical Combat Proficiency Test again. He has never scored higher than 100 out of the 500 possible points. The average on the final is 400, with 300 needed to pass. He returns with not a bead of sweat on him despite the 100-degree heat--in fact, he may never have scored above the air temperature any time he has taken the test--and a score of *385,* well above passing and well beyond credulity. "Peyser's records," says CPA Stan, thinking of the rifle score of "expert," the Tactical Practical he is about to breeze through, and the PCPT he has just miraculously completed, "have all the compelling believability of the Warren Commission report."

The word had been sent down from Colonel Treandley's office that no one from our battalion was to be recycled. Not even Private Peyser. Not even the Great Green Blob would be allowed to spoil Colonel Treandley's record. But Peyser, if he knows, is not showing it. He is going along with the joke, and for one last moment we can see him, at a distance, visible only in silhouette, struggling against the rigors of "left shoulder arms."

The secret is out: the Army doesn't care. No matter what you do, it'll pass you--lie, prostitute itself, expose itself, betray itself--if you promise not to go AWOL. That's all. No effort is required, just a little inertia or cowardice.

The Army's forward regurgitation of Private Peyser breaks Drill Sergeant Conboy's spirit. He realizes that his efforts, energy, yelling, threats, instruction and guidance were meaningless. No matter what he would do or wouldn't do, the Army would do as it pleased. He feels the crushing insignificance that only bureaucracy can bestow on one.

"I'm gonna get out of this mo'fo'in' Army and join the rodeo again," he says. "Maybe I'll go to South America. At least there you can choose when you want to die."

The rest of the platoon feels frustrated as well, after each man has put out for eight weeks to pass the tests, learning that the effort was pointless. They will vent their feelings in another way later.

The last empty threat: We are told that we must "GI" the barracks and clean our weapons or else we will not leave Fort Bliss. The barracks remain a pig sty and the weapons get a cursory dipping in gasoline. Boo!

BEAR-BAITING, ARMY STYLE

"Is this your shaving cream?" Private Ricardo asks me in the latrine. "Yes," I reply. It is the third can I have bought this week. I average about two or three a week and at least two bars of soap and one or two toothpaste tubes. I am constantly leaving things in the latrine, and they are constantly fleeing as soon as I leave, not there when I return.
"May I borrow it?"
"Okay."
He starts to walk away with it.
"Hey, wait a minute How much do you need anyway?" I ask innocently.
"The whole thing," he replies matter-of-factly.
"Oh. Wait a sec. What for?"
"Come look, man."
I follow him into his wing of the barracks to Private Peyser's bed, where, on the top bunk, Private Peyser sits, bound by sheets used as ropes, with his arms pulled behind his back and his legs lashed to the bed in front of him, making him look like a befuddled Gulliver, trapped by underwear-clad Lilliputians He is covered with what looks to be the contents of at least fifteen cans of shaving cream. My can is added to the rest, and since it is self-heating, is squirted into his drawers. It is handed back to me by Private Ricardo, empty. Private Peyser sits resignedly through the ordeal, and at its end is released, rising slowly off the bed like an animated sundae, and waddles toward the door.
"I'm going to the CO," he threatens as another trainee tries to

restrain him.

"Let him go; they'll only laugh."

He walks into the blackened company area like a moving snowdrift, and makes his slow sad way up to the Charge Quarters. He doesn't know, nor do we, until we discover it, to our delight, that the CQ intercom is on, and we can hear every word spoken in the CQ office.

As soon as he enters the office, the Charge Quarters, Drill Sergeant Brown, looks at him and says, "Pea-zer, what-did-you-do?"

"I didn't do anything."

"Why are you in your underwear in this office?"

"They covered me with shaving cream."

"You probably deserved it."

"I didn't do a thing."

"You're always woofin' people." (Woofing, in Drill Sergeant Brown's language, means to pester or spoof.)

"I didn't deserve it. They're crazy." Actually, I thought we were rather methodical. "I'm not going to sleep down there."

"You get down there or you'll be AWOL." Sergeant Brown then tells him what I would never have given him the credit for knowing: how the barracks must feel about Peyser's free ride, and how he's lucky that he hasn't had his throat slit.

Norman moves gloomily out of the CQ office and back to the barracks, where, explaining that he wants to go to bed, he showers and changes. As he showers, buckets of hot, cold and filthy water are hurled in at him. Finally in dry clothes, he slips into his bed to find about six pounds of shaving cream under his covers and between his sheets. He changes again, protesting that he is now wearing his last pair of underwear. They are filthy and full of holes. For this announcement he is tossed into a cold shower. He dries himself off as best he can and walks his weary way back up to the CQ office, where we hear the senior duty officer berate him for entering in his shorts, dripping wet.

He returns to the barracks to find that all of the lights are on. As he steps through the doorway they all snap off. He halts and crouches low, expecting some sort of assault, tiptoeing warily to his bed, looking around fearfully.

He discovers his bed newly made with fresh sheets. "Aha," he announces to the crowd drawn about him, as he rips off the blankets and sheets, expecting to uncover some new treachery. The new treachery has been a play on his paranoia, as he stands there, the fool once again, holding perfectly good bedding in his hands. The crowd in the darkness begins to moan and hoot low ghostly sounds--"Woooo, hoooo, oooooh." I expect Rosemary to be delivered of a child at any moment.

He remakes the bed amid raucous teasing and laughing, settling in it at last, nearly an hour after the pranks began. As sleep creeps up on him a soaking wet sheet is dropped on his face. He gathers up his bedding and walks to the door, weeping and stumbling half-asleep into the night, looking very sad indeed as he disappears--his underwear-clad body ambling up to the CQ headquarters until it becomes a lump of staggering whiteness, then but a point of whiteness, like a fading star, and then nothing, gobbled up by blackness--in a lugubrious walk up the Hill.

He is sad, sad and beaten. And yet, by the perverse logic of Army life, he is lucky. Any other company long ago would have beaten him up, shaved his head, or burned him at the stake. He hasn't even been recycled, let alone punched out by a drill instructor. The boys at Charlie Company Sur-le-Mont are vengeful because his undeserved passing made us all look like fools. We believed the Army, and for the most part played by the rules. We worked and ached, led on by fear, now proved ground-less. And we pushed on for the reward of "passing," as if somehow basic training were a test of fitness. But we have seduced a nymphomaniac. Our efforts are so much wasted sweat in the face of Private Peyser's free ride. The massive frustration and anger that has welled up in the platoon manifests itself, in the irrational way these things do, in actions symbolic of the meaninglessness of the entire eight weeks. The platoon relieves itself in a childish way rather than a murderous way--a fitting way.

Wednesday

PETTY REVENGE

Given the daily order to practice marching for the big "graduation" parade with the rest of the company, which will officially squirt us into the Army beyond, I choose instead to flee to Company Headquarters to help type some forms. We are typing, it seems, the Postmaster's forwarding instructions for the soon-to-be-departed personnel. I grab, in my own childish way, one last chance for personal retribution against the several devils of my existence.

Private Williams, my squad leader, who will be staying at Fort Bliss to learn missile repair, will, by virtue of his overweening hawkishness, receive his mail by way of Fort Ord. Big Martin's Baby Boy Barton Wasserman's will arrive at Fort Huachuca by way of Fort Polk, as will Jimmi Jackson's--whom I don't really know, but have despised ever since I heard his name called at the first mail call. The mail sergeant studiously mispronounced all of our names (those he could read), with a southern drawl that made the malediction doubly so, until he came to "JimmiJackson," which he rolled off his tongue as one word--the archetypal Southern White Boy's Name. Private Peyser's mail will take its time coming back to Fort Huachuca from the APO in Tokyo. At least three Mexicans, victims, perhaps, of a subconscious racism on my part, will await the return of their mail (if it ever is returned) from the Fleet Post Office in Gibraltar.

LOVE IS STRANGE

I demand a break of an hour, because the Protestant chaplain is giving a talk on "love and marriage," half of which is one of my favorite topics, and which, knowing Army chaplains as I do, promises to be a classic. I am not to be disappointed.

He speaks: "Sometimes you meet a girl who races your motor, as a young girl I know used to say. In fact I asked her just before she got married whether he still raced her motor and she said:

"No, he's burned my bearings out.'"

"It's easy to keep that spit-shined shoe out front. But there comes a time when it's got to be reshined."

"When your motor's racing, you're not thinking." I used to get letters from my mother, whenever I had fallen in love with a blonde at college, telling me that I "shouldn't mistake lust for love." I was usually pretty careful not to.

At last a truth: In our society there is a give-away to a girl's priorities--her hair curlers. If she's wearing them when she's out with you, watch out." Not a laugh from the crowd.

He rattles on cheerfully and glibly like a salesman, making no real point, but instead, passing off as advice endless chaplain-to-American-boy-type jokes. It will do for wisdom in this Army. And like a salesman, he is, in the end, passing off a bill of goods for which he will never be responsible, never be called to account for. He gives no warranty on the homilies he passes on, or on the lives he affects.

Love is neither much too much, nor much too very, very, to ever be in a Webster's Dictionary. There love is defined, briefly, as: 1) strong liking for, feelings of ardent affection; 2) Eros or Cupid, the God of love; 3) as in love of learning; 4) as in Love of Country; 5) in tennis, no points, nothing. Ant.: hate. To this hitherto complete list the chaplain adds, "when two people are willing to use the same toothbrush."

As if to circumscribe the less grisly aspects of such bonds, he attempts a verbalization of the more ethereal aspects of mutual fondness:

"There are times when you come home," he explains to those of us who may never have done so, "and you need a little cheering. Or you're feeling good and she asks, 'Did you have a good day?' Or maybe you're feeling low and she cheers you up with a 'How you feeling?'" And if that's not loving you, then Johnny didn't plant little green apples and Hubert doesn't vote in Minneapolis at election time.

"But no matter what," he concludes in a dazzling flash of

Freudian wit, "she's Number One on your Totem Pole."

WARNING: NOTHING AHEAD

It has been eight weeks since we took "the oath on the plain," and eight weeks since the Army began to make us into soldier types. It is coming to an end now, with a whimper that is highly fitting for the non-event. It is true that all our talk these days is about "when it's over," but, like everything else, there is no planning. We know it will happen, regardless of our efforts. A ceremony will mark our ejection, and ejection may be a poor word, as we are really being thrust deeper, but it will be a nothing ceremony. Even the Regular Army and draftees, originally gung-ho, have been remade in our image, and now merely want it to be over with, the sooner the better. I suppose I will have to announce at some point here, when it is over, as it may otherwise be hard to tell. But as the Pentagon would say, "We can see the light at the end of the tunnel."

PLUS ÇA CHANGE

Field First Drill Sergeant Rawlins, refusing to the last to do anything correctly, takes the entire company on a five-mile bus trip to the parade field as Lieutenant Tanner runs screaming and waving his arms furiously behind the bus, trying vainly to stop it. Lieutenant Tanner is supposed to issue travel money to the men who are being sent across the country, and must return the un-issued cash in two hours. The troops will be back in three.

Field First Drill Sergeant Rawlins giggles as he tells CPA Stan, "By the way, you're not shipping out." It seems that Field First Chipmunk-Cheeks Rawlins misplaced CPA Stan's medical waiver for the PCPT, and the Army thinks that CPA Stan hasn't taken the test. A frantic call to the Medical Officer elicits another waiver form, but by late afternoon it is still being processed at the Army's leisure, somewhere in the brigade or Battalion Headquarters. CPA Stan puts in a desperate call to the Protestant chaplain. The Jewish chaplain is altogether too renowned for saying "Don't worry, what's another few weeks in the course of a lifetime?," while the Protestant chaplain is one of the co-owners of the Army, and is always inviting us to turn to him in an emergency. CPA Stan puts it to him in a "show me a miracle" challenge, making the whole thing rather more a religious than a bureaucratic question. Within the hour word is returned that an officer has been assigned to escort CPA Stan's records from one desk to another until the processing is completed. Unfortunately that officer is Beep-Beep, and he doesn't understand what he is supposed to do.

Private Vardon discovers that the Military ID he gave to Field First Drill Sergeant Rawlins to have corrected eight weeks ago-- it had an erroneous digit in the social security number--has languished on Rawlins' desk all the while and hasn't been acted on. "I haven't had the time," Rawlins explains. He did, however, have the time to send in a form to the Army declaring that Vardon's ID was, in the Army's terms, "fraudulent," and as a result, Vardon has been denied national security clearance, which not only denies him access to the beer hall but also automatically lifts his fifteen-day pass--an Army bonus given to those who are bound for Fort Ord and Nam. He is automatically confined to quarters instead. He declines to call the chaplain, because he doesn't want to disturb the man. The next day, July 4, he will, as a result of his kindness, be unable to find the chaplain, who will have split for the weekend. Changing an ID takes about two weeks at Army speed, during which Vardon will be confined to his quarters except for details.

There is one sure way of telling that the Big Day is approaching, despite the utter lack of portent in the air. The parking areas, and even the nonparking areas, are filled with carloads of local families, ten and twelve to a car, all come to visit sons in the service. They never leave the cars, and, often as not, soldier son gets in with the mob.

The best-laid traps. The last night before graduation we plan to descend on our favorites, à la Peyser, and do them in. We plan to tie Privates Peyser, Stein and Rackles to the tennis courts, and shave Private Wasserman's head. But fatigue catches up, and we sleep instead, as usual.

Thursday

THIS LITTLE PIGGY STAYED HOME

The Big Day is upon us.

Privates Peyser and Stevens are awakened an hour early and told that they will not go to graduation, but will stay behind, in fatigues, on KP, which is, I suppose, fitting. It is Private Peyser's tenth trip to the "Pits." He protests and tells Field First Drill Sergeant Rawlins that he will not go to KP. Rawlins tells him, in reply, that he doesn't have to go if he doesn't want to, and that the Army will even supply defense counsel for his court-martial. He relents and dons his personal KP apron for the last time.

Keeping the spirit that we have upheld for eight weeks, the third platoon oversleeps by an hour. We are told to clean up the barracks and, for the last time in Basic Combat Training, charge furiously away from work.

I AIN'T MARCHIN' ANYMORE

Texas cowboys and New York "Vietnik-Egghead-Creep Freaks" bid each other farewell ritualistically but meaninglessly. Addresses are exchanged--"In case any of the Texans ever bring their cows to market in New York and in case any of us ever get stuck in Texas again," says CPA Stan.

The bus to the parade field, where we will be officially "graduated" cruises down the hill, while the private sitting next to me tells me about his orders to Nam and how excited he is by the prospects of it all (very). We pass a movie theater where "Hell in the Pacific" is playing, and I wonder who is in charge of the scenery for this bus ride.

We are unloaded back at the Reception Center, which was our first glimpse of Bliss eight weeks ago, and now looks oddly foreign. We are the first company to return there not to tease the new recruits about their hair and the allegedly hard times ahead of them. We tell them that it is easy, and boring, and that we envy them their hair; which it is, it is, and we do.

THE GRADUATES

This is It, the moment we have allegedly been waiting for and working toward for two months.

In a last fling at martial order, Field First Drill Sergeant Rawlins tells us that, since some of us are wearing tee-shirts under our khakis and some are not, the ones wearing them will have to remove them. "Take them off and carefully lay them down in front of you," he says.

"Oh, no!" shouts a voice. "Someone will steal it!"

"We'll leave a tee-shirt guard," says Rawlins. Two dozen men volunteer.

"It's not fair," shouts CPA Stan. "Why should we have to take them off? Why can't the ones without them go back to the company and get them?" CPA Stan is not wearing a tee-shirt. Half of the tee-shirted men finally comply. In a last fling at defiance of martial order, the other half simply ignore the order.

Across the field we march, the only grassy area I have seen on the entire base. It is quickly apparent why grass grows here. Rice could grow here. It must be constantly watered, The ground yields beneath our feet with a disgusting swish-swishsquish. We look, for at least a moment, like real soldiers, pressed and sharp in our dress khakis. But the impression is relieved by the sleighbell jingling of our dog tags; a herd of reindeer in khaki suits. Good Humor wagons and Swiss bellringers all in formation.

We stand at attention for a few moments, listening to a speech that is as audible as a bus-station announcement, crackling across a hundred yards of parade field. The anonymous officer at the microphone yields to another, and then a third. Twenty minutes and five speeches later our entire company fidgets and scratches as Lieutenant-cum-Captain Applesauce strides up and down our ranks saying, "Good. Good. You're looking sharp, men. Real troopers." As he passes in front of CPA Stan, still nodding and telling us how sharp we look, CPA Stan announces, "You're fuckin' nuts." Without a hitch in stride, the CO keeps saying, 'Good. Good. Looking sharp there." He passes in front of Private Wasserman, who has the bottom three buttons of his shirt undone and is scratching his stomach with abandon.

"What are you doing?" demands the CO in angry horror.

"I'm scratching my stomach. What does it look like?"

"This is a parade!"

"I know. This is an itch."

"I'm telling you to stop."

"Good. Tell my uniform to stop itching." The CO walks away and passes in front of me. Next to me, Kid McDonald, once a war-eager volunteer, watches the ceremony with a silent snarl on his lips.

"Cap'n," says the Kid as the CO turns to look at him, "this Army sucks so big it . . ." He doesn't finish. He doesn't have to. He has reached the Thomist point of "greater than which cannot be conceived."

"And you?" asks Lieutenant-cum-Captain Applesauce, looking me in the eye as if to ask what my comment will be.

"He just loves parades," says Private Wasserman.

"And me," I answer lamely. "And me."

The band breaks into a lusty fanfare and launches into a rather tentative "You're a Grand Old Flag." The flags of all fifty states, and significantly, the Republic of Vietnam, and Mexico (Mexico?) are paraded forth, fluttering almost triumphantly in the sunshine. Old Glory leads the pack, and a brief emotional surge of pride and patriotism wells inside me at the sight as the colors flap in flowing grandeur.

The list of honors is read, somehow more audibly than the patriotic perorations that preceded it. Our company, Chargin' Charlie, known in the land as Pussy Company, comes chargin' in last in every field of endeavor. Last in the battalion, last in the brigade; and my platoon, bottom-heavy with Reservists, a proud last in the company.

"We won! We won!" shouts CPA Stan as he hears us named for every booby prize.

I shake my head. If only Norman could be here to see this. "He'd be so thrilled."

"And the winner of a special award," announces the far-off voice, "Company C" (of my battalion and brigade--us), "for the lowest number of AWOLs in the Training Center." Maybe in the whole Army. Two hundred of Charlie's finest break into loud, disrespectful laughter.

"I'm proud of you men," says the CO.

A formerly kill-crazy Texan, who volunteered to go to Nam even though two of his brothers are there--which may be why-- calls out, "Stuff it, babe," and the CO does a prompt about-face and looks away from the company. We continue laughing.

Suddenly the CO calls, "Right face." Nearly all of us get it correct on the first try, and we began to march. A "left column, harch," and we are headed straight for the speaker's stand.

CPA Stan begins to chant, "Rush the stand. Rush the stand. Let's get the son of a bitch." A "right column harch," and we are passing in review, out of step and ragged, sloshing through ankle-deep water, a mob more than a column. A Mexican breaks ranks and starts to run into the crowd after a girl. Two friends of his, thinking perhaps that he has snapped at the sight of a woman, leap after him. Ten others lunge at them as the spectators look on horrified. It is Private Ricardo, going over to his wife. The men fall back in as the mob swirls past the reviewing stand, under the gaping gaze of the reviewing officers. Only Lieutenant-cum-Captain Applesauce and Field First Sergeant Rawlins pretend to be parading, proudly and stiffly walking ahead of us.

The crowd is the one depressing note. They have been watching us from their folding chairs, splashed in pastel shorts and painted shirts, fanning themselves, snapping pictures, oozing ceremonial patriotism. The People, celebrating our elevation into warriorship. I am caught up in that nasty image until we all march off past them and I see that yes, they are sweaty, noisy and excessive, but, in the end, they are parents and sisters of, not soldiers at all, but merely the boys who have gone through this meat grinder. They are not thanking the Army at all, but telling Johnny that they are proud of him for having survived the immutable forces. They are, after all, not so bad as I tend to think. They are here for the ceremony, a fitting way to spend the day before the Fourth. And if they are more with the spirit of this day than we, it is merely because we know how little it means, while they are protected from reality by their romanticism.

The reviewing stand is behind us now and we have made it. We are graduates of Basic Combat Training, entitled to wear a red-and-yellow National Defense ribbon, the best-trained, best-equipped, best-fed and best damned fighting men in the world, ready to do any task, eager to defend Old Glory's honor, determined not to tell anyone the truth about the level of our ordeal--ready to say, "It was a rough fight, Ma, but we made it."

We made it. We passed, graduated, flew up, hit the big time. They put us through the mill and we played by the rules. And now the result: a company of men, many once dreaming of heroic military deeds, convinced of the Army's crashing stupidity, and, yes, from the most hawkish Texan to the most compromised Reservist, sure of the stupidity of the Vietnam war. Maybe it was our refusal to take it all seriously, or the ineffectualness of our commanders, but we have held onto our selves. And now our orders will scatter us, like pollen, throughout the Army, spreading the news that a little laughter is a subversive thing.

As we leave the parade field, Lieutenant-cum-Captain Applesauce calls "Halt." "Men," he yells, "Congratulations. You're graduates of Basic Combat Training. You're soldiers now." No hats are tossed in the air, but there is some hand-slapping and V-flashing. A few joyful noises are raised to the Lord, most audibly and joyfully, "Fuck the Army!"

REVELATION

The curtain rings down on Private Peyser in a simple ceremony in the barracks.

He requests that Pvt. Sandos pay him back the five dollars that Sandos owes him and obviously has very little intention of paying back. It should be noted that Private Peyser loaned him the money the day after payday, making the prospects of collecting rather dim, at least. And it should be noted that Private Peyser returned Private Sandos' "security" as soon as Private Sandos asked to have it back. And it should be noted that Private Sandos is one of the less tolerable of the Mexican crew, making the entire transaction a mistake, at least, and a misplaced kindness and trust at best, and about to make Private Peyser a fool at least, as usual, at his best.

Private Terry, looking for an opening, intercedes in the discussion and tells Peyser, "Anything you have to say to Sandos, you better say through me. And you'd better shut up, because I'm going to punch you out if you say a word." In the trade it is what is known as a five-dollar lesson. The better part of valor being to chalk up the five dollars as a lesson and walk away.

Yet Private Peyser has his own instincts, and so he replies to Private Terry by saying, "I don't believe you." I understand that he intended it to mean, "I don't believe my eyes. Are you really standing there saying such things?" But to Terry it was a clear enough statement of doubt about Terry's intentions. Truth is revealed to Private Peyser--the truth about the massive animus toward him in the platoon, which Terry represents--in a (nearly) blinding flash, as both of the lenses of his eyeglasses are smashed, his wind knocked from him, his stomach caved in, his legs buckled, his lacteal glands exercised by Private Terry's fists, as he attempts to squeal "You've got to be kidding."

The first sergeant calmly tells Private Peyser that he may indeed press charges of assault if he would like to spend the next three months at Fort Bliss while preliminary paper work is taken care of, languishing on KP, that he would need Private Sandos as a witness for his side, and that, by the way, it won't be reported in the morning report--as the shaving-cream incident wasn't either--and, as you were, will officially not have happened, and Goodbye.

Glumly he leaves the first sergeant's office, and Fort Bliss, older than when he arrived, schooled in the potential of other people's hostility toward him and his own effect on people, and no closer to competence, maturity or adjustment.

Peyser goes back to finish packing. The buses are here. The buses! We're shipping out. Only ten minutes to go. CPA Stan, permitted to go to graduation but not permitted to leave, accosts Lieutenant Tanner, who knows the Army's systems, and with one well-placed telephone call is sprung loose from the red-tape trap. He will leave with the rest of us without his records. But Private Meshack Shadrak-"Mike"-Vardon remains, perhaps forever, trapped in the maze of Army regulations and screw-ups. We are all ready to leave except Private Meadows, who, immediately after the graduation ceremony stepped into his wife's car, never to be seen again. His orders had him on the conveyor belt to Vietnam.

We get on the buses, chartered Greyhounds, and Peyser sits across the aisle from Private Nelson and *me*. Despite our chirpings of release, he is a much sadder person than when he entered the American Army. No different really--he is the one who held onto most of himself, while we became, for a time, what they wanted--just more tortured, like an idiot who has been forced to understand his handicap, an ogre made to stare at a mirror and see his disfigurement. I am dozing and dreaming, and I awake thinking of Private Norman Peyser, somewhere in New Mexico. Like many other things, I'm not sure where.

Norman is sleeping, a finger firmly in his nose.

CPA Stan gets into the aisle and begins to sing "The Star

Spangled Banner." From the back of the bus, in a distinct Texas drawl, a voice booms, "Hey, man, Ah'm sleepin'. You want to shut the fuck up?" Then, "Please?"

Looking mock-horrified, CPA Stan replies, "But there's a war going on, and we're soldiers in the United States Army. It's our Natural Anathema."

The voice answers, "Stuff the war. Stuff the Army. Ah'm sleepin'!"

CPA Stan taunts him, "Where's your patriotism, you big tough Texan?"

The Texan's voice slowly drawls, "Aw c'mon, man. Not now. Can't y'all leave a body in peace?"

On its way to Huachuca-in-the-wilderness, the bus flashes past an advertisement for U-haul trailers, proclaiming, "We're moving to a new life." Someday soon, baby blue.

CIVILIANIZATION

We stop for supper on our way to Sierra Vista, Arizona, home of Fort Huachuca, in a town that, by the sign on the terminal door, is named Greyhound, New Mexico. The restaurant and town are pure American West, except that everyone seems to be Chinese. Its real name, I learn, is Lordsburg. "Sounds like it was named after a Jewish God," says CPA Stan. Several of us dash to a dry-goods store to buy civilian duds. I linger in fresh Levis before a mirror, admiring my resurrected self.

It is here, halfway between somewhere and nowhere, that the dividing line can be perceived.

Here is where those of us in the Reserves are at our farthest point out, beginning the long slide home, our deepest penetration. From now on our remembered Army yesterdays will be more than our imagined Army tomorrows. I remember an odd notion I had when we came in, For the first time I could remember, I and the other members of an entering class were not greeted with the traditional warning that one of the men on either side of each of us would not be around next year. There is no need to remind men of metaphoric mortality when they are dealing with the real thing. And 80 percent of us were. There were only a handful of eastern Reservists, twenty in all, and an equal number of Guardsman and Reservists from the South and Texas. But the teams were simply New York Reservists versus Texans. Some of us facing mortality, the rest of us facing nothing more challenging than Texans.

THE METAPHOR DISCARDED

I have come through it, and it was not so hard, so tedious, so torturous that it could not be borne, be fun and even be challenging--though stupefying and stultifying all the while. I am, I suppose, in spite of it all, somewhat pleased with myself. I arrived believing that this was the American Dare, and if it is, I have won. And if it is not--if Basic Combat Training as a personal existential challenge is, as it seems to be, nothing more than a bunch of crap--then I have only wasted eight weeks of my life. And in the process I have killed a myth that troubled me and might one day have troubled my children. For whatever it means, I can tell them, "I've been there. And back."

And in Lordsburg I tarry over dinner, thinking about a questionnaire sent to me by a girl doing a graduate school thesis on the McCarthy campaign (she had sent it, it seems, to many of the workers in the vineyards). I begin to compose an answer to her questions, thinking to myself about Gene and Bobby and hope, and it seems so long ago that I knew any of the three.

And finally, I suppose, to draw an arbitrary line of demarcation, I rise to leave, about to begin the second leg of Army Games, taking the first step from neutral ground, toward Fort Huachuca--a side trip on the road home.

I get on line to buy an ice cream on a queue that stretches into the men's room, and let my mind wander over the eight weeks I have survived. I will not tell you that I am different, or even the same. I am me, still.

THE ONTOGENY RECAPITULATES

I remember a line from Grace Slick of the Jefferson Airplane: "War's good business, so give your son, but I'd rather have my country die for me."

I believe in beginnings and endings and markers and monuments. Eight weeks ago, on the first sleepless evening of my soldierhood, I wrote to my newborn nephew, to pass the time I wrote about my father's life, and his life, and mine, as my father had written me upon my arrival in the world. He had written about The War, which he had just come back from.

My father's other war ended the evening he put me on the giant jet plane that would take me to the Army.

In his eyes were tears, and by not hiding them he told me something about manhood that would protect me from the Army's twisted notion of masculinity. There was a tightness in his grip as we walked down the airport corridor, his arm around me as if he would not let go. It was as if to say that the true ambition of gentle, strong men is to make the world safe for little boys to dream in, that the sin of man is that we force children to accept compromise of their spirit as the dues of civilization.

We shook hands in the fluorescent tunnel, where sterility mocked all sentiment. He leaned over and kissed me and withdrew quickly down the hall.

He had fought his first war in World War II and his second in daily battles for civilization ever since; tiny brave actions that mean everything but come quickly to naught. He had fought, he believed, to release his son from the tyranny of history and man's habits, to free his own little boy from the habit of war and the tyranny of armies, and he had not, despite all his strength and purpose, carried the battle and borne the victory.

He had made me a promise when I was young that I would never have to wear a uniform or risk my life to take another man's. And that promise had been broken, in spite of him, by a world that doesn't stop for fathers and sons, that regularly breaks promises built on the flimsy fabrics of love and hope and human energy. Such a world must be changed, he once swore.

I remembered then as I boarded the plane something I had read one gloomy day: "There are three things that are real: God, Human Folly and Laughter. The first two are beyond our comprehension. So we must do what we can with the third." Surely God could stand for death, and human folly, the perverted service of war. But what, I recall thinking as I entered the plane, could we make laughter stand for?

And now, measuring ourselves against what we might become, we fight yet another war against the demons in nature and our human nature, for another generation of sons.

I am on line for ice cream in Lordsburg, still searching. Above me, saying something about it all, I'm sure, is a vending machine: "Korona Prophylactics--Wear 'Em With a Smile."

I cannot tell you I have come to conclusions.

EPILOGUE

Eschatons come and Eschatons go. The end of time presages the coming of a new time. We came back from the Army to begin our lives. When we boarded the plane that would take us home the ground crew was loading a long shallow box which must have held skis or fur coats. One of the boys embarking with me nodded to the box and placed his hat over his heart. Shaking his head, he said to me, "He was a good soldier."

Fittingly, the plane touched down in New York with a screech and a roar: noises of New York's healthy madness. The sun fluoresced on the smoggy air.

The City. The Big City. It had made us what we were and what we were not. The Texans knew us by its brand: we laughed too loud and too often. The Army knew us by its antibodies: we had weathered The City and were immune to bullshit. We were self-centered, provincial, ethnocentric, and cocky. But then, in their regional ways, so was everyone else. When it gets big enough, they call that feeling nationalism and kill people for it.

We had studied the rhythms of the Americans and maybe learned a thing or two, and in the end decided that the game was not worth playing. It was a stupid game with silly stakes, worthwhile only if you believed in it and let it get the better of you.

We were leaving the Green Dimension, returning to a present we left behind only four months before. It was four months of trying to pretend we were Americans, as good and bad as any others. Now we were merely weekend warriors, having bought life at a very cheap price, back for six years of probation, letting men with worn-out egos attempt to terrorize us; men who hope that there will always be a need for armies, so that they can feel some strength and frighten little boys.

"What shall we do?" an aide is reputed to have asked Field Marshall Von Runstedt, as the armies of the Reich collapsed. "What shall we do?"

It is said that he replied, "Make peace, you fools. Make peace." As we walked to the baggage claim area to collect our duffles, two federal types scanned the faces, looking for dope smugglers: people who would subvert American Youth. Many of our duffle bags contained grass, smuggled in by Green Berets on a training trail that dipped into Mexico. And we carried a more subtle kind of subversion in our minds. We were going home to a different kind of war--for sunshine.

"Okay, let's go" I heard one of the federal types say to the other. "There's none here."

The other one looked at the green-suited troopers picking up their duffle bags and nodded. "Yup," he said, "just these soldier boys. Just good American boys." I smiled at the praise.

The soldier walking next to me took a deep breath and said, "Here we go," and plunged toward the glass doors that separated us from the mob of anxious relatives.

There they were beyond the glass: the mothers and sisters and girlfriends, fathers and friends and brothers; the new cars, resumed careers and lifetimes. Only this last ceremony remained before we became Americans, and I took a deep breath myself: hats off and hug your mom, kiss the girls and get some Coke, we're home.

Acknowledgments

WHILE ALL mistakes of fact, tone, emphasis and interpretation are entirely my own, I would like to acknowledge the aid, encouragement and friendship of the many people who comforted me professionally and personally. In some sort of categorized chronology, they are: the men recently of Company C in my necessarily anonymous battalion and brigade in Basic Combat Training at Fort Bliss, United States Army Training Center, El Paso, Texas, and at the Supply School and Electronic Warfare Center, the Strategic Communications Command, Fort Huachuca, Sierra Vista, Arizona, and especially the men of the 146th General Supply Company, Fort Totten, New York, particularly serial numbers ER10910529--16 inclusive, who shared this adventure with me. Our color was olive, but never drab.

A future inquisition might also want to enrack the following civilians: Richard C. DeBold, who woke me up many times and many ways; Betsy Wade of *The New York Times,* who started me off on my errant way; Mrs. Arthur Hays Sulzberger and Punch and Carol Sulzberger, who gave me an early hand; Abe Rosenthal, Arthur Gelb and Mort Stone of the *Times,* all of whom mobilized my guilt and helped me move at last; Don Forst of Maddick Manuscripts, who helped me break the ice; whoever it was who pulled me down the mountain at Mad River Glen when I broke my leg; Shelly Zalaznick of *New York Magazine*, who lateraled me to a halfback coming the other way for a ten-yard gain, and Dick Kluger, then of Simon and Schuster, now of Atheneum Publishers, soon to be in my will, who took a few extra turns at bat for me; Michael Korda and Suzanne Little, of Simon and Schuster, who put up with me and put me up, and Diane Neustadter, who reserved this space; John Cushman and Jane Wilson of Cushcurt Industries, who understand; my publisher, Peter Schwed, who gave me a home, and my incredible almost-as-told-to editor, William Hackett Simon, who fulfilled his military obligation on weekends with my manuscript.

And there are, most especially, those people who are my friends, who occupy with me this parenthetical phrase in an ongoing comedy:

June B. T. and Stephen A. 0. Golden; Lucy T. and Commodore Marcel M. D. Brysk; Ann S. Halladay, Claudia P. Viek, Cathy J. Sulzberger, Robert I. Horowitz, Eric Lax, Jay A. Schmitz, and David R. Chapple; Ronald S. and Baby Cheryl Frank, Phillip F. Strassler, and Lanny Rominger; Timmy and Missy Williams (and Fair 'n Square), Dr. and Mrs. David A. W. Wilson, Sir Ray and Shirley Hulsart, and Mr. and Mrs. John Gregory Dunne, all of whom do not suspect how great their contribution has been: they came with open faces.

And Donnie Lee Bailey of Texas. I don't know who he is, beyond three simple facts: he lived in Texas, he died in Vietnam, and his lifetime was the peace between two wars. On November 15, 1969, I carried a candle for him from Arlington to the Capitol, past the house of his Commander in Chief.

But most of all, for nothing might have been without them, David and Sharon Wilson, Christina S. Brundage and Queen Isabella King Watts, patrons of the arts, friends who saw me through the night. No court-martial papers would be complete without these names.

ABOUT THE AUTHOR

Since the original publication of *The Sunshine Soldiers* in 1971, Peter Tauber has been a journalist, novelist, humor columnist, ski coach, stand-up comic, presidential campaign speech-writer, internet satirist, political analyst, editor, consultant and university lecturer.

His celebrated best-selling first novel, *The Last Best Hope*, was a Book of the Month Club Main Selection and cited by the New York Times, and others, as among best of the decade.

His articles for *The New York Times Magazine* have included pivotal stories on Muhammad Ali, Jay Leno, Maya Lin, Tom Lehrer, Gary Hart; he has also covered AIDS vaccine research and The Central Park Jogger Case and written for the *Times* about California as "Our Manifest Disney" and the many identities and conceits of Aspen, Colorado.

He was a writer for NBC's *Saturday Night Live* and also *Our House*; and was creator-producer *of The New! Improved! Facts!* a late-night topical satire for CBS, produced in Canada.

He was a columnist for *The Los Angeles Herald-Examiner*; and was a contributing editor and wrote the "Idylls of the Mind" column of humor in science, for *The Sciences*, the magazine of the New York Academy of Sciences.

In the 70s he had a brief career as a night-club comedian, performing with such future stars as Jay Leno, Andy Kaufman and Robin Williams. He also taught skiing, appeared on every network talk-show, and spoke to political policy groups and on campuses coast to coast

As a free-lance he has written Op-eds, features, and long-form projects from the explosion of Sports-Entertainment merchandizing, "You Gotta Have Balls" to the East German Stasi's secret tapes; as well as political analysis and satire in *Playboy's Oui, Penthouse, Evergreen* and the *Caucus for Television Producers, Writers & Directors*; and has had an editorial hand in a half-dozen books by others, on subjects as varied as the crisis in the New York City schools to literary detective-work and *Caldicott*, poems by Robert Funt.

For *Family Circle Magazine* he has written on the frequently missed-diagnosis of Cushing's Syndrome and other adrenal disorders in women and "hidden" female ADD, as well as wilderness survival techniques and outdoor emergency care, and children with "Brittle-Bone Disease"; also teaching young Americans how to understand the costs of freedom and celebrate our constitutional heritage.

He has been an unregenerate political consultant, analyst, speech-writer and campaign advisor since 1968.

In 1987 he was brought to Buenos Aires by the Argentine government to give how-to advice on running succesful and clean presidential campaigns. That same year he wrote the Carnegie Hall all-star rock concert *Tribute to Harry Chapin* fund-raiser for the homeless and hungry, which remains a staple of PBS' Beg-a-thon weeks. His scripted campus "debates" in the late 1980's between aging 60's activists Abbie Hoffman and Jerry Rubin, Yippie vs Yuppie, was a capsule history of the Baby Boom generation's myths, realities, delusions and commercialized narcissism.

In 1992 he went to Alaska in winter to speak on the coming Clinton Era as "The Baby Boom's Blind Date With Destiny" for Anchorage and Juneau foreign policy groups ---and stayed to cover for the New York Times "the Great Alaskan Christmastime Reindeer Massacre" on an island in the Bering Sea's Bristol Bay; then returned when the lights were on that summer to train with and write about the National Ski Patrol.

With the coming of the Internet he has done e-social satire and political analysis as *Type Radio* and *The RockDove Daily Droppings*; and on AOL as *MsoftGates* and *FawltyTaubers*--- selections from these essays are to be published as Virtually Yours. His next novel, *Isaac's Time* and a non-fiction account of middle-aging baby-boomers in the clutch of HMOs, *The Worst Ride in the Theme Park* (described as "The Sunshine Soldiers get hip(s) again...") are now considerably overdue.

He was Artistic Advisor for film & television at the Aspen Winter Arts Conference and Festival and for two decades a fellow at the University of Colorado at Boulder's annual Conference on World Affairs, the first Fellow of New York State's Millay Arts Colony and a ten-time Fellow at the MacDowell Colony in Peterborough, NH; and been involved with the direction a variety of educational, cultural and civic event organizations.

He is, however, proudest that he was cited in 1996, by New York City's Mayor Rudolph Giuliani, for giving life-saving emergency medical assistance to a stricken neighbor.

Peter Tauber was born in the Bronx, NY, and graduated from the Bronx H.S. of Science and Hobart College in Geneva, New York, in 1968. He has lived in Vermont, Southern California, Colorado, Lake Tahoe, Seattle and Alaska.

He resides currently in New York City and has only one ex-wife.

RECENT COMMENTS
On *The Sunshine Soldiers*

(A note from the publisher: Look at the dates on the remarks below. Clearly *The Sunshine Soldiers*, first published in 1971, has a remarkable staying power and relevance. They appeared as reader's comments on *Amazon.com's* Reader's Review Pages. *Courtesy of Amazon.com. All rights reserved.* RCD.)

"It is great to hear that every person who has picked up this classic period-piece has loved it as much as I have. I found my copy in my parent's attic in our suburban New York City home. My father was in US Army in the late 50's and I'm sure he purchased it to remind him of his own days of basic training at Fort Dix, New Jersey. I have to say that it was one of my most memorable reads during my high school years. It is a funny and insightful story of an urbanite's journey through army basic training in scorching Tests during the height of the Vietnam War. The story is tinged with wit, sarcasm and a sense of hopelessness surrounding our involvement in that most unpopular of military conflicts. It also showed the brutal mind games that must at times be played out by both the establishment (DIs) and the recruits. Peter Tauber, the author, is truly a gifted and eloquent writer and I wish that he would pen more wonderful books like "The Sunshine Soldiers." Everyone who reads it will most definitely enjoy it."
. . . Jonathan,. February 10, 2000

"Got my hands on this in 1981 when in basic training when a girl I left behind sent it to me having not read it, thinking I might enjoy it based on something someone once told her. I read it and thoroughly enjoyed it. It was accurate and drop dead hilarious."
. . . A reader from DC area.. August 10,1999

"Still one of, if not THE, funniest book I've ever read. Reprint this book!" . . . A reader from USA. February 20,1999

(Comments on *The Sunshine Soldiers*, continued.)

"One of the most hilarious books I've ever read! I actually bought this book 3 times. Apparently the people I lent them out to must've also enjoyed them enough to ever return them! This book actually kept me sane through Basic Training, 1973,at Fort Dix, NJ. I lost my first copy during Basic (borrower went AWOL, obviously inspired from the passage) second copy lost during barracks shakedown (probably confiscated as questionable reading material) and the third copy, tattered and worn, is probably in a used bookstore in Southeast Asia!! This book is a must read for anyone who has, or is about to experience the life lesson of Army Basic Training! Pick up this book, if you can find it.. I'm STILL looking to buy another copy of it! This one WON'T get out of my sight!!!"

. . . Ron Correia, Auburn, NH   January 3, 1999

"I read the Sunshine Soldiers while in Army Basic Training at Fort Ord, CA in 1972. It opened my eyes to what was ahead, and helped me keep my sense of humor. I loaned my copy to another soldier, and never saw it again. I've been looking since."

. . . Tom Valenta, Las Vegas, Nevada   November 7, 1998

"When I was in Boot Camp in 1978,1 was loaned a copy and it really hit home. Over the years I've lost copies of this book and after finding another, it's always a great joy to reread it. Very funny."

. . . sfree, Kissimmee, FL   September~ 12,1998

"It wasn't until after I was discharged from the Army in 1972 that I read this book. I picked it up because the title and the cover art caught my eye. I think it was the peace sign.. little did I know I was picking up a book about the very same basic training company I was in. I always wondered what the man was doing constantly writing in that journal of his. In retrospect it was hilarious, and dead on the way it was. For years I've wanted to thank him for a great read, a great memory. If you can ever find a copy of it...you'll have a great time with it."

. . . A reader from Guam   April 12, 1998

"I was a college senior in the Fall of 1969 ready to graduate at the end of the semester when the Draft Lottery was started and, guess what, I won with #21 1 joined the Army National Guard on December 15,1969 and reported to Fort Bragg in North Carolina on March 13, 1970 for

(Comments on *The Sunshine Soldiers*, continued.)

Basic Training. It was an experience that I will never forget. When I read "Sunshine Soldiers" in 1971, I said to myself, "This guy was really there with me!" I wish I had the book today, but I lent it out to a "friend" who never returned it (sound familiar?). My son is now 18 and I wish I had a copy for him to read just so that he knows what to expect if he ever wants to join the military."

    ... Al Short, from East Northport, NY January 16,1998

"While not a work of literature in the true sense of the word, The Sunshine Soldiers is a period piece worth the trouble to find. When I was in the army in the early 1980s, and miserable, a friend sent it to me. The recounting of Tauber's own time in basic framing served my need to be affirmed; it told me that basic training is hard on others, too, and that my own hardships were probably not unique. The language is clear, direct, valuable, the story interesting and amusing and the between-the-lines cynicism memorable."

    ... cbuki from Washington, DC December 18,1997

"I bought Tauber's book while stationed at the 130th Gen Hosp in Nurnberg Germany in 1972. He accurately portrays basic training during the time period between the end of the draft (#35, first lottery) and VOLAR. Recently picked up copy in used book store and it brought back many memories of my basic training at Fort Campbell, KY in 1972. if you are an aging boomer who never was in the service or Nam and you never inhaled, you probably won't get this book. If you were in any of the above, you will get it and understand it."

    ... Ozark Mtn from Rockaway Beach, Missouri December 9,1997

"I loved this book. I was on the verge of joining the Navy, and Mr. Tauber's irreverent look at Basic training was an eye-opening experience. It is a very funny book, filled with loony real-life characters and examples of crazed military thinking. Anyone who has gone through military basic training will get a kick out of this book. I wish I still had my copy!"

    ... A Reader, Rohnert Park, CA September 30,1997

Reviews of the First Edition

"Peter Tauber's beautifully observed and hilarious diary of basic training as it is practiced in 'the new action army' is the most likeable work of lightly serious non-fiction I've read since *The Strawberry Statement*, a cool devastation of an institution one would have thought too thoroughly battered by this time to be worth expending any more ammunition on. Every draftee should equip himself with *The Sunshine Soldiers* and, just to even the contest, the Army should issue it to every officer and noncom who must deal with the troops. As for me, I stand in some small awe of Tauber's achievement."

-----Richard Schickel, *Harper's*

"Lord, to think what twenty-odd years has done to Pvt, Hargrove."

-----George Plimpton

"Does for Basic Training what *Up the Organization* tried to do for the corporate scene---blow the whistle on the whole stupid, phony, wasteful, counterproductive charade just by telling it like it is. Right on, Peter Tauber"

-----Robert Townsend, author of: *Up the Organization*

"For anyone who recalls his own military service with any reverence, it makes harrowing---if at times hilarious--- reading

-----E. Roy Ray, *Business Week*

"*The Sunshine Soldiers* is the most reasoned, and the best anti-military, pro-human book since *All Quiet on the Western Front.* Its humor is as black as that in *Catch-22,* and its grasp of military 'reason' is as complete."

----- Eric Lax, *The Texas Observer*

". . . .the spirit of *The Sunshine Soldiers*--a daybook accounting of two months of basic training at one of the West's most unpleasant bald spots, Fort Bliss-- is a blend of *Lucky Jim and Catch-22.*"

----- Robert Sherrill, *New York Times Book Review*